April 23, '96

Dear Tsiporah,

Thank you very
much for inviting
me to speak.

With Best Regards,

In memory of my father, Jack Brown
To my wife, Tsippy and our children,
Jack and Jennifer

My sincere gratitude to:
my publishers Murray, Ilan and Dror Greenfield; to Hayim Zeldis, Marty and Pat Ween who painstakingly reviewed the manuscript; to Barbi Yellin and Steven Klein for their artistic talents; to my friend Irwin Cooper, to my wife Tsippy for not only assisting me with my research but without whose support this story of Berurya's life would not have been written.

SACRED FIRES

Berurya: A Daughter, A Wife, But First A Woman

by

Ronald N. Brown

gefen
publishing house

Typesetting: Marzel A.S. - Jerusalem

Cover Design: Gil Fridman / Gefen

Library of Congress: TXU 355-081

ISBN 965-229-126-9

Edition 9 8 7 6 5 4 3 2 1

Gefen Publishing House Ltd.   Gefen Books
POB 6056, Jerusalem   12 New St., Hewlett
91060 Israel   N.Y., U.S.A. 11557

Printed in Israel

Contents

A Time of Martyrdom

Usually a slight breeze from the Mediterranean offered the people of Caesarea temporary relief from the oppressive summer sun. Today, however, the air was as still as a messenger anxiously awaiting to bring back word to his master. The skies were crystal clear. Since early morning people had begun gathering in the courtyard. Now they stood shoulder to shoulder, so close that one could almost feel the breathing of the person behind. A few of the onlookers whispered to each other, but all eyes were focused on the pole and the pile of wood.

Four figures entered the front of the courtyard. The first, a Roman officer, carried a rolled document in his left hand. Two Roman guards, escorting a man, followed a few steps after. The prisoner, held securely by his guards, was brought to the pole. The guards lashed his hands behind the pole and bound his feet together. Unraveling the document, the officer began to read the charges. When he had finished reading, he closed the scroll and proclaimed: "Rabbi Hananiah ben Teradyon, for the crimes you have committed, you will be burned alive!" A wave of shock and disbelief swept through the crowd. As the murmuring swelled, the Roman soldiers stationed around the courtyard's perimeter made their presence more evident.

Then the Romans brought out a Torah scroll and placed the first section against the rabbi's chest. Slowly, they circled, enwrapping him in layer after layer of parchment. The Torah for which he had lived would now be used to bring about his death. Next, they carried out bundles of twigs and tied them about his body. Tufts of wool saturated with water were placed over his heart. And finally, his body was soaked down so as not to burn rapidly. Teradyon's disciples stared at their teacher with mingled anguish and reverence. Quickly, the Quaestionarius swung his torch and kindled the wood. As black smoke rose upward, the rabbi's students urged him to breathe deeply so that flames would end his life swiftly. "No," shouted the rabbi, "only God, Who gave me my soul, will take it away at the appointed time!"

Among the crowd of onlookers, one person pushed his way forward impatiently. Wrapped in a cloak and with his face concealed, it was impossible to distinguish his features. As the man broke through the front row, his eyes and the feverish eyes of Rabbi Hananiah ben Teradyon met. But it was not a man; it was Berurya, his daughter. "Father...." Berurya called out.

As she well knew, a special relationship existed between her father and herself. It was far more than the love and affection between parent and child. Berurya was Hananiah ben Teradyon's first-born. If, before her birth he had hoped for a son, like the pain of childbirth which a mother quickly forgets, this desire of the rabbi had vanished from the first moment he cradled her in his arms.

As Berurya grew, it was her father who had first recognized her extraordinary mind. Other rabbis respected Hananiah ben Teradyon's knowledge and wisdom; Hananiah admired his daughter's exceptional intelligence. He alone knew her potential. From childhood, Berurya could effortlessly recite from memory vast amounts of teachings. Complicated discourses, which at times eluded even the most promising of Teradyon's students, were mastered by Berurya with little difficulty.

Had this been all, it would have been sufficient for the rabbi. But Berurya was also blessed with beauty – an exotic beauty which made her appearance different from that of other women. It was not any particular physical feature but rather the striking combination of all which drew the eyes of admirers. From her father, she inherited her olive-colored skin and expressive brown eyes. From her mother, Berurya inherited her full, sensuous lips, long straight black hair, delicately shaped ears and nose, and her commanding height.

Except for his wife, no one had been dearer to Hananiah ben Teradyon than his daughter. And Berurya had always loved, respected, and admired her father.

"I cannot bear to see you suffering like this!" Berurya cried out.

With enormous effort, Hananiah called his daughter's name, "Berurya, Berurya!" as if at once to draw her closer and warn her not to approach the fire.

Hearing her father's voice and gazing at the searing flames, Berurya recalled the time when, as a young girl, she and her father had studied late into the night. A single flame had flickered in the oil lamp on the table before them. Her father had risen from his chair. "Berurya, it is very late. You must sleep now. We will study again tomorrow."

Berurya had cherished those study times. She would have stayed awake for longer had he not bidden her to sleep. But she had obediently stood up and hugged her father before leaving. He had kissed her forehead tenderly.

As Berurya the child left the room, she had looked back. There the rabbi had stood, bent over the lamp. He had blown out the flame and at once all went black. Only the smell of smoke remained.

Suddenly, as the flames leapt higher, singeing the tufts of wool, Teradyon writhed in agony. Berurya shut her eyes and turned her head away. The Quaestionarius picked up the wool that had been soaking in water. Beads of sweat on the rabbi's forehead streamed down the side of his face. Droplets of water hit the rabbi's body. "Berurya," whispered Hananiah, "go home! The Romans ... want to execute your mother and take Penina away." Berurya shuddered: she could no longer bear to watch. The Quaestionarius stood back in awe: not once had he heard the screams of anguish he was used to hearing. Shoving her way back into the crowd, Berurya looked one last time.

"If only –" But it was too late. Tiny scraps of blackened Torah parchment sailed up into the sky with the smoke.

"If only," thought Berurya, "I could embrace him again and tell him how much I love him." Still moving through the crowd, she heard her father's last words: "Hear O Israel, the Lord is our God, the Lord is –" There was a pause, as if he were gathering the last strength left in his body. Then she heard the word "One" and then there was silence. The smoke thickened. Berurya wiped her eyes. She had to be strong. There was no time for emotions. They would have to wait. Now she had to warn her mother and sister. At last, she burst out of the crowd. Bilha, the woman who had cared for Berurya since childhood, was waiting by the donkeys. Berurya grabbed the garment beneath her cloak and ripped the fabric. Bilha began to weep. "Bilha, my father is dead. We must return at once to Sikhnin. I'll explain to you on the way."

As Berurya rode away, she resisted the temptation to look back. Staring down at the dirt track, she imagined her father's face, his dark and piercing eyes. All she could think of was his last word, "One".

Two days had passed since Bilha and Berurya left Caesarea. The journey back to Sikhnin was slow and wearisome. The intensity of the sun in the lower Galilee, while not as fierce as on the coast, still made traveling in the afternoon ill-advised. Bilha kept thinking about finally sleeping in her own bed. Every muscle in her body ached. "Berurya," said Bilha, "why can't we stop and rest? A few minutes cannot possibly make a difference."

Berurya did not answer. She too was exhausted, but she was used to pushing herself beyond her body's endurance. She knew that physical strength allowed one to prevail over another. But strength of will allowed people to prevail over themselves! Berurya felt that she must warn her mother and sister as soon as possible.

Bilha looked around. The land was mostly brown, with scattered patches of green. Only the thistles that grew between the rocks seemed to flourish in the hilly terrain. "Berurya," Bilha shouted in exasperation, "I need to stop!" Berurya, who had been riding a short distance in front of Bilha, halted abruptly. Quickly, she got off her donkey and turned it around.

"Bilha, dismount!"

"First, you push me to exhaustion and then you rush me to rest! Make up your mind, Berurya."

"Bilha, soldiers are coming! We've got to hide! We passed a cave back there, just beyond that boulder. We'll hide in it until they pass by."

As they led the donkeys down the slope, thorns scratched the skin above their sandals. Once inside the cave, Bilha said: "Berurya, I'm not sure that I can –"

"Shhh," whispered Berurya, "I was right. There are Roman soldiers! Be silent."

They could hear the soldiers speaking.

"Antoninus, what is the first thing you'll do when we get back to Caesarea?"

"The first thing, Marcus? Get some of this dirt off my body!"

"And the second thing?"

"The second thing, my friend, will be to find a woman, and drink enough wine to forget I was ever here!"

As the soldiers' horses drew nearer, Berurya felt her heart race. If the Romans spotted them, there would be no escape. Berurya bent, and pressed back against the cave wall. Bilha, crouching behind her, glanced down. "A snake!" gasped Bilha. Berurya covered Bilha's mouth with her hand. "Don't move! Don't say a word!"

Antoninus reined in his horse. "Did you hear that, Marcus? It sounded like a woman's voice coming from that cave." Antoninus dismounted and started toward the cave. Berurya breathed with difficulty. If her heart pounded any louder, it would surely reveal their hiding place! And if they were discovered, what would happen? Berurya assumed the worst. She and Bilha would be raped, perhaps even killed. "I won't make it easy for them," Berurya resolved. She spotted a loose rock nearby. Slowly, so as not to make a sound, she bent down and picked it up. Holding the jagged rock tightly in her soft, smooth palm, she prepared herself to smash the Roman's head. "Any second now ..." she thought, as she held her breath.

"Antoninus," Marcus shouted, "you've been out in the sun so long that you're imagining women's voices! Come on back and let's go!"

The other paused. "It wasn't my imagination," he said. "I did hear a voice."

"Okay, you heard a voice. I'm not going to argue with you. Just let's get out of here."

Antoninus mounted his horse. "Right now I think I need a drink even more than I need a bath."

"Trust me, Antoninus, you need both!"

They laughed and rode away.

Berurya dropped the rock. The snake was gone.

"Come on, Bilha, let's move."

Coming back to Sikhnin was reassuring. The town was cradled between two rolling mountain ranges. Part of it was built on one of the lower slopes. A steep, serpentine path connected these homes. Berurya's family lived at the foot of the mountain. As a young child, she would often climb up past the houses and sit under a solitary fig tree. There she would pretend to be the Prophetess Debra, who judged the children of Israel as she sat under a palm tree. Berurya's memories of childhood were mainly good ones. Her father would always take her to the *Beit Midrash* where he taught Torah to his pupils. Once, she overheard him tell her mother that she, Berurya, was blessed with a mind and acumen which far surpassed many of the great scholars of the generation. Berurya knew she was intelligent. Not only could she remember precise details but her reasoning power was remarkable.

Berurya's brother, Elhanan, was also very intelligent, but he was overshadowed by his sister. And Berurya had a penchant for study. No matter what the material, she applied herself with the selfsame determination. The more challenging the subject matter, the greater her perseverance. Elhanan had far less patience. He wanted things to come quickly. When he studied, a part of him was somewhere beyond the walls of the *Beit Midrash*.

On one occasion, Shimeon ben Hanina journeyed to Sikhnin to inquire about a difficult point of Jewish law. The Rabbi was absent at the time and so he asked Berurya and Elhanan. They offered different opinions. When word of the incident reached the great Rabbi Yehuda ben Bava, he observed: "The daughter answered more correctly than the son." This could have led to jealousy but did not since the children truly loved each other.

Penina, the youngest child, was more like her mother – delicate as a flower. Even when very young she was extraordinarily sensitive to the feelings of others. The child whom other children teased was the one whom Penina befriended. In defense of the victim, she would quote the sages: "Do not do unto others, as you would not want them to do unto you." Whether she really understood the saying at five was questionable, but the compassion she felt was genuine.

The sun was sinking behind the mountains when Berurya and Bilha arrived in Sikhnin. The isolated trees dotting the mountain tops were silhouettes against the scarlet sunset. Finally, they were home. Berurya paused. How should she tell her mother and sister about the way her father died? She had to think of something! She pushed open the door and went in. Then she stood frozen in disbelief. The house was in shambles. Tables were overturned, chairs broken, glass strewn about the floor. "Bilha, light a lantern! –"

Bilha handed Berurya the lantern, and took one for herself. Cautiously, Berurya climbed the steps to the bedroom. It was wrecked. She went downstairs again.

"What happened?" whispered Bilha.

Before Berurya could answer, someone called her name.

"Berurya, is that you?" The voice sounded familiar. "It is me, Shulamit. I saw the light – I thought it might be you –"

"Shulamit," Berurya said to her next-door neighbor, "what happened? Where is my mother? Where is Penina?"

"You had better sit down."

Suddenly, Berurya felt cold. She lifted an overturned chair and sat.

"Two days ago," said Shulamit, "many heavily-armed soldiers marched into Sikhnin. They took us totally by surprise. Somehow, they knew exactly where your house was and surrounded it. Some entered. There was a terrible ruckus – things breaking and glass smashing! Then we heard your mother scream: 'Don't take my daughter!'

"Two Roman soldiers came out, dragging Penina by the hair. Her clothing was in shreds. She was shrieking! They put her on a horse and a Roman shouted: 'This Jewish bitch will go to Rome and work in a brothel to pay for the crimes committed by her father, Hananiah ben Teradyon! Punishment has already been meted out to his wife!'

"Before we knew it, the soldiers had left with Penina." Shulamit took a deep breath and continued: "We found your mother on the floor, dead. A soldier must have struck her and she fell, hitting her head on a sharp edge. She probably died instantly. We buried her right away. Berurya, why would anybody harm your mother? What crime could your father have committed for the Romans to murder his wife and disgrace his daughter?"

Bilha, who was weeping, walked over and put a hand on Berurya's shoulder. Berurya did not move. She kept staring at the glass littered over the floor.

"Is there ... anything I can do?" Shulamit asked.

"No," murmured Bilha. "We'll be all right for now. If we do need help, we'll ask you. Thanks."

Shulamit left the house with her head bowed. "If only we could have done something –" she muttered.

Berurya sat motionlessly. Then she lifted her head and gazed around the room as though she were seeing it for the first time. And then she clenched her fists and began pounding them on her knees. Suddenly, Berurya rose to her feet and screamed: "Murderers! Murderers!" She spun around to Bilha. "Murderers," she said hoarsely. "They murdered my father and my mother...."

Slivers of broken glass glittered as the first light of morning stole into the room. Berurya was still in the chair. Bilha had covered her with her cloak. Slowly, Berurya got up, let the cloak fall to the floor, and walked to the window. The air was fresh and crisp. She breathed in deeply, paused and then slowly exhaled. Standing there, she began to recite the morning prayers. Her lips moved but the sound was barely audible. Every day of her life, three times a day – evening, morning, and afternoon – she prayed. This day was no exception. Bilha entered and waited quietly for Berurya to finish.

"Berurya," said Bilha gently, "what ... will we do?"

"I haven't thought things through yet, Bilha. But one thing is certain: I must get Penina out of the brothel."

"But they took Penina to Rome! What can we do?"

"What can I do?" Berurya echoed. "Whatever must be done! If necessary, I'll go to Rome and bring Penina back!"

"When do we go?"

"We!?" interrupted Berurya. "Who said anything about you going? This will be dangerous."

"Berurya, I've been with you ever since you were a baby. I'll never let you go off alone –"

"Bilha," said Berurya quietly, "I'm going for a walk...."

As Berurya walked down the main street, shopkeepers opened their stores. As a result of the war, the economy had suffered gravely. The inhabitants in the Galilee were better off than their brethren in Judea, but the war had affected them as well. Prices – especially food prices – had risen considerably in the past few years. Many crops had been destroyed during the war and when Rome began confiscating Jewish land, countless farmers found themselves reduced to tenants on what had been their own soil. Only towns mainly inhabited by non-Jews had fared well; for them, life went on as usual....

Berurya was ascending the dirt path that led up the slope of the mountain. A group of children ran in the opposite direction, chasing after metal hoops. They guided the hoops with wooden sticks and the first one down the hill was the winner. Berurya remembered racing down the same hill with Sha'ul. She had beaten him and he had not liked the idea of losing to a girl. She could picture his angry expression.

"If my hoop had not rolled off the road into the ditch, I would've beaten you easily!"

Berurya had shown him no pity. "You're lucky you lost to me! My little sister just learned to walk and she's already faster than I am –"

Sha'ul muttered under his breath and walked away.

Berurya was weary. "Just a little farther," she told herself. And then her favorite tree was in sight, waiting for her like some patient, old friend. Berurya sat down, and rested her back against the trunk. She felt utterly alone. What would be if she could not locate Penina? Penina was now the only family she had left.

Berurya heaped a few pebbles into a pile next to her. With her finger, she drew a circle in the dirt around them. Staring at the pile, she thought of Elhanan. She remembered how often she had overheard him advocating force against the Romans.

War was inescapable when Emperor Hadrian arrived in Jerusalem and proposed changing the city's name to Aelia Capitolina. The mere thought of a shrine dedicated to Jupiter on the very site where the Holy Temple once stood was repugnant to the Jewish soul! This time, unlike the time of the first war with Rome, the Jews were resolved to be better prepared. Intentionally, they forged defective weapons which they knew would be rejected for the Roman army; these same weapons were then repaired, and would be used by the Jews at a later time.

Elhanan and his father had disagreed about war with Rome. Elhanan said: "The Romans only respect physical might. They live and die by the sword. They ridicule us for our beliefs, and mock our traditions. It's time to end their amusement! Let them mock us no more! What Judah Maccabbee and his followers did to Antiochus Epiphanes, we can do to Hadrian. May his stinking bones rot!"

On the other hand, his father had a more tempered perspective. "If we struggle with an enemy who wanted to uproot our faith or forbid us the study of Torah, I could agree with you. Without Torah, life itself has no meaning. Then we would fight. But our situation is different. Armed resistance is not the solution. Just remember: in a storm, it is the unyielding tree which is uprooted, while the blade of grass which bends, stands upright again when the winds die down." But neither Elhanan nor his father could persuade the other.

In the meantime, the roads of Israel were increasingly unsafe. Brigands roamed the countryside, terrorizing the people. While some of the brigands banded together to fight the Romans, others simply plundered unsuspecting passers-by.

One day, Elhanan learned of the whereabouts of certain brigands who had battled against the Romans. His father forbade his joining them. Each day they argued bitterly.

Elhanan was determined. Late one night, after everyone had gone to sleep, he left. Two weeks later, word reached them that Elhanan was dead. Apparently, the brigands he joined had attacked a group of Jews and murdered them. Realizing their true nature, Elhanan left the next night. To protect the location of the secret hide-out, the brigands murdered Elhanan. They stuffed his mouth with pebbles – their warning to informers.

Three days later, Elhanan's body was brought home. At the funeral, little Penina clung to her mother. Rabbi Hananiah ben Teradyon permitted no eulogy, because his son had disobeyed him. Instead, the rabbi quoted from Proverbs: "And I have not obeyed the voice of my teachers, not bent my ear to those who instructed me! I was almost in all evil, in the midst of the congregation and assembly."

Berurya had been bewildered. She loved her brother; part of her, the part that grieved, wanted to weep. Yet she sensed that her father would disapprove, and so she had held back the tears until she was alone. Like her father, she too cited a verse from Proverbs: "Bread of deceit is sweet to a man, but afterwards his mouth shall be filled with gravel."

Elhanan's mother sobbed for weeks, and mourned for years. Though neighbors tried to comfort her, she refused to be consoled. "When my parents died," she said, "I cried. I buried them. I mourned for them. And then life went on. When my Elhanan died, I buried a part of myself with him. As long as I am alive, I will mourn for my son and cry for myself."

Berurya scattered the pebbles and erased the circle. She stood and thought: "Had Elhanan heeded father's advice, he would be alive today. Had father known what the Romans would do, he would have permitted a eulogy and allowed himself to shed a tear. Poor Elhanan! His death proved nothing. He stood like a mighty tree, but toppled in the storm."

Slowly, Berurya walked home. It was mid-morning and quite warm. Berurya was about to turn into the street leading to her house when she stopped. The *Beit Keneset*, the synagogue where her father so often prayed, would most likely be empty at this hour. In the adjacent House of Study, the *Beit Midrash*, students were usually immersed in their study of Torah, but since her father's imprisonment, the number had declined.

Sikhnin's Beit Keneset, *while by no means the largest in the Galilee, was nonetheless impressive. The two-story structure was taller than any other building. The facade faced southward, toward Jerusalem. Of the three front entrances, only the larger, center one was crowned by an ornate arch. At the center of the lintel, stood a seven-branched candelabrum on a tripod base set in relief. Surrounding this* menorah *was a geometric design, depicting a wreath of vines. The large stone ashlars created an imposing edifice.*

Berurya walked up the three front steps and stood in the entrance. Inside, two parallel columns of seven pillars ran the length of the room, creating aisles to the right and the left. At the other end of the room, was a raised platform. It was from there that the Hazan *chanted the liturgy. The Torah was read in the* Beit Keneset *on Monday and Thursday mornings, on Holy Days, on the occasion of the New Moon, and twice on the Sabbath – morning and afternoon. In spite of the regularity of Torah readings, the Torah and the ark in which it was housed, were kept in a separate room, and brought in only when needed for the prayer service.*

Berurya walked through a side door, which led to the adjacent room, the much smaller *Beit Midrash*. Here, in this room, her father had spent the greater part of his days. The *Beit Midrash*, although smaller in size than the *Beit Keneset*, was of equal importance. Study had always been at the core of the Jewish religion. Remove the Jews' right to pray, and you cut off their communication with God. Remove the right to study, and you cut off God's communication with the Jews. Berurya sat down and stared at her father's chair. It looked desolately empty. He had known that his life was in danger, he had been warned; and yet, in spite of all this, he had defied Rome and paid the terrible price.

Being a martyr and dying for one's convictions, Berurya thought, was not the worst fate. Far worse was to pass through the years of one's life and fail to understand what it meant to live. The martyr's life ended prematurely. Yet it was that final act of defiance, the defiance of death itself, which extended meaning beyond the grave....

Berurya recalled that a few weeks before the Romans executed her father, Rabbi Hananiah had journeyed to Tiberias to visit Rabbi Yosi ben Kisma, who was gravely ill. Lying there in bed, Kisma was overjoyed to see his friend and colleague. At first, the conversation was casual. Each inquired about the other's family, and the well-being of mutual friends. Then the conversation turned to politics, as it inevitably does during troubled times. Teradyon had hoped to avoid the subject, fearing that any excitement would harm Kisma's health. Kisma, however, was determined to pursue a political discussion.

"Hananiah," he said, "I speak to you as if to my brother. I believe that we cannot defeat the Romans. It must be obvious to everyone. Just consider what they've done! They have destroyed the Temple in Jerusalem. They have defiled and burned the Holy of Holies. Their swords have downed the flower of our youth. They have murdered the righteous amongst our people. More than half a million of our people have died following the banner of Bar Kokhba into battle. Yet, in spite of all the pain and suffering the Romans have inflicted, they survive – and even prosper! Why is there no retribution from Heaven? Why? Let me tell you what I believe...." Kisma sighed deeply and then went on: "– I believe ... that we are being punished – and that Rome is the implement of the Almighty. To oppose Rome would be to oppose Heaven itself! Hananiah, I am worried. Not for myself, but for you. They tell me that you continue to teach Torah, that you defy the Roman decree prohibiting the gathering of groups in public. Why do you insist on antagonizing them? Do you want to become a martyr?" Kisma lifted a hand, "I implore you as a friend," he murmured, "stop teaching Torah so that you may live!"

In a soft, barely audible voice Rabbi Hananiah replied: "If my sin is teaching Torah, then I am sure ... that Heaven will forgive me."

But Teradyon's answer annoyed Kisma. "Hananiah," he protested, "I'm serious. This is not something to be taken lightly. You defy an official Roman decree. Do you grasp the consequences?"

Rabbi Hananiah decided to end the conversation. So he prayed for Kisma's recovery and departed with the words of Deuteronomy: "As the Lord my God commanded me...."

Kisma understood.

A few days later, Rabbi Yosi ben Kisma died. The Romans arranged an impressive funeral with full honors. All the dignitaries in the city came. Every official paid his last respects. Never had so many Romans praised a Jew, and a rabbi, no less!

After the funeral, a number of Romans came upon Rabbi Hananiah as he was publicly teaching Torah to a small group. That was clearly an act of sedition! Teradyon was openly and brazenly defying Rome! An example had to be made. So the Romans took Teradyon, and the Torah from which he was teaching, back to Caesarea. There the rabbi would be tried; there he would be executed. And there he would become a martyr....

Berurya stood and walked over to her father's chair. She tried to picture him sitting there, teaching his disciples, but all she could see was the expression of agony on his face as the flames seared his skin. Tears welled up in her eyes, she wiped them away quickly with her fingers. Then, for the first time ever, she sat down in her father's chair. It would have been improper to do so while he was alive, but now that he was dead, it was different. Maybe, just sitting in the chair, she could somehow come closer to the memory of his love. But the seat was cold. There was no warmth, only pain. Berurya bowed her head and wept uncontrollably. She could no longer restrain herself – nor did she wish to. "I miss you so much," she sobbed brokenly, "I miss you so very much –"

At length, Berurya wiped her face. "I will never cry again," she said aloud. "I will never allow my emotions to control me. I will be like my father: strong, courageous – and even more! This is my vow to God!"

When Berurya returned home, Bilha had already finished cleaning up the house. As they were about to eat, there was a knock at the door. Bilha opened it. Standing there, out of breath, was David, Yehezkel's youngest son. Bilha brought the child to the table, and motioned him to sit and catch his breath.

Yehezkel and Berurya's father had been close friends. That was unusual, considering that most of Teradyon's friends had been scholars with whom he shared common interests. While Yehezkel was a devout man, he was certainly no scholar. His great delight in life was eating and, being fairly affluent, he freely indulged his enormous appetite. Yehezkel's full, round face always beamed. Nothing in life ever seemed to bother him. However, what Teradyon admired most about Yehezkel was his generosity. More than any other inhabitant of Sikhnin, Yehezkel gave money to support scholars, widows, and orphans. He had insisted on paying for the silver ornaments which decorated the Torahs, as well as on purchasing the scrolls which were used in the *Beit Midrash*. The man was not only generous with his money, but he also made his home open to visiting scholars. He demanded that they eat and spend the Sabbath in his home. Since so many students came to Sikhnin to attend Rabbi Hananiah ben Teradyon's lectures, Yehezkel become well-known amongst the rabbis.

David caught his breath and was able to speak. "Berurya," he rattled off, "Father sent me here to tell you that Rabbi Meir is staying at our house. He asked if you could come. But only after dark, since Rabbi Meir's whereabouts must be secret. So come to us tonight." Without waiting for an answer, David rose and ran out of the house.

As the two women ate, Berurya recalled the first time she met Rabbi Meir several years ago. Meir had been a student then. He had studied primarily with Rabbi Akiva, but also with Rabbis Ishmael and Elisha ben Avuyah. Berurya's father had been particularly impressed with Meir's brilliance, and had told Berurya that this student's knowledge of Jewish law far surpassed that of all the others.

Late that night, Berurya slipped quietly from the house. A sliver of a moon was barely visible. The stars, like a thousand candles flickering in the dark, glimmered in the heavens. Berurya knocked softly on Yehezkel's door. From within, a deep voice responded: "Who's there?"

"It's Berurya, Yehezkel. I've come as you asked."

The door opened. "Berurya, my daughter," Yehezkel boomed, as he gestured with a sweeping motion of his arm, "please come in." As Berurya entered, she noticed someone sitting in the corner of the room. Yehezkel led Berurya over to him. Berurya assumed the visitor was Rabbi Meir but, the room was so dimly lit that she could not discern his features.

"Rabbi Meir," said Yehezkel, "this is Berurya, the daughter of the departed Rabbi Hananiah ben Teradyon."

"Please forgive me if I do not rise," Rabbi Meir said slowly, "but I have traveled for many days with almost no sleep. I am exhausted, but I must talk to you before I rest."

Yehezkel and Berurya seated themselves. Rabbi Meir cleared his throat. "Yehezkel told me about your father's execution, the murder of your mother, and the abduction of Penina. I cannot convey to you... the sorrow I feel." He sighed and went on: "What words could possibly ease your pain? I never knew your mother or sister. I consider your father to have been one of the great sages of our generation. Anyone who had the privilege of studying with him ... knows the truth of what I say."

Rabbi Meir rubbed his forehead. "During the past few months, I have heard about, and personally witnessed, acts of cruelty by the Roman authorities – acts which I did not believe they would ever commit. Among the first of the rabbis to be executed were Rabban

Shimeon ben Gamaliel and Rabbi Yishmael. Since each wanted to
be spared witnessing the other's death, lots were cast to determine
who should die first. The lot fell on ben Gamaliel. Without warning,
the executioner raised his sword, and with tremendous force brought
the blade down on the back of the rabbi's neck. Severed from the
body, the head fell and rolled over the floor to the very feet of Rabbi
Yishmael, who wailed: 'The pearls of wisdom spoken by this man...
Where is the Torah with its reward?'

"The Romans delayed Rabbi Yishmael's execution. Apparently,
the daughter of some Roman official had seen Rabbi Yishmael and
was so taken by his handsome features that she petitioned for his
life to be spared. But the execution was not rescinded; in fact, the
Romans ordered that the skin of his face be flayed while he was
alive. As they raised the razor-sharp knife to his face, they teased
him. 'Do you still trust in your God?' they mocked. When the knife
cut into his skin, Rabbi Yishmael cited a verse from Job: 'Though
they slay me, yet will I trust in Him.' Moments later he expired."

Meir stared silently into the darkness. Again, he raised his fingers
to his forehead and temples, as if to erase the memory from his mind.
Then he continued: "The Romans considered my own teacher, Rabbi
Akiva, to be their greatest threat. While other rabbis either opposed
or remained silent about Bar Kokhba, Rabbi Akiva openly supported
his rebellion and went so far as to proclaim him... the Messiah! At
first, the Romans imprisoned Akiva, as if they were unsure about
what to do with him. His students were allowed to visit him in prison,
so he continued to teach. Finally, the Romans decided to execute
him. The death they chose for him was no less painful than that of
his colleagues. They used iron rakes to comb off the skin from his
body. The pain was certainly excruciating, but once again Akiva
denied the Romans the satisfaction of winning. He used his own
death as a means of teaching his students that one must love God
with all one's strength. By his own example, he taught them that the
love of God extends to the point that one is willing to die for God,
if need be...."

Berurya glanced at Yehezkel. Even in the dim light, she could see how grim he looked. She wanted to touch his arm, but restrained herself.

Meir said: "Many others have been killed. Now they are looking for me."

"Why do they want to kill you?" asked Berurya.

"The Romans have realized fully that the greatest threat to their authority is not the sword ... but rather the spiritual resistance which emanates from the sages. The power of faith is ... a formidable weapon. At times, it has even defied the logic of the battlefield! The Romans have concluded that if they prohibit the ordination of rabbis, which denies the Jews new religious leaders, they need not fear another uprising. Their decree states: 'Anyone who ordains will be killed. Anyone who is ordained will likewise be killed. And the city in which that ordination takes place will be destroyed.' As you can imagine, this poses a grave dilemma. On the one hand, we know that we must defy the decree. But on the other, to do so means the death of hundreds, perhaps thousands of innocent men, women and children. Even if we chose a site in the countryside, the Romans would still destroy the nearest city.

"Rabbi Yehuda ben Bava found the solution. Even though I had already been ordained by Rabbi Akiva, he asked me and four others to meet him at a certain location between Usha and Shefar'am. Rabbi Yehuda had calculated that this location was the exact midpoint between the two cities. He also knew that the Romans would adhere strictly to their own laws. Therefore, since the ordinations were not inside either city's boundaries, the inhabitants would be spared.

"So there we were, the five of us, standing in a valley between two mountains. Someone had informed the Romans. More than three hundred soldiers arrived. It was after the ordination, and Rabbi Yehuda pleaded that we run for our lives. At first, we refused. 'At least, flee with us,' we begged. 'No,' he said, 'I will stand here, like an immovable rock. That will enrage them, and give you the opportunity to escape.' He was right. Slowly, the Romans approached on horseback. A signal was given and they dismounted. They formed concentric circles around Rabbi Yehuda, each soldier bearing a lance. On command, the lances were lowered, pointing at the rabbi like spokes of a wheel. The Romans closed in, but Rabbi Yehuda ben Bava did not move an inch. He kept his eyes focused on the commanding officer, who was still on his horse.

"The metal tips pierced ben Bava's body and blood spurted in all directions. Rabbi Yehuda dropped to his knees. A second circle of lances tore his body. Now, he pitched forward on his face. The officer ordered a third circle of lancers to mutilate the body.

"By then, we were safely away from the Romans. We split up, and went our separate ways. Since then, I've been moving from town to town to avoid the authorities. Some of the rabbis are in hiding here in Israel; personally, I believe it's better to leave the country until things return to normal."

Berurya stared at the speaker. "Rabbi Meir, where is the one place the Romans would never think to look for you?"

"I don't know," replied Meir. "Maybe in Alexandria or in some small town in Asia Minor."

"No," said Berurya firmly. "The one place the Romans would never think of looking for you is in Rome itself!"

The suggestion surprised Meir, but after some consideration he said: "You're probably right, Berurya. That would be the last place they'd expect to find me."

"Perhaps," Berurya went on, "you could accompany Bilha and me to Rome and help us free Penina." Meir reflected on her words and then said: "I suggest that you go home and get a good night's sleep."

"Does that mean you agree?" asked Berurya.

"Yes. We'll begin to make preparations tomorrow." Meir rose from his chair and turned to his host. "Yehezkel, dear friend, I am utterly worn out and must sleep now. Please excuse me."

Berurya was visibly elated. Yehezkel walked her to the door. "Berurya," he said soberly, "aren't you worried about your safety? Doesn't the thought of Rome frighten you?"

"No, Yehezkel," answered Berurya, "it's just the opposite. Every day that I'm here is another day that my sister must suffer. Like my father and the other rabbis, I do not fear the Romans. Maybe I once did, but no longer. Listening to how the Romans have devised such cruel tortures has only strengthened my resolve." She gestured. "Consider my father's death. What could be worse? What could be more painful? Yet he was not afraid. His last word was 'One'. His only fear, if you could call it that, was of 'the One', of God. There was no room left in him... to fear Man." She pressed her host's hand. "Good night, Yehezkel. Thank you for being my friend."

2

The Prostitutes of Rome

Yehezkel concluded all the arrangements swiftly. A week later, Rabbi Meir, Berurya, and Bilah left from the port of Acco and, after an uneventful journey, arrived at the port of Ostia, not far from Rome. There, they were met by a servant of Flavius Iulianus, the contact who might help them free Penina.

Flavius Iulianus was a member of one of the wealthier Jewish families of Rome. This family, however, was the exception. As he told newcomers, the economic condition of the Jews in Rome was bad; in fact, most of the Jews were impoverished. The Jewish quarter was located in Transtiberline, a region near the Tiber river. Much of Rome's Jewish population had been brought to the city as slaves after Pompey's capture of Jerusalem in 62 B.C.E., and again in 67 C.E., when the Temple was destroyed during the reign of Vespasian. Whenever they were able, the Jews already living in Rome would ransom the Jewish slaves who had most recently arrived. The Jews born in Rome no longer spoke Aramaic, the language of their brethern in Israel; their languages were those of the Diaspora: Latin and Greek.

Berurya knew that the ties between Yehezkel's family and the family of Flavius Iulianus went back several generations. Supposedly, they were related somehow, although no one remembered the exact genealogy. Flavius' father had been a widely respected physician who saw to it that his son married into the right Jewish family. According to the agreement between the two families, Flavius and Annia would marry when Annia became fourteen. Now, they had two daughters and a son, all of whom were married with families of their own.

What impressed Berurya when she was in Rome was the city's magnificent architecture, evident everywhere, from the delicate beauty of its gardens to the grandeur of its triumphal arches. Rome seemed to be the marble statues of heroes and emperors, the massive stone structures in which human beings sought exotic entertainment. Rome was striking even to those who had reason to hate her!

As the three travelers passed through the streets, Berurya noticed the great diversity of race, dress, and language. People from all over the world – Parthians, Cilicians, Germans, Cappadocians, Egyptians – mingled in Rome. It was amazing, Berurya thought, how people with such dissimilar features could all be descendents of Adam and Eve!

Flavius' servant led the three through streets along which itinerant vendors shouted out their wares, and merchants conducted business from their stalls. Berurya saw houses that were small and crowded together. She asked the servant and he told her that real estate was expensive and that it was more economical to build vertically. She noticed that the houses were irregular, both in height and in footage; overhanging, wooden balconies extended from many of them. Bilha pointed to two women exchanging a pot from balcony to balcony. The servant explained that, adding to the tumult, today was nundines. Once every nine days, the country folk came in from the surrounding areas to sell their produce, and to buy whatever they needed. They brought what they had to individual markets – cattle, pig, fish, vegetable, bread and fruit – located along the banks of the Tiber. Merchants sold their wares outside the baths, theaters, and the circus, since crowds frequented these public establishments.

At length, they arrived at Flavuis' home. The servant led Berurya, Bilha and Rabbi Meir through the vestibula, the graceful portico between the facade of the house and the front door, into the atrium. Flavius and Annia greeted them warmly. The four of them conversed in Greek. Since Bilha did not understand the language, she contented herself with looking around the magnificent room.

Flavius explained that the atrium was the main room in the Roman house: everything of importance took place there. Now, Berurya gazed around her. The double doors through which they had entered were plated with ivory; they were locked by a large, transverse, wooden bar. On the walls of the atrium hung several family portraits. The floors were quite different from those in Sikhnin: they were paved entirely with smooth blocks.

Berurya and Bilha followed after Annia. Exiting the atrium, they entered the cavaedium, a courtyard in the center of the house. Off the cavaedium were the storage rooms for wine and foods, as well as the servants' quarters. The bedrooms were smaller than the visitors might have expected. The beds, made of bronze, were so high off the floor that a stepping stool was needed to get into them. Veils were drawn over all the windows, mainly to block out the sun's rays. The last room they saw was the triclinium, or dining room. It was brightly painted. In the center was a low table, surrounded on three sides by couches. Annia said that people ate reclining on their sides and propping up their heads with their left arms. Then she led them back to the atrium, where Rabbi Meir and Flavius were still immersed in conversation.

At once, Flavius turned to Berurya. "I was just telling Rabbi Meir," he said, "that I've given the servants the day off. They'll all probably end up at the gladiatorial games. How anyone can watch people being slaughtered for sport is something I will never fathom!"

"Exactly what sort of games are they?" questioned Rabbi Meir.

"They vary," replied Flavius. "Sometimes the contest is only between two opponents. One is armed with a trident and a net, the other with a short scythe. Or the battle can be between several combatants. It is told that Trajan once arranged a spectacle involving several thousand prisoners of war.

"The Coliseum you passed on your way here was built by Vespasian, or, actually, I should say by Jews. It seats about 80,000 spectators. Jews were forced to build it, and to lose their lives in it."

Flavius sighed and went on: "The gladiatorial contests are announced by their sponsors before they are held. Posters are displayed everywhere, even in outlying areas; they list the names of the combatants. Famous gladiators draw huge crowds."

"Do all the games ... end in death?" Berurya asked quietly.

"Not necessarily," replied Flavius. "Sometimes the decision is left to the spectators. If they like the loser and feel he fought valiantly, they'll raise their hands with thumbs folded under the fingers. This is the sign for leniency. On the other hand, if they feel the man was cowardly, they'll stretch their thumbs out and point them at the gladiator, indicating that they want no mercy to be shown. Under the seats, there is a sort of cave called the spoliarium. Using hooks, slaves drag the bodies into the caves temporarily. I do not understand how people can enjoy such horror."

Flavius fell silent. His eyes narrowed and he said: "Berurya, Yehezkel informed me that your sister has been placed in a brothel here in Rome."

"Yes," Berurya said grimly.

Flavius moved across the room. "I have connections," he said, "and I know where she is. I have a plan to free her, but it is a dangerous one. Furthermore, no matter how much I personally want to help out I cannot be implicated in any way." He smiled sadly. "You see, I live in two worlds. On the one hand, I help my fellow Jews whenever possible; on the other, I'm also a Roman – and my loyalty to Rome must never be questioned! I can accomplish things only from behind the scenes."

"Flavius," Berurya broke in, "you needn't apologize! Just tell us what we must do."

Flavius folded his arms across his chest. "Penina is being held not far from the Circus Maximus," he said. "The only way to get her out is to bribe the lipo, the proprietor of the brothel. In turn, he must bribe the aedile, the government official who collects the taxes levied on prostitutes. You'll have to go twice. First, Rabbi Meir must go with a friend of mine and deliver the bribe. Then later tonight Meir and Berurya will go back for Penina." He unlocked a large chest, opened, and pointed: "Here are three sacks of gold coins. They should be more than sufficient."

"Will they suspect us of being Jews from abroad?" asked Berurya.

"Dressed as you are, probably. You must alter your appearance. You have to look as though you live in Rome. Rabbi Meir, I'm sorry, but you'll have to shave your beard and dress in one of my togas." He continued, "And tonight you'll put on a lacerna. It's a cloak that's fastened by a clasp at the shoulder. It has a hood."

Flavius turned to Berurya. "You'll have to pretend that you're a prostitute. Then you'll be able to enter and leave the brothel without inviting suspicion."

Berurya was taken aback. "Pretend I'm a prostitute!? But I know nothing about them! How they talk, dress, behave! Isn't there another way?"

"No," said Flavius.

"Don't worry," said Annia. "Here in Rome, prostitutes come from every level of society. While most are slaves, some have even been the wives of prominent Roman citizens, who managed to sneak away by night. You're very beautiful – don't be concerned. You'll carry off the deception without a problem. I'll see to it that you look like a prostitute. Men's imaginations will do the rest."

"Rabbi Meir," said Flavius, "you've got to hurry. My friend is coming soon. You have to be at the brothel before the late afternoon, when they open for business."

Flavius' friend arrived within the hour. Flavius handed the sacks of gold to Rabbi Meir. When the friend and Rabbi Meir left, Flavius went out of the room. The three women remained. At first, they sat patiently. Then Berurya began to pace back and forth.

"Are you worried about going to the brothel?" Bilha asked.

"I'm not worried for myself," Berurya answered, "but I am concerned about Rabbi Meir. The Romans may discover his identity, and execute him. I'd be responsible. It was my idea that he come to Rome."

"Don't worry," said Bilha. "Rabbi Meir can take care of himself."

"Perhaps ..." Berurya murmured.

Suddenly there was a knock at the door. Berurya froze. Flavius opened the door; Berurya could hear him talking. Moments later he entered with Rabbi Meir. Meir was smiling – it was one of the few times Berurya could recall him that way.

"Everything went off perfectly," said Rabbi Meir, seating himself. "In fact, it was easier than I expected. The man took the money and when I told him it was for Penina, he looked like he was relieved to be rid of her."

"Did you see her?" Berurya asked.

"No, I wasn't allowed to go inside. He just told me to return by myself tonight and take Penina away."

Annia cleared her throat. "Berurya," she said, "let's begin your transformation. With a change of your hair style, some make-up, and the right attire, you'll look as if you'd been born in Rome!"

The three women rose and left the room.

"Flavius," said Rabbi Meir, "I didn't want to worry Berurya, but something makes me not trust that lipo. Everything seemed ... well, a little too easy."

"You could be right," said Flavius. "That's why Berurya must be the one to actually find her sister. You distract the lipo for as long as you can. If anything goes wrong, there should be a back exit by which you can escape."

About an hour later, the women reentered the room. When his wife and Bilha came in, Flavius glanced in their direction but continued talking. When Berurya entered, Flavius stopped in mid-sentence, gaping at Berurya's stunning beauty. Annia had transformed Berurya into a Greek goddess: tall, slender, and sensuous. The toga emphasized the curves of her lithe, ripe body. Her hair now flowed freely down her back. Skillfully applied make-up accentuated the features of an already exquisite face.

Flavius nodded his approval. "If I was a young, single man," he said, "I'd ask you to marry me this minute, Berurya!" Looking at his wife, he winked. "But I'm already happily married! Right, Annia?"

Berurya stared at Rabbi Meir. "Not even one comment," she thought. "It is as if I'm not even in the room. I know I'm attractive. Why doesn't he say anything?"

Annoyed with Rabbi Meir's indifference, Berurya went over to speak with Bilha; Rabbi Meir's eyes followed her every movement. "She is beautiful, very beautiful," he thought.

"It is getting late," Flavius announced. "Time to go."

At the door, Flavius warned: "Remember, that you're going to a dangerous area – be careful!"

As they walked, Berurya said: "Rabbi Meir, I want you to know how grateful I am ... for all your help. If it weren't for you...."

"There is no need to thank me, Berurya. Whatever happens, you must know that it was my decision."

When they arrived at the brothel, Rabbi Meir turned to Berurya. "I'm going in first to distract the lipo. While I'm talking to him, you must find Penina and leave through the back door."

"What about you?"

"Don't worry about me," said Rabbi Meir. "I'll be all right. We'll meet at Flavius' place."

Rabbi Meir disappeared into the brothel. Berurya waited a little while, drew a deep breath, and walked into the brothel. "If I act as if I belong here," she thought, "then no one will suspect me. But how do I act as if I belong here?" Berurya walked into the first room and froze. On the walls around her were erotic paintings: pictures of naked men and women engaging in sexual intercourse in various positions. Suddenly, a hand siezed her elbow. Behind her, was an enormously fat man who reeked of perspiration and alcohol. The Roman opened his clenched left hand and displayed three copper coins in his palm. He muttered something in Latin. Instinctively, Berurya pulled away. She whirled around, glared directly into his eyes, and without uttering a word turned her back and headed towards an ornate curtain. She yanked it aside, stepped forward, and shut it behind her. Then she leaned her head against the wall and listened intently to hear if the Roman was following. All was quiet.

Berurya moved slowly down the corridor. As Flavius had described, the prostitute's name was above each door. Berurya did not understand Latin, but she knew the letters of the Latin alphabet. Silently, she pronounced the names: "Sabina ... Alexe ... Aurelia ..." She went on, "Flora ... Valeria ... Eugenia ... Panina ..." Berurya halted. Panina?! That had to be Penina!

She called out in Aramaic: "Penina, it's Berurya, your sister! Open the door. Quickly –"

There was no answer. "Penina," she repeated, "it's your sister, Berurya. Open up!" Berurya held her breath. Maybe she was wrong. Maybe it was someone else, whose name was similiar to Penina's. But as she was about to move on, the door opened a crack.

"Penina? Is that you? Open up! Hurry!"

The door swung open. It really was Penina! Berurya grasped Penina's shoulders and embraced her fiercely. But Penina did not respond. Berurya pulled back. "Penina, don't you recognize me?"

Wearing only a plain cloth garment which fell to her knees, the frail girl stood there, silent and blank-faced. "Penina, it's me ... Berurya! Don't you remember me? Don't you remember Father and Mother!? I'm here to take you back home to Sikhnin! Please – say something!"

Penina stood motionless. Only a single small tear glistened in an eye. Yet Berurya felt that the one tear, the one drop of water, was sufficient to drown out the noise of the mightiest river. At once,

Berurya removed her cloak and wrapped it around Penina. Walking with an arm around the petrified girl and guiding her, she whispered: "Don't worry. Everything will be fine. I've come to take you home."

At the far end of the corridor, there was a door. Berurya raised the cloak's hood and covered Penina's face. Behind them, she heard men's voices. Were they talking to her? Were they following? She kept moving with Penina. "Please God protect us," Berurya said silently. She kept repeating the words until she and Penina were out the door and a good distance away from the brothel.

Rabbi Meir waited for the lipo to return. He had informed the rabbi that he had to take care of something and would return momentarily; then he would take Rabbi Meir directly to Penina. Cautiously, Rabbi Meir stepped over to the window. He drew the curtain back a little. A few yards away, the lipo was talking to several Roman soldiers. They turned and made for the brothel. The rabbi knew that he had been betrayed! The lipo gestured. Two of the soldiers ran toward the rear of the building. Rabbi Meir felt trapped! How could he escape? He realized that he could not stay where he was. Instantly, he ran back into the corridor. There were steps leading up to the second floor. He could either climb the stairs or try the back exit. No, the soldiers would already be at the exit. His only chance was to hide. Meir dashed up the steps and walked down the corridor. The soldiers would not be far behind. Where to hide? On each door, was the word "occupata". He raced down the corridor. Only one room was unoccupied. Perhaps it was empty and he could hide in it? He flung the door open. A prostitute was sitting on the bed: his sudden entrance startled her, and she jumped up. Rabbi Meir motioned for her to be still. In the corridor, he could hear the soldiers banging on the doors. There was no time. He only had one of Flavius' coins left. He tossed it at the girl. Her eyes opened wide when she saw it: apparently it was far more than she had expected! She smiled, and began to undress. Quickly, the rabbi unlaced the straps of his sandals and extinguished the lamp. He dropped his clothing to the floor, and got into bed with the prostitute, turning himself so that his back would face the door.

The prostitute put a hand on the nape of Meir's neck and began curling his hair with a finger. She drew closer, and kissed him. At that instant, the door swung open. A Roman soldier stood in the doorway with drawn sword. Enraged by the intrusion, the prostitute sat up and began screaming at the soldier. The soldier mumbled a word or two, and closed the door.

Rabbi Meir sat up in the darkness and set his feet on the floor. The prostitute pressed her warm body against his back. Rabbi Meir grasped her wrists, and gently pulled them away. He rose and picked up his clothes. When he had finished dressing, he sat down on the floor. His back was against the wall, and his knees were pressed to his chest. Now he could only wait. The prostitute was dumbfounded. She lay quietly in bed, watching him and clutching tightly the coin he had given her.

Rabbi Meir did not move for what seemed an endless time. Finally, in the early hours of the morning, he got up. The prostitute was fast asleep. He got safely out of the brothel, and slipped into the night. As he walked, Rabbi Meir spotted a sketch posted on a wall. He could not believe it! Before his eyes, was an etching of his face. The Roman authorities had posted a reward for his capture!

But what if the Romans had connected him to Flavius? He felt that he could not return to Flavius' house now. He would have to flee Rome. He sighed. Flavius' house was but a short distance away. So near and yet so far! Rabbi Meir turned and headed in the opposite direction.

Berurya had remained awake and waited the entire night. But Rabbi Meir did not appear. Flavius entered the atrium. "There is nothing you can do now, Berurya," he said. "If you value your own life and that of your sister's, you must leave Rome immediately! My servant will take you to the port, and you can board a boat bound for Israel. If Meir has managed to escape, he won't be able to return to Israel as long as Emperor Hadrian lives. I'm sure that Meir has friends who will help him."

Berurya thanked Flavius and Annia warmly for their help. At the door, Berurya paused and said "Shalom!" That was the one Hebrew word she knew Flavius and Annia would understand. "Shalom!" they answered.

3
Return to Sikhnin

Berurya knew that the political situation in Israel had gone steadily from bad to worse. Tinneus Rufus, the Roman governor, was determined that the Jewish people would never again pose a threat to Rome. Initially, Roman law condemned certain rabbis to martyrdom. But now it was a crime for anyone to practice Judaism. This new period, called Sh'mad, or destruction, bound the Jewish people like a sacrificial lamb on the Roman altar. Jews were forbidden to observe the Sabbath, to eat unleavened bread on Passover, during the holiday of Tabernacles they could neither dwell in booths, nor shake the Lulav as traditionally prescribed. Jews were forbidden to light candles on Chanukah or to read from the Scroll of Ester on Purim. Laws had been passed forbidding ritual immersion for women after menstruation, the donning of Tephilin (phylacteries), the affixing of the Mezuza to the doorpost of the house, the observance of the laws of tithing. The Romans even regarded the Jewish rituals prescribed for mourning and divorce as criminal behavior. Rabbis could not be ordained. The prayer Sh'ma, proclaiming the oneness of God, was proscribed. The study of Torah was illegal. The age-old performance of Jewish rites and ceremonies now had become transgressions punishable by death.

Since returning from Rome, Berurya and Bilha cared for Penina as best as they could. They did not inquire about the ordeal, nor did they discuss anything which might evoke painful memories. Perhaps, when the time was right, Penina, would on her own initiate a discussion. For now, she remained silent. She rarely spoke, and spent most of her days in her room clutching the doil she had played with as a child.

Berurya often reviewed her life as a woman. She always felt strengthened because Jewish law defined and regulated almost every aspect of life. For example, as she well knew, the *mitzvah* of procreation required a minimum of two children, although there was disagreement among the sages as to whether one's obligation is fulfilled by having a son and a daughter or two sons. Berurya had been firstborn. A year later, Elhanan had been born. There would have been another child born after Elhanan, but their mother had suffered a miscarriage early in the pregnancy. For whatever reason, the last pregnancy had been the most difficult. Penina had been born five years after Berurya.

Being a daughter, as well as the youngest child, Penina's relationship with her mother was closer than those of her siblings. After Elhanan's death, Penina's mother became overly protective of her youngest. What she had once allowed Berurya to do as a child, she no longer permitted for Penina. She often said: "I've mourned a son, and it is more than I can bear. I cannot mourn again." Murdered suddenly without warning, she had never known about the death of her husband, nor suffered the pain of Penina's abduction. Ironically, her words came true: she never mourned again.

Berurya and Bilha were part of the life in Sikhnin which was, for most of its inhabitants, mainly a matter of routine. At dawn, people rose from their beds, and the men set out directly for work. Whether in the fields or in a shop, each day began with the recitation of the Sh'ma *and the* Shemoneh Esreh.

People customarily ate two meals a day on weekdays, and an additional meal on the Sabbath. Daytime was divided into four parts: the first meal was eaten in the first quarter, although some finished this meal as late as the end of the second quarter. The second, and final meal, was eaten at dusk, either at the conclusion of work or upon arriving home. There wasn't much to do at night; after a long and arduous day, most people welcomed sleep.

Bilha enjoyed the market place. In the Garden of Eden, Eve had learned that food and knowledge were often inextricably bound together; now, the market place provided Eve's descendents with both staples of life. Everyone talked. Some stories were like cheap dried figs. They passed quickly from mouth to mouth, without much attention being given to what was said. Other tales, like the more expensive fruits, were picked with care. Like the seeds in fruit, these dear stories contained points of information about family and friends. A third category of story was most dear, like the meat that was purchased no more than three or four times a year for special occasions; they were accounts that affected the life of the entire people. In these, there was no need for embellishment. After the information was digested, there remained the discussion as to what had to be done.

One morning, Berurya braided her hair and pinned it to the crown of her head. She put on the head-covering and told Penina that she was going with Bilha to the market. She promised to return shortly.

When they reached the market, Berurya and Bilha made their way through the crowd to the carts of vegetables. Berurya examined a few cucumbers, but she was really listening to the conversations of the women nearby. Some complained about the exorbitant taxes the Romans had levied; others retold stories of violence they had heard from friends and relatives in nearby villages. One woman said: "My cousin told me that several Jews in Beit Shean were crucified for eating Matzah on Passover; others were executed for defying the order not to circumcise their sons." "May Hadrian's name be wiped out and his memory obliterated!" a woman responded bitterly. "I myself heard that two Jews were publicly executed in Caesarea last week for wearing phylacteries."

"What's so unusual about that?" a woman interjected. "Jews are executed everyday for observing the commandments of the Torah!"

"I didn't say the punishment itself was unusual," the first woman responded. "It was the way that the Romans carried it out! They sharpened reeds, and inserted them under the nails of the victim's fingers and toes! The next victim's fate was even worse. They stripped him to the waist. They shoved iron balls in the fire, and when they were white-hot, inserted them under his arm pits. And then they lowered his arms!"

Berurya had heard enough. She found Bilha and pulled her out of the crowd. "Let's get out of here!" she said.

"But I haven't finished shopping," Bilha complained.

"Forget it," Berurya insisted. "You'll come back another time."

Berurya had often been revolted by the cruelty of the Romans; this execution had reminded her of her own father's death.

On the way home, Berurya thought about Rabbi Meir. She had heard nothing of his whereabouts, but somehow she felt he was safe. This was not the first time he had been away from Israel. Rabbi Meir was renowned, and would be cared for by Jews in Diaspora communities. But what if he'd been caught? What if she never saw him again?

At one point, Berurya handed Bilha her basket and told her to go on alone. "I'll be at the *Beit Midrash* if I'm needed," she said.

"But Berurya, you know what they're doing to people who are caught teaching Torah! They won't show any leniency because you're a woman!"

Berurya shook her head. "I won't be intimidated, Bilha. Nor will I live in fear. If it's the will of Heaven that I die for Torah, so be it! There are things in life over which we have little control; there are also more things in life over which we willingly surrender control. Self-imprisonment is worse than Roman incarceration. Living life as they decree is a punishment not only for us, but for generations yet to be born as well. I'll be a slave to no man; I'll be a servant to God alone, and so I'll always be free! Go home, Bilha. I've been away from the *Beit Midrash* for too long. It is time for me to take up where my father left off."

Bilha did not argue. Long ago, she had learned that Berurya had a will of iron. Once she was determined to do something, there was nothing in this world that could dissuade her.

Quietly, Berurya entered the *Beit Midrash* and sat down unnoticed on the bench in the rear. Only a few old men had gathered in the room. Berurya listened as they mourned over the suffering of the last years.

An old man stood up and exclaimed passionately: "When I was a young child, we lived in Jerusalem. I can remember the day the Romans broke through the walls of the city and set everything ablaze! Titus strutted into the Holy of Holies with whores and desecrated God's House! Then orders were given to raze the Temple to the ground. All of us wept. The entire nation mourned.

"I saw all of this as a small child. A few years ago I thought there was at last a glimmer of hope. Hadrian promised that we could rebuild the Temple. But the hope was short-lived. Instead of a Temple to the Lord, Hadrian erected a pagan house of worship, a hideous abomination to the Jews! And he decreed that circumcision was forbidden. Circumcision, the first commandment that God gave to the Patriarch, Abraham! How could Jews fail to obey the word of God? We had no other choice ... but to rebel! And we fought with courage! So many of us fell. So very many – young and old, men and women. They died sanctifying the name of God.

"Now, I am old. I will never set foot again on the soil of Jerusalem. All through my life I have witnessed endless suffering and misery and I keep asking myself one question: 'Why do the wicked prosper, while the righteous are trampled under foot? Why?'"

The old man's words moved the others. Everyone nodded, as if to say, "You are right! There is no justice in the world!"

Berurya could no longer restrain herself. She got up, strode to the front of the room, and slammed the palm of her hand on the table. All eyes turned to her. Her cheeks flushed with anger. "How dare you!" she cried out. "How dare you presume to understand the ways of God! How dare you question God's justice! What is the span of a mere seventy or eighty years as against the over-arching plan of God? Must I remind you that our destiny has already been recorded? Did not the Patriarch, Isaac, proclaim: 'The voice is the voice of Jacob, but the hands are the hands of Esau.' What do those words mean? 'The voice is the voice of Jacob, but the hands are the hands of Esau'. They mean, my friends, that Jacob, the father of our people, survives through the voice of prayer. They mean that Rome, Esau's descendents, must live by the weapons of war. Which way is stronger? Which will prevail?"

Berurya paused for a moment, and then went on: "The Torah tells us that when Esau learned how his brother, Jacob, had stolen his blessing, he swore revenge. Consequently, Jacob was forced to leave home and spend the next twenty years being cheated and deceived by his uncle, Laban. When at last he came back home with his wives and children, he learned that his brother was approaching with four hundred men. Esau was now in a position to make good his threat!

"Jacob responded in three ways. First, he sent presents to Esau, hoping to assuage his anger. Second, he divided his camp in half. This was a strategic response: if one camp was attacked, the other might escape. Finally, Jacob prayed. And the voice of Jacob was the strongest defense of all."

Berurya gestured, "That night Jacob was alone. Suddenly, unexpectedly, an angel of God descended and wrestled with him until the first light of morning. During the struggle, the angel struck Jacob in the hollow of his thigh, causing him to be lame. But Jacob refused to let go until he had received a blessing! And Jacob was blessed! His name was changed. No longer would he be called 'Jacob' but rather 'Israel'.

"And that is our name: 'Israel'. Its meaning is that we have striven with God, and with men, and have prevailed. Yes, we have been struck in the hollow of our thigh! How many thousands have fallen in battle! Yes, we have been wounded; but in the end, we will survive! We are Israel, the voice of Jacob! No matter how powerful the enemy, no matter how numerous their forces, no matter how sharp their swords, we will prevail. And when the morning light once again shines on Jacob, on Israel, we will be blessed."

The room was silent. All knew that Berurya, the daughter of Rabbi Hananiah ben Teradyon, had spoken!

4
The Dream

At dinner that evening, Penina was absolutely silent. Nevertheless, Berurya and Bilha spoke about the events of the day as if nothing were wrong. Berurya felt they should behave normally, no matter what. When dinner ended, Penina rose and went to her room. Most evenings, she remained in her bedroom until the next morning.

When Bilha finished clearing the table, she said: "Berurya, I'm worried about Penina. Will she always be so?"

"I don't know. She must have experienced such horror that she can't bear to think about it. I remember that when we were younger, and something troubled her she would come in and throw her arms around me. She'd cry, and I'd tell her that everything would be all right. I wish it were that way now."

"You should go to sleep, Berurya. I'll take care of everything."

"Thank you. The truth is that I'm exhausted."

Berurya walked slowly up the stairs. In front of Penina's door, she paused. There was no sound. Penina was probably asleep.

In bed, Berurya thought about the next day. First, would come Torah. Every morning was devoted to study. That was always the most important thing of the day. Fortunately, she had the inheritance left by her father: money was not a concern to keep her tossing at night. In the morning, there would be the problem with Penina again.

Berurya might be forced to take care of the girl for the rest of her life!

Then Berurya's thoughts turned to the *Beit Midrash*. For weeks now, she had been wrestling with a dilemma. Since his death, her father's students had been without a teacher. If Berurya had been a man, she would have continued in his place without question. But she was not a man: many people, women as well as men, would object vigorously. Ironically, it would not be a matter of her sincerity, piety, or knowledge! Instead people would say that it wasn't fitting for a woman to do what was traditionally the task of a man.

"Foolishness," she thought. "I will teach, at least for the present. If I run into opposition, it'll come from the ignorant and not the learned. That's how life usually goes; the emptier the jar, the louder the noise."

Suddenly, there was a blood-curdling scream from Penina's room. Berurya sprang out of bed and ran to her sister. Penina, her body shaking, was sitting up in bed. Berurya sat next to her, and put her arms around her. Penina was soaked with sweat. She whimpered like a wounded animal and rocked back and forth. Then she began to sob wildly. Bilha appeared in the doorway. "What can I do?" she murmured.

Berurya shook her head. Gently, Berurya stroked her sister's forehead. "Don't worry, Penina, it will all be fine." At length Penina calmed down. "Berurya," she said hoarsely, "I ... had ... a horrible nightmare! I was stretched out on the floor, with my wrists chained to the bed. My room was totally dark. Suddenly, the door burst open! I saw the silhouette of a Roman soldier. He entered, drew his sword, and hurled it into the corner of the room. The sword had stuck in the chair and blood gushed out! I realized that the chair was mother's. The soldier hurled his lance at me. It stuck in the floor, between my legs. I tried to scream, but couldn't. I discovered ... that I no longer had a mouth!

"Then, I found myself in an open field covered with flowers. Everything was peaceful... and beautiful. I felt as if I were a little girl again. Suddenly, I ran. Someone was chasing me. I glimpsed the man's face, but the features were blurred. I sensed that he was closer. I looked back and tripped. I rolled over and sprawled in the grass on my back. I couldn't move. The man stood over me. He wore a mask. Suddenly he tore off the mask. It was my father! I was overcome with joy! 'Father, father...' I screamed.

"But now the man pulled off a second mask. It was Elhanan! I called his name, and lifted my hand. He grasped it to pull me up. But then he tore off yet another mask! I stared directly at the Roman who raped me in my room. He laughed. His laughter became deafening. That's when I woke up."

Penina continued to speak. Her words rushed out like a torrent of water through a wadi; she did not seem able to speak quickly enough. In detail, she described all that had happened to her from the time the Romans took her to the point of her rescue. Berurya did not interrupt.

At last, Penina finished. She was silent for a time and then questioned Berurya about the dream. "What does it mean?" she asked softly.

Berurya reflected. She cleared her throat. "The blood spurting from mother's chair is related to mother's death. It was a monstrous thing for you to have seen. The room in the dream is... the brothel, to which you were 'chained'. The soldier's spear had to do with being raped."

Berurya gestured. "In the second part you were back in a nicer period of time when you were a little child with father and Elhanan. They were the two men whom you loved dearly. The Roman was a totally different sort of man. His laughter degraded you.

"Penina, I believe that in time you will meet a man like father and Elhanan, someone who'll be kind, gentle and understanding. You are a fragile flower whose petals have been crushed. But some day, you will blossom again."

"Thanks, Berurya. I want you to know that ... I feel safe when you're around."

"I'll always be here for you, Penina."

Suddenly, Penina lay back and closed her eyes. Berurya leaned over and kissed her forehead. "Good night, little sister. Sleep in peace."

5

Betrothal

The seasons succeeded each other in the town of Sikhnin. It was 138 in the Common Era. Three years had elapsed since Hadrian began his campaign of persecution. Many went to their deaths for their faith; many more lived for that faith. For most people, life went on routinely. Given time, people get used to almost anything. Routine provides its own sort of comfort ...

Penina's nightmares were now behind her. After several months, she could sleep calmly through the night. Nevertheless, Berurya maintained her watchfulness.

At dawn, Berurya rose promptly and immersed herself in study. She often sat to the night, oblivious of time, until the light of the lamp flickered out into darkness. Her utter devotion reflected the words of the Psalmist: "...in His law doth he meditate day and night."

One morning, as she was concluding her prayers, there was a knock at the door. It was unusual for anyone to call at this hour. When she opened the door, the strong sunlight made her squint. She could barely make out the figure of a tall man. She shaded her eyes.

"Shalom!" said the man. The voice was unmistakable.

"Meir!" Berurya exclaimed. "Meir!" she repeated. It was the first time she had ever said his name without using the title "Rabbi".

"Aren't you going to invite me in, Berurya?"

Berurya composed herself. "Rabbi Meir, please come in." Her words were now measured, but her heart pounded. How often had she thought of Meir, wondering if he were still alive! And now he was back – he had really returned!

"Rabbi Meir, isn't it dangerous for you to be in Israel? If they recognize you ..."

"Obviously, you haven't heard the news –"

"What news? We've heard nothing."

"Hadrian is dead!" Meir said. He waited for the full impact of his words to sink in. "Hadrian is dead," he repeated. "A new Emperor sits on the throne in Rome: Antoninus Pius. Hadrian's decrees haven't been rescinded yet, but there's a real chance that things will get better." He smiled and waved a hand. "The *mitzvah* of circumcision is no longer a crime! Many of the rabbis who went into hiding are already returning."

Penina came in. "Rabbi Meir!" she exclaimed. "How wonderful to see you!"

"It's good to see you too, Penina! You're looking well, thank God!"

"Things have been better for the last few months. But tell us about yourself! Where were you? How did you live? How did you get out of Rome?"

"Penina, one question at a time, please." He paused and then continued: "This wasn't the first time I was abroad. As a matter of fact, many years ago, before the Bar Kokhba war, I traveled with Rabbi Akiva throughout the Diaspora. This time, I sought out some of the communities I'd met then. They were as hospitable now as they had been before. I supported myself by working as a scribe – a scribe is never at a loss for work! There's always something that must be set down, from copying a Torah to composing *Ketubot* for couples who want to marry. Some day, maybe, I'll write your *Ketuba*, Penina."

Penina blushed deeply. She stared at the visitor. "Rabbi Meir," she said, "while you were gone, did you ... miss anybody in particular?"

"Penina!" said Berurya sternly. "How dare you ask such an impertinent question!"

"That's all right," smiled Meir. "In fact, I was very homesick. Sometimes, I felt like the generation which was exiled after the destruction of the first Temple, about whom it is written: 'By the rivers of Babylon, there we sat down, and we wept, when we remembered Zion....'"

"But Rabbi Meir," persisted Penina, "you know what I mean! Did you miss some ... person?"

"Enough, Penina!" admonished Berurya. She turned to the visitor. "Rabbi Meir," she said, "please excuse me – are you hungry? Let me offer you something."

"No, thank you. I've come to Sikhnin only long enough to see a few friends, and now I must go to Usha."

Though she tried not to show it, Berurya was disappointed.

"Before I leave, Berurya," said Meir, "I'd like you to take me to the *Beit Midrash* where your father taught."

"By all means," said Berurya. "I was just about ready to go there and study. Give me a minute to get my wrap and scarf."

When Berurya left the room, Penina said quietly, "Rabbi Meir, you can tell me. Don't you think my sister is wonderful? She would make a perfect wife! Whom else do you know who is so beautiful and so intelligent?" She continued, "She is understanding. And she's a good listener. I guarantee that you'd never be bored with her! Let me think ... what else. Well she's generous ... and kind ... and loving. She is witty; she can even be hilarious. I remember that when we were children, in the evenings when the family had gathered for dinner, Berurya would mimic many of the pompous men and women in Sikhnin. She'd give each one a nickname that was not very flattering. Father would laugh until his sides ached. Now, if you get right down to it, how many women are there in the world who are brilliant, beautiful, modest, kind, loving, understanding, respectful, knowledgeable, funny ... all in one? And not only that, but ..."

Penina stopped to catch her breath. Berurya entered.

"What are you so happy about, Penina?" she asked.

"Nothing," answered Penina: "Nothing at all."

"I'll be back from the *Beit Midrash* soon," Berurya said.

"Take your time."

The early morning air was still brisk, but the sun was warm on the skin. "Is it true that as a child you mimicked people?" Meir asked.

"So my little sister has been telling tales, eh? What else did she have to say?"

"Somehow," said Meir, "I think that she'd like us to get married."

"She actually said that!"

"No," observed Rabbi Meir, "I said that."

Berurya did not respond, and the two of them walked on in silence. Then Rabbi Meir said: "As I told you, I've got to go to Usha today. Several rabbis will be there to discuss important points of Jewish law. The economic situation alone warrants that we enact some new measures. Beyond such enactments, the meeting will probably set the stage for the return of the Sanhedrin. If rabbinic leadership is to be effective in the future, then Usha is the key."

Suddenly, Meir halted, and turned to Berurya. He recalled meeting her first as a young child in her father's house. Even then, she was witty, intelligent – sometimes impertinent – but always intriguing. In Yehezkel's house, he had been impressed by her courage and determination. In Flavius' home, dressed in a toga, she had been ravishing. He forced himself to look away. But Berurya confronted him. Her warm, brown eyes shone brightly.

"Berurya," he said in a whisper. "Will you ... be my wife?"

Berurya had often imagined how it would be to hear Rabbi Meir ask her to marry him. Now, the actual question took her by surprise. She failed to speak.

"If your father were alive, I'd have spoken to him first and asked his permission. I'd have told him how much I respected and admired his daughter: her courage, intellect, tenacity, wisdom ..." He sighed. "Berurya, if you say 'yes' we can be betrothed this very day, before I leave for Usha."

Rabbi Meir fell silent. He felt uneasy, uncertain. Had he talked too much? Was this the wrong time? Had he – "

Berurya smiled. "Do you know a good scribe?"

Rabbi Meir laughed. "Know a good scribe? Yes! But you'd probably do better with me – I'm much less expensive!"

Berurya reached for Meir's hand; pressing each other's fingers, they stood where they were on the path. "Do you still want to go the *Beit Midrash?*" asked Berurya.

"No. I think my mind's too preoccupied."

Meir accompanied Berurya back to her house. "There are a few matters," he said, "that I've got to attend to immediately. But I'll return as soon as possible, and this afternoon we'll be betrothed." Meir stood for a few moments and gazed at Berurya. It wasn't proper for him to kiss her before their wedding. But the way Meir held her hand in the palm of his, caressing the back gently with his thumb, expressed his tenderness and affection.

"Meir," Berurya said to herself. "Rabbi Meir and his wife, Berurya! That sounds as if it were meant to be."

Berurya entered the house; Meir departed. Once inside, Berurya leaned her head against the door. Penina came in to the room. "I'll bet that he asked you to marry him, didn't he!?"

"No," retorted Berurya. "He wants to marry you!"

"You're joking! He did ask you to marry him. I knew he would! I just knew it." Penina could no longer restrain herself. She lunged forward and embraced Berurya with such force that, had her sister not been leaning against the door, she would have fallen to the floor. The two began spinning around in a dizzy circle. "I think I'm happier than you are!" Penina cried out.

Berurya shook her head. "I don't think that's possible!"

The door opened. It was Bilha, returning from market. "I bought some fruit and vegetables," she grumbled. "With prices so high, it's amazing that we can afford anything at all."

Before Bilha could put the food on the table, Penina grabbed her and whirled her around.

"Stop that! Stop it at once! Fruit is expensive enough, without you crushing it! What's gotten into you? You're acting like a silly child!"

"I am afraid it's all my fault," said Berurya. "Rabbi Meir was here. He... asked me to marry him."

"He asked you to be his wife?!" Bilha shrieked, dropping the food to the floor.

"Bilha, the food!"

"Forget the food! Tell me everything that happened – and don't leave out a single detail!"

People perceive time as passing slowly or quickly. Neither is true. The day is divided into segments called hours, based on the sun's position in the sky. According to the lunar calendar, the month is divided into days, in accordance with the shape of the moon. The stars, as the ancients declared, follow their own courses in the heavens, but like all else in heaven, they too return to the point at which they began. The whole of nature appears to be on a recurring journey; there is neither beginning nor end – only unending repetition.

Berurya often reflected that the Jew lived in different dimensions of time. Six days a week, he measured time like everyone else. Six days a week he worked, he created, he built in the present moment. But his thoughts, his expectations were focused on the Sabbath, the day of rest. When the Sabbath finally arrived, his attitude towards time changed. No longer was time perceived as though it was composed of grains of sand slipping through an hourglass; on the Sabbath, he viewed it as a gift from God, not to be squandered. The Sabbath was not the absence of activity, but rather the presence of the holy. If the weekdays were filled with people's dreams of what they might achieve, then the Sabbath was God's dream of what people might be. In the sight of God, a thousand years are but as yesterday when they have passed. In the sight of Man, a thousand hopes are pinned on tomorrow, which may never come. Time passes neither slowly nor quickly. For some, the tragedy was not that too few grains of sand were allotted them in life, but rather that they themselves, like the sand, slipped emptily through the hourglass of time.

6

Passages of Time

Weeks turned into months. Each day, Berurya immersed herself in the study of Torah. The intricacies of *Halacha*, Jewish law, had to be repeated over and over, until at last they were imprinted on the pages of the mind and could be retrieved as easily as from the pages of a book.

And Berurya studied Midrash, or hermeneutics, the intellectual key which unlocked the doors of Scripture. The word of God as revealed in the Torah had various levels of understanding; it could be read for its simple meaning, or the words – or even the letters themselves – could be poured over to unearth the deeper, esoteric meanings. Berurya probed for the greatest depth!

One day, as Berurya returned from the *Beit Midrash*, Penina came running towards her sister.

"What is it Penina?"

Penina had trouble catching her breath. "A letter for you," she said.

Berurya read it quickly.

"It's from Meir."

"What does it say?"

"It's dated the first of Kislev," said Berurya. And she read it aloud:

My Dear Berurya,

For the months that I've been here in Usha, I've thought about you on countless occasions. I've wanted to tell you that what we are doing here is of great significance ... to say nothing about the importance of what is happening here and the impact it will have on Jewish life. When I'm not with my colleagues, I'm busy with the difficult and arduous task of compiling the *Mishna*. There is an ocean of oral traditions, handed down to Moses at Mt. Sinai, which must be systematized and arranged in some logical fashion. My teacher, Rabbi Akiva, is the one who began this monumental task and I feel that I must make my small contribution, as well.

In my discussions with the other rabbis, I perceive that I've gained their respect and admiration. All my years of study with different teachers, have permitted me to resolve even the most difficult of problems. They even quip that the etymology of the name, 'Meir,' means appropriately 'to shine or to brighten,' since I shed light and understanding on the words of Torah. I'd like to also mention that the rabbis here have expressed their joy regarding our forthcoming wedding, and many of them plan to attend the ceremony. I thank God for all the good things with which I've been blessed!

In a little over three weeks, we will be celebrating Chanukah, the festival of lights. At that time, I will be standing next to you under the *Huppah*. Not only will the lights of Chanukah blaze as we stand under the bridal canopy, but the light of our life together will shine like a canopy of stars ... Meir.

Berurya folded the letter and put it away.

"Well," said Penina, "we don't have a lot of time, do we? There is so much to prepare for the wedding. The food! Who will be invited? What will I wear?"

"Penina, relax! There's plenty of time. The first thing to do is to buy cloth for our dresses. Your job will be to help Bilha plan the meal."

As the days moved steadily on, Berurya thought much about the underpinnings of a Jewish marriage. According to Jewish law a woman could be licitly acquired as a wife by means of kesef *(something of value),* sh'tar *(writ) or* be'ah *(cohabitation), although the last was highly frowned upon. The object of value might even be a cup of wine or perhaps even a coin. The marriage document, the* Ketubah, *included: the basic dowry (200 zuzim or 100 zuzim, depending on whether the bride had previously been married); an additional sum the groom added to this dowry; a documentation of the wife's possessions; and the groom's pledge to honor, nourish, and provide for his wife. The entire process, beginning with the betrothal (referred to either as* Erusin *or* Kiddushin) *and culminating in the marriage ceremony* (Nissu'in), *could take up to twelve months. During this period, the betrothed woman did not cohabit with her husband, and remained with her parents. Later on,* Erusin *and* Nissu'in *were combined into one ceremony. The* Ketubah *itself was most often written on betrothal; however, marriage was effected only when the groom brought the bride into his house or into the marriage chamber (*Huppah). *While the formulation of the* Ketubah *had changed over time, the relationship between bride and groom remained similar to that described by the Prophet Malachi: "... she is your companion and the wife of your covenant."*

7

The Wedding Night

The sun had set. Torches, set high upon poles, lined the four sides of the main square in Sikhnin. As the guests began arriving, there was a sense of high excitement. Many of those attending had known Berurya from the time when she was a little girl and had fond memories of her father and mother. Meir's guests were distinguished rabbis and scholars. These colleagues came from all over – Rabbi Yehuda, Rabbi Nehemia, Rabbi Yosi, Rabbi Shimeon bar Yohai, Rabbi Eleazer the son of Rabbi Yosi HaGalilee, Rabbi Eleazer ben Ya'akov, and many others.

It was an extraordinary wedding. In the clear night sky, the stars seemed to burn with added brightness, as if they too shared the happiness of the marriage between Berurya and Meir!

In the center of the square, the *Huppah* was erected. Rows of tables formed a large square. Following the ceremony, the people would dine on delicious food, the likes of which they only enjoyed on holidays. At least two oil-burning lanterns sat on each table. The smell of freshly baked bread, as well as the aroma of lamb which had been seething in a vegetable broth for many hours, permeated the air.

The guests wore their finest clothes. In keeping with the accepted code of modesty, women kept their hair concealed under attractive kerchiefs and colorful headcoverings. Before the ceremony, the only musical instrument played was a single *Chalil*. Berurya had chosen the flute because it could range from the joy of a wedding to the sorrow of a funeral. After the ceremony, there would be flowing wine, dancing and singing. Several instruments would lend to the gaiety. But perhaps the real reason for the initial solo flute was Berurya's sorrow that her father and mother would not be there to share her joy. Had they been alive, her mother surely would have wept. Berurya could picture it in her imagination. The tears on her mother's cheeks, tears of joy for her daughter's happiness. And her father... how proud he would have been!

How many times had Berurya dreamt that her parents were not really dead. Sometimes she felt that life itself was a dream, and that the images of night which appeared with such clarity and seemed so real were in fact the only things that were real. Who could say that this life was no more than a corridor or vestibule, through which we pass on a journey to another life far different from anything we imagine? Perhaps, when we sleep, the door separating the two worlds opens ever so slightly, and those on the other side call out to us in dreams? If the spirit of man is a candle of God, perhaps the stars that fire the heavens are souls that have returned home? The brightest star, Berurya liked to imagine, was her father, now looking down from heaven as his daughter was being married.

Rabbi Meir was clad handsomely. He wore a pure white robe. Over it, he wore an *'avnet*, a type of belt, which crossed his chest. The *'avnet* was adorned with gold and bedecked with pearls.

According to custom, scholars and rabbis wore a talit over their garments. The talit of the sages – such as the one Meir put on – was a long cloak which extended down to the ankles, with fringes attached to each of the four corners. The basis for the fringes, or tsitsit, was found in the commandment in Numbers, Chapter 15, to put fringes on the corners of the garments. People other than scholars and rabbis also wore the talit; although the ones they wore were not as long as those of the rabbis.

Rabbi Meir stood erect under the *Huppah*; his tall figure was
impressive. Penina and Bilha helped Berurya, who wore a long white
dress whose edges were embroidered delicately with gold thread. On
her feet were soft, leather shoes, or impilia. Under her bust, she had
on a leather belt; it was blue and decorated with semi-precious stones.
About her neck was a catella, a chain of designed metal links strung
on a linen thread. She had her hair up; an ornate pin held it in place.
Her face was hidden by a veil. Both Penina and Bilha were all but
overwhelmed by her beauty.

Soon the entire square was filled. Yehezkel and his wife Miriam
tried to get close to the bridal couple, but the press of well-wishers
made it impossible. "Yehezkel," said Miriam.

"What?" Yehezkel questioned impatiently.

"I can't see what's going on!"

"What is there to see! It is a wedding, like any wedding."

"Don't give me a cute answer! For once, do what I ask, without
an argument!"

"All right, Miriam, all right. I can't see much from here because
the view is blocked. But even if I could see, Berurya and Meir are
facing the rabbi, so I'd only see their backs. "Wait ... just a minute!
I think he is lifting her veil! Yes! He is!"

Yehezkel's voice was choked. "Imagine, Miriam," he went on,
"here we are at Berurya's wedding! How time flies by! One minute,
you watch a little girl playing with other children and the next, that
little girl has grown up and has children of her own! It is a pity the
wisdom we get from life can't be taught to us when we're young."

"Yehezkel," Miriam smiled, "the truth is that people do try to
teach us when we're young but we can't fully understand and
appreciate until we've matured, and are ready to comprehend for
ourselves. It is easy to give a child knowledge, but wisdom... that is
something else. Wisdom has to take time."

"How is it you know so much?"

"Because I'm married to such a wise man!"

Yehezkel stood on his toes to get a better view. "I think that the ceremony is over. Yes, it is. Rabbi Meir and Berurya are husband and wife!"

Tears came into Yehezkel's eyes. Miriam reached up and gently wiped them away. She took his hand in hers. "I'm fortunate to be married to a man like you, Yehezkel," she said. "More than all else I love your tenderness and your compassion."

Then the joyful wedding music began.

The guests had departed. Penina and Bilha were asleep. In her bedroom, Berurya sat at the small table where she kept her cosmetics. She reached back and unfastened the clasp of the pin which held her hair. Slowly, she pulled the pin out and put it on the table; she tilted her head back and shook her head. Her long, straight raven-black hair dropped almost to the small of her back. With a hand, she pulled her hair to the front. Then she picked up one of several combs and with smooth strokes, combed her hair as she always did each night. As she tended to her hair, she thought about the beauty and dignity of the wedding and about the sanctity of the institution – only the absence of her dead parents and brother had tinged it with sadness.

She finished combing her hair, untied the straps of her shoes, and let them slip off. She unfastened her belt and breathed more easily. Standing, she removed her dress. She picked up a bronze mirror from the table and gazed at her face. "Not bad," she mused. "Some people might even think I'm pretty." She tilted the mirror so that she could view her body. She was tall, with long, slender legs. Her waist was narrow, her stomach flat. She was a little self-conscious about her bust. While Penina had a boyish figure, Berurya was buxom, as had been her mother. Initially, she had worn a *pesikya*, tied around her breasts over her undergarments. Her mother had told her that she herself had worn the band as a young girl and that binding the bust retarded the development of the breasts. Berurya hated wearing the *pesikya*, but her mother said that it was worth the discomfort.

However, after several years Berurya refused to continue wearing it. If God wanted her to be fashioned that way, let it be that way! She put the mirror down. "Not bad at all."

Berurya undressed completely. She took a small glass bottle from the table: it resembled a miniature vase, rounded at the bottom, with a long, narrow, extended neck. The glass itself was powder blue. Berurya pulled out the stopper and put the bottle to her nose. The scent was Berurya's favorite; it was made from a mixture of the finest flowers immersed in oil.

Berurya placed a finger over the mouth, and turned the bottle over; she massaged the oil sparingly on her neck and chest. She chose a new gown, slipped it on and got into bed. "Meir will be coming upstairs now," she mused. She was right. She heard his footsteps on the stairs. He halted at her door and knocked gently.

"Berurya, is it all right for me to enter?"

"Yes," Berurya replied, pulling the sheet to her neck.

The door opened; Meir entered and closed the door. Silently, he went to the oil lamp and extinguished the flame. Berurya heard him moving in the darkness. How nervous she was! It was odd: she was knowledgeable about so many things, but her knowledge of sex was purely academic. She was well versed in Jewish law as it pertained to sexual relations between men and women, but she was ignorant of the emotions that were involved. Intellectually, she understood that sexual intercourse was pleasurable, that Judaism presented the intimacy between husband and wife in absolutely the most positive light, but she was concerned that the first act would be painful. How much would it hurt? What if she were to pull away? Would Meir be upset? She felt helpless, weak. She closed her eyes and drew a deep breath.

Meir came to the bed, pulled the sheets away and stretched out beside her. Moments after, he rolled onto his side and faced her. Gently, he caressed her forehead, and then her cheeks. Through the open window, moonlight streamed in upon them.

"Berurya."

"Yes ..."

"You're very beautiful."

"Really, Meir?"

"Really! Berurya, you're the most beautiful woman in Sikhnin – in all of Israel!"

"Now I know you're not serious."

"But I'm very serious! I thought so from the moment I first saw you."

Berurya put her hand on his cheek and caressed it.

Meir took the hand and kissed it. "Berurya," he murmured, "I can't tell you how much I love you!"

Berurya smiled, but did not speak.

Meir went on: "It is said that a man should love his wife as much as he loves himself, but respect her more than he respects himself! There is no woman alive whom I respect as I respect you! And love ... the word has a new meaning when I think of you! It's almost as if I can never use it unless it's tied to your name."

Gently, he drew closer. He saw, as he embraced her, how the light of the moon, like a transparent veil, glowed on her smooth, olive skin. And it seemed to him that it wasn't an earthly veil meant to conceal, but a pane of luminescence meant to reveal. Only this light separated them; and then, as Meir's lips pressed against Berurya's, the veil was swallowed into shadow.

8

Outside the Sanhedrin

Before the destruction of the Temple in Jerusalem (70 C.E.), the Sanhedrin, or High Court, met twice a day to adjudicate ritual, judicial and political matters. The court was permanently situated in "The Chamber of Hewn Stones in the Temple," the place from which the Law went forth to all Israel. Tradition has it that before the fall of the Temple Rabbi Yohanan ben Zakkai met with Rome's military leader, Vespasian, and petitioned him to spare the sages and allow them to reside in Yavneh. Permission was granted. The ramifications of this decision were crucial, for had the Temple been destroyed and the Torah gone unstudied, who could say for certain that Judaism would have survived.

Yohanan ben Zakkai was succeeded by Rabban Gamaliel II. As a descendent of Hillel, the latter was accorded the title of Nasi, heir to the Patriachate. His father, Rabban Shimeon ben Gamaliel I, was thought to have perished at the hands of the Romans during the great destruction.

Under Gamaliel's leadership, the Sanhedrin was re-established at Yavneh. Gamaliel died before Hadrian became emperor. During the years of turmoil, there was a hiatus in the dynasty for over thirty years. When the sages first met at Usha in 138 C.E., it had been too dangerous for the heir-apparent, Rabban Shimeon ben Gamaliel II, to assume the title of Nasi and preside over their discussions. Two years later, the political climate had changed.

In addition to the Patriarch, there were two other positions of prominence governing the Sanhedrin: the Av Bet Din (President of the Court) and the Hakham (Chief Counsel). Rabbi Nathan, the son of the Babylonian exilarch, was Av Bet Din; the Hakham was Rabbi Meir.

It was customary for all to rise when the Nasi entered the room alone, and again when the Av Bet Din and the Hakham entered together.

Usha was situated to the west of Sikhnin, not far from the Mediterranean sea. The surrounding terrain was mountainous. It was in Usha that the rabbis met to plan the reconvening of the Sanhedrin.

Berurya's and Meir's house in Usha was smaller than their house in Sikhnin, and not unlike most dwellings in the Galilee. Homes were square in shape and divided into two rooms. The larger chamber, the *triclinium*, measuring ten by ten cubits, served as a combination dining- and guest-room. Behind the *triclinium*, was the smaller *kiton*, or bedroom. Homes were built of stone, with flat, wooden ceilings. While the wealthy could afford floors of stone or marble, in the majority of homes, the ground was simply covered with plaster. The wealthy could afford their own privies; most people had to use public baths and privies.

The courtyard was an integral part of a dwelling. It served various needs and functions. Part of it might be fenced off, to keep out animals. The kitchen was situated in the courtyard. Each day, fresh bread was prepared in a stone oven. The cistern was there, as well. When it rained, mainly in the winter months, a drainage system directed the rain water from the roof and the courtyard into a hole in the cistern; the water collected was used for drinking and for laundering clothes.

After endless hours and weeks of arduous work, Rabbi Meir and his colleague, Rabbi Nathan, agreed that they needed a rest. Even one day of rest, they felt, would make a difference. They took a day off and the next day walked together, as they did every morning, to the Sanhedrin. Rabban Shimeon ben Gamaliel would not be there yet, but most of the other scholars would be waiting.

Rabbi Nathan was a few steps ahead of Rabbi Meir. As they entered the room, the rabbis did not stand up as custom dictated. One row at a time stood up for Rabbi Nathan and sat immediately after he had passed; even less respect was accorded to Rabbi Meir. As he walked, only the individual he passed stood up and at once sat again. Rabbi Meir and Rabbi Nathan were baffled. They stared at each other, unable to explain the change in protocol. As they seated themselves, it was announced that the *Nasi*, Rabban Shimeon ben Gamaliel, was about to enter; instantly, everyone stood.

The seating of the Sanhedrin was arranged in concentric semicircles, like an unelevated amphitheater. The *Nasi* passed down the center isle, stepping with the stately gait of a prince. It was obvious to Meir and Nathan what had happened. In their absence, the *Nasi* had changed the protocol; the move was a political gambit designed to increase the stature of his office by diminishing the respect paid to the *Av Bet Din* and even more so, to the *Hakham*. Meir was livid; he felt it to be a personal insult and an affront to him as a scholar. How dare the *Nasi* humiliate him before the Sanhedrin! However, Meir, remained silent.

That evening Meir told Berurya what had happened. "Berurya," he said, "this isn't just a matter of honor, it is a question of which we value more, the study of Torah and pursuit of knowledge – or the need to pay tribute to a prince? This man is the Patriarch, only because his great-great-great-grandfather was Hillel! But Hillel was recognized for his wisdom, not for his lineage. Israel needs leaders whom people will respect for their wisdom and knowledge of Torah, and not descendents of scholars, whose only respect derives from a ruling that others must stand in their presence. The Torah says: 'You shall rise up before a hoary head, and honor the face of the old man ...' When Shimeon ben Gamaliel is old, then will he deserve the respect due the elderly. Presently, he is still too young."

Berurya listened in silence. She knew Meir was right, but she wasn't sure what could or should be done. "Meir," she asked, "what do you intend to do?"

"I have a plan. I've already discussed it with Rabbi Nathan and he is in full agreement. Tomorrow, we will arrange for one of the rabbis to request that Rabban Shimeon ben Gamaliel give a discourse on Tractate Uktzin."

"But he's not familiar with it," said Berurya.

"That is exactly why he'll be asked. When all the other scholars realize how little he knows, we'll call for his removal as Patriarch! Rabbi Nathan will become the new *Nasi*, and I'll get the position of *Av Bet Din*."

"What happens if the other rabbis oppose you?"

"I'm prepared for that as well. I've invited a number of rabbis to come over this evening. Rabbi Nathan and I picked them because we felt they would support us if it comes to a vote. If we've got strong support initially, it will convince others, who are undecided. In any event, it is worth the risk."

That evening Rabbi Meir and Rabbi Nathan discussed their plan with several other rabbis. All of them agreed that Rabban Shimeon ben Gamaliel had indeed overstepped his authority, and that he had no right to surreptitiously alter protocol when Meir and Nathan were absent. But as to publicly humiliating the *Nasi*, some were reluctant. After hours of discussion, the rabbis, with the sole exception of Rabbi Jacob ben Korshai, agreed that drastic measures needed to be taken.

That night, Berurya and Meir spoke into the early hours of the morning. Meir was convinced that he was doing the right thing. He anticipated a battle. Rabban Shimeon ben Gamaliel would surely fight him all the way on the issue; Meir was not really certain about how much support he had in the Sanhedrin.

The next morning, the *Nasi* was announced. Everyone stood. Rabban Shimeon ben Gamaliel took his place and muttered, "Be seated." Everyone sat down. At that point, Meir motioned to one of the other rabbis, who promptly rose to his feet and said: "*Nasi*, I'd like to request that you lead this morning's discourse on the Tractate Uktzin." The rabbis who were unaware of the plan were surprised by the request. Those who were with Meir and Nathan focused their attention on the *Nasi*. How would he react? What could he possibly do?

There was dead silence in the chamber. No one moved. The *Nasi* sat there, his hands folded together over his mouth. At first, he stared directly at the rabbi who had asked the question. Then, slowly, he turned his eyes to Rabbi Meir. Then the *Nasi* stood up and began his discourse.

Rabbi Nathan whispered to Meir: "He knows the subject! How can it be!?"

"Obviously, someone who met with us last night prepared him: it was probably Rabbi Jacob ben Korshai."

"What do we do now?" asked Nathan.

"Nothing. Absolutely nothing," replied Meir firmly.

Rabban Shimeon ben Gamaliel finished his discourse. He paused for a moment, and then said, "Last night, I learned about a plot to discredit me with this august body. It wasn't simply a question of honor." He pointed a trembling finger. "The two men over there, Meir and Nathan, have conspired together to remove me from my office!"

The *Nasi* shook the finger at Meir. "Is your lust for power and your need for recognition so great," he cried out, "that you are willing to besmirch the office of the *Nasi* and humiliate him publicly!? May I remind you that embarrassing someone in public – as you had hoped to do – is tantamount to murder and that the person who does so has no share in the World to Come! May I remind you that when Miriam slandered her brother, Moses, God punished her with leprosy, and that she was shut out of the camp of the Israelites for seven days!" He clenched his fists and raised them. "This, Meir and Nathan, will be your punishment! You will both be excluded from this camp until we deem it proper to open our doors to you again."

The *Nasi* lowered his arms and stood motionless. Meir and Nathan rose and walked out. The door swung shut behind them.

The next days were difficult. Each morning, Meir and Nathan arrived at the Sanhedrin, but were not permitted to enter. They communicated with the members by writing notes, and passing them into the chamber.

The rabbis were separated into two camps: those who supported the *Nasi*, and those who wished to reinstate Rabbi Meir and Rabbi Nathan. Rabbi Yosi expressed the sentiments of the latter eloquently in a single sentence: "The Torah is without and we are within!"

At length, Rabbi Nathan went to reconcile his differences with Rabban Shimeon ben Gamaliel. But Meir refused. Late one evening, there was a knock at his door. Rabbi Meir opened it and found Rabbi Yosi standing before him. "Meir, my friend," said Rabbi Yosi; "I've just learned that you are to be excommunicated! You'll be placed under *Herem*, and no one will be permitted to speak with you."

Meir was speechless.

Berurya said, "Yosi, please come inside."

"Thanks, Berurya, but I must go. If I hear anything, I'll notify you immediately."

Rabbi Yosi turned and departed. Berurya closed the door, took Meir by the arm and led him over to a chair. Meir sat down. He uttered one word: "*Herem*."

Meir sat in the chair most of the night, devastated. There was no punishment worse than excommunication. You met colleagues and friends and they passed you by as if you didn't exist!

It was almost dawn. Berurya approached her husband and gently rested a hand on his shoulder. Meir looked up. "It's over," he said. "I've lost."

Berurya was always supportive of Meir. She had listened attentively when he and Rabbi Nathan had spoken about dethroning the *Nasi*. She had her own doubts, but had held her peace. She had consoled her husband when Rabban Shimeon ben Gamaliel excluded him from the Sanhedrin. She had known then what must be done, but hadn't been asked her opinion and thus remained silent. She was Meir's companion and his confidant; she had always been a shoulder to lean on. But she had never seen him like this before: beaten, defeated. She knew she had to speak her mind. Now, she had to be his strength!

"Meir, look at me," Berurya said firmly.

But he seemed not to hear her.

"Meir," she repeated more loudly, "look at me!"

He raised his head.

"Meir, you have to fight back! If you succumb now, you'll always be treated like some whipped animal, cowering in fear!" Her eyes blazed. "Meir, are you listening to me!? You've got to find the specific charges against you, and know who's behind them! On what grounds do they wish to excommunicate you? You haven't done anything wrong – anything! Is it supposed to be a question of honor? But this is the Sanhedrin! Its purpose is to guide the Jewish people through these troubled times. Its glory is only as great as its greatest scholar! You're the *Hakham*, Meir. You are the scholar – not in name only, but in reality! The title wasn't given you because you're someone's son or a descendent of some sage. You earned the title because of who and what you are, not because of what you represent!" She squeezed his shoulder. "Meir," she said hotly, "confront them! Confront them all if need be, but confront them! You were right in what you believed and did. You are Rabbi Meir, never forget it! And if a scholar is to be judged, then he must be judged only by the acumen of his mind; if a scholar is to be judged, he must be judged by his peers. Remember, Meir, that as a scholar you stand above them all, alone. They cannot excommunicate you. Face them, Meir! Now!"

The intensity of her words and the fire in her eyes touched Meir's spirit. "You are right, Berurya," he said. He stirred in the chair and rose to his feet. "You are right about everything, with one exception. I do have an equal: you!"

Berurya embraced him and they stood together, in each other's arms, for a time.

When it was time, Meir and Berurya walked to the Sanhedrin together. A student was guarding the door. Meir stepped up to him.

"Let us pass!" he commanded.

The student stepped aside.

Meir and Berurya entered. Berurya stood in the rear; Meir strode to the front of the chamber. The great room fell silent. Meir stared at the *Nasi*, and then at his colleagues. He lifted his head and said in a ringing voice: "So you intend to excommunicate me do you!? Well, your words have no meaning! None at all! I refuse to obey this court until and unless you enumerate the specific charges against me! I refuse to obey you or be excommunicated until and unless I know exactly who is my accuser! To those who would punish me, I say: stand up now, so I can see your faces!"

Not a person in the room moved.

That very afternoon, Meir was reinstated: the rabbis of Usha voted not to excommunicate any sage. To have the last word, however, Rabban Shimeon ben Gamaliel ruled that the scholarly statements made by Rabbi Meir or Rabbi Nathan be recorded anonymously. Meir was designated as 'others say' and Nathan as 'some say.'

9

Changes In Life

Rabbi Meir and Berurya decided to leave Usha a few days before the Sanhedrin officially recessed. They packed their belongings and fastened them securely on their donkeys. The last few days had been draining and Berurya felt the strain. She was also anxious to return to Sikhnin.

As they rode out of Usha, Berurya's thoughts turned to Penina and Bilha. She wondered how they had managed. She was confident that Bilha could care for Penina, but she worried about her younger sister. "She has suffered terribly," Berurya thought. "She deserves some happiness."

Suddenly, Berurya felt a sharp pain. Meir saw her expression.

"Berurya, is something wrong?"

"It's nothing, Meir. Probably cramps."

Meir reflected for a moment, and then said: "I had some good news —but now I'm not sure ..."

"What do you mean, Meir?"

"Some of the community leaders in Tiberias have asked me to spend a couple of weeks there, teach in the *Beit Midrash*, and give a discourse on the Sabbath."

"That is good news."

"But there is more: I'm almost certain that they'll ask us to live there permanently."

"Really?" said Berurya. "This is unexpected! But what about Penina and Bilha? What'll we do with the house in Sikhnin?"

"Frankly, Berurya, I'm concerned about your health. I'll probably decline the offer."

"You'll do nothing of the sort, Meir! There's no need to worry about me. I just need a little rest. You should go to Tiberias."

Meir was uncertain. He wanted to travel to Tiberias, but Berurya really looked worn out. "We'll talk about it later," he murmured.

As evening fell, they arrived in Sikhnin. They rode slowly toward the house; the door swung open, and Penina dashed out. "Someone is happy to see us!" Berurya said.

Meir smiled as well. They dismounted.

Penina ran to Berurya and flung her arms around her sister's neck.

"Maybe I should leave more often! Obviously, I've been missed," laughed Berurya.

"Berurya, Meir, I have wonderful news," Penina burst out. "Our neighbor, Menahem, wants to marry me!"

"The same Menahem who teased you when you were a little girl?"

"Yes, Berurya, that Menachem!"

Berurya hugged her sister tightly. "Penina, Penina, what wonderful news!" Arm-in-arm, the two walked up the path.

"Tell me about Menahem," said Meir.

"Menahem? Menahem is wonderful! He is marvelous! He is special."

"I know that you like him, Penina. But tell me something about his family, his background, about what he does for a living."

"Well," said Penina excitedly, "Menahem is the youngest of five children. You might say that Menahem is simple – not in a negative sense, but in the way he views life. He works as a blacksmith. He's not a scholar like you, Meir, but he has a heart of gold. He is tough and powerful, but he's also gentle and soft ..." Penina sighed. "He told me he loves me. He said he always liked me – even when we were kids. He'd always tease me; I thought he didn't like me, but it was just his way of getting my attention. Meir, once you meet him, you'll see how special he really is."

"I don't doubt it," said Meir.

The three of them entered the house.

"I hope we're not too late for dinner," Berurya called out.

Bilha dropped the utensils in her hands and embraced Berurya. "It's so good to see you," Bilha said tearfully. "We've missed you terribly."

"We've missed you too," said Berurya.

That night, they all talked – for hours and hours. Berurya talked about what had happened in Usha. She described Meir's confrontation with the Sanhedrin in detail, and dwelled on the dramatic moment when he demanded to know who his accusers were and what the charges were. Penina and Bilha listened intently. They wanted to know about all the rabbis and their wives, about Usha and its inhabitants. Berurya always avoided gossip but this time she indulged Bilha.

Abruptly, Penina said: "We're terrible, Bilha! Berurya has come all this distance. She is exhausted and we're keeping her up with our questions. Berurya, you'd better sleep. You look utterly worn out. We can talk tomorrow."

Berurya didn't argue. Meir had gone to bed hours ago. As Berurya climbed the steps, she felt the searing pain again. She leaned on the wall. The pain disappeared as quickly as it had come. "I'm tired," Berurya thought.

The next week, Meir and one of his students set out for Tiberias. Berurya had convinced him that she was in good health and that the trip was important. Before he left, Meir met with Menahem and found that he was everything Penina said he was. He would make her a perfect husband. Meir also met with Menahem's parents and discussed the conditions for the marriage with them. One day before Meir departed, Penina and Menahem were betrothed.

Berurya watched Meir and his student ride off. It was early morning. When they disappeared, she went into the house and sank into a chair. She felt weak and nauseous. Bilha came in. "– What is the matter, Berurya?"

"I don't know. Sometimes ... I have pain. I'm tired all the time. And now, I feel nauseous."

Bilha stared at her and smiled.

"Why are you smiling? Does my illness amuse you?"

"Illness?" exclaimed Bilha. "You've invented a new word for it, have you?"

Berurya's eyes opened. "Bilha," she said hoarsely, "you don't mean to tell me that you think I am pregnant?"

"Those are the symptoms, my dear. When did you have your last period?"

"About seven weeks ago, I think. Or maybe before. I just thought... that I was late."

"God willing," said Bilha softly, "you're going to be a mother."

Berurya's eyes filled with tears of joy.

Bilha touched Berurya's shoulder. "I haven't learned to read your thoughts."

"I can't wait to tell Meir! But I'll wake Penina this minute!"

Berurya went upstairs. Seconds later, Penina's shouts rang through the house.

The next two weeks seemed to pass at once quickly and slowly. Slowly, when Berurya counted the days until Meir's return. Quickly, because her days were filled with things to do. She continued to teach in the *Beit Midrash*. She enjoyed teaching almost as much as she enjoyed learning. Meir and Berurya had attracted a large following; students came from great distances to study with them. It was difficult to say who was the better teacher. Each was demanding – and expected nothing less than excellence from the pupils. Each had a splendid reputation.

Finally, Meir returned. He held Berurya tightly in his arms and kissed her.

"I've missed you," he said softly.

"I've missed you too."

"I have some wonderful news for you," Meir smiled.

"I have wonderful news for you too!"

"Let me tell you my news first," Meir said unable to restrain himself. He released her from his embrace and took her hand. "They want us to come and live in Tiberias! Actually, it's not Tiberias, but Hammat, a little town about a mile to the south. It's beautiful there! The *Beit Midrash* and *Beit Keneset* are like none that I've ever seen and it faces Lake Kinneret. They'll provide us with a house. And the students! Berurya, think of all the students we'll have! We'll be able to train disciples there as we never could here."

He gazed into her eyes. "Now, tell me your news."

"I'm pregnant."

Meir's face lit up; his entire body trembled. "I'm going to have a son! I'm going to have a son!" he cried out. "A son! A son! What I've always wanted!"

Berurya was astonished. "But how can you be sure you'll have a son, Meir? It might be a daughter."

"No, Berurya," retorted Meir: "I don't want a girl! I want a son!"

Berurya was stunned. It was a reaction she had never believed possible in Meir.

10
The Other

Berurya convinced Meir that they should remain in Sikhnin until Penina's wedding. After Menahem and Penina were married, she and Meir would go to Hammat. Meir agreed reluctantly; he was anxious to begin his new life in Hammat.

Meir described Hammat at length and in detail to Berurya. He told her that it was located directly south of Tiberias, on the southwest shore of the Kinneret. The two towns were so close to each other that they appeared to be one elongated city. The Kinneret was pear-shaped, and lay almost 700 feet below sea level. Steep mountains surrounded its fresh, greenish-blue waters. "From above," Meir said, "it looks like a turquoise tear that dropped from heaven!" The temperature in the area varied considerably from the mountain-tops to the shore of the lake below. In the summer, the skies were cloudless; the heat and humidity were so oppressive that people didn't venture out during the mid-day period. At night, the earth cooled and there was a breeze from the lake. "And when the moon is reflected in the lake," Meir smiled, "the Kinneret pulls the harp-strings of lovers' hearts."

With Penina and Menachem, Meir discoursed about the history of the area. He told them that Tiberias was built around 18 C.E. by Herod's son, Herod Antipas, and named in honor of the then Roman Emperor, Tiberius. For a time, Tiberias was considered unclean by the sages because graves were found within its borders; later on, it was declared to be clean, and so it was permissible for Jews to live there. The streets of Tiberias were set up in a rectangle, approximately 1500 meters by 300 meters. Four long roads ran the entire length of Tiberias, transversed by six parallel streets, each one of which led to the Kinneret.

Tiberians did not take part in the Bar Kokhba revolt; in fact, trade relations between Rome and Tiberias flourished there, even during the worst times. The economic situation was thus considerably better than elsewhere. In Tiberias and Sepphoris a wealthy class of merchants had even emerged; their riches became proverbial. It was said that, like members of royal families, they would shave on Friday every week!

Hammat, Meir told his sister-in-law and her fiance, was not as large as Tiberias, although – like the former – it had its share of marketplaces and public baths. Some of the synagogues in Hammat were identified with specific Jewish communities. Jews from Babylonia, for example, might prefer to pray with other Jews who had also resided there at one time.

Above all, Hammat was renowned for its hot baths. Mineral waters, springing from far below the earth's surface, were considered to have therapeutic value. People with various afflictions found their way to the hot baths of Hammat in the hope that they would be cured. Others came simply to enjoy the pleasure of the hot water.

The *Beit Keneset* in Hammat, to which Meir had been invited, was the largest and wealthiest in the area. It was an imposing structure, built on a site higher than the surrounding buildings. As in Sikhnin, this *Beit Keneset* had been designed in the shape of a basilica, with colonnaded aisles and stone benches running along three of the walls. The columns were made of smooth marble and rested on high pedestals. The Corinthian capitals were elaborately graceful. The chamber had fine light which came in through windows set high in each wall.

Up front, was a large block of stone carved out to form a chair; it had a back and arm-rests. This seat of honor was called a *Cathedra*, or "seat of Moses". The top of the chair's back was rounded; in its center, a rose was carved. At the base of the stone, chiseled in Aramaic, were the words: "May he be remembered for good. May his portion be with the righteous."

Before the *Beit Keneset* was a large courtyard which led to the portico. To the left of the courtyard was the *Beit Midrash* and a storage-room where the scrolls of the Torah were kept until needed for the prayer service. Several other rooms were used for study.

Outside the building was a staircase that led to a second floor gallery. Above the main entrance, the lintel was decorated with a seven-branched Menorah encircled with a garland of acanthus: geometric designs appeared on each side. Hammat's *Beit Keneset*, was faced to the south, toward Jerusalem, as were many in the Galilee.

After the wedding of Penina and Menachem, Berurya and Meir moved to Hammat. Their new home was quite large. The bedrooms were spacious, larger than those in Sikhnin. Students who came along with Meir and Berurya would be accommodated; their meals would be provided for as long as they studied at the *Beit Midrash*. Most of the students were unmarried and so could devote themselves entirely to study.

Berurya and Meir settled down in Hammat. With each passing week of her pregnancy, Berurya found it more difficult to maintain the routine to which she had been accustomed all her life.

Bilha found it difficult to adjust to the new surroundings. Her old friends were left behind in Sikhnin; she perceived the people of Hammat as being less friendly. Eventually, she made new friends. From them she heard the gossip which she so sorely missed.

Berurya detested gossip. It was a religious transgression, since the person discussed was often injured as a result. Occasionally Berurya lectured to Bilha on the evils of gossip, but to no avail; there was something which Bilha found appealing about listening to other people's misfortunes. Bilha knew that much of what she heard was not entirely accurate, still it did not seem to matter to her. It was assumed that the relator of gossip had the right to embellish his story somewhat, especially if it made the tale more tantalizing.

The best gossip, Bilha believed, dealt with people whom you knew. It might revolve around the sexual escapades of an unfaithful spouse, or around family problems such as a wayward offspring. The greater the discrepancy between appearance and reality, the more intriguing the gossip! It was always interesting to learn about someone who committed adultery and Bilha could not resist a story about someone who professed to be righteous and God-fearing, but in truth was neither. She also derived a certain satisfaction in learning about people of influence and wealth who had their share of problems.

Berurya had reached her last month. Her pregnancy was uneventful, for which she was grateful. During the entire term, Berurya had used a *Mokh*, a contraceptive device similar to a tampon. Rabbi Meir had some time ago ruled that three categories of women should use a *Mokh* during intercourse: a minor, a pregnant woman, and a nursing mother. Both he and Berurya felt that if intercourse in any way might be injurious to the health of a young woman, to the fetus, or to a mother still nursing her child, then precautions had to be taken. Other sages, however, disagreed with Meir's ruling.

As Jews, Berurya and Meir believed that, generally speaking, procreation was first and foremost a *mitzvah*, a commandment from God. Beyond that commandment, the rabbinic attitude regarding sexual intimacy between a husband and wife was favorable. Sexual pleasure was never taboo: on the contrary, it was a gift from God meant to be enjoyed.

Berurya now wished to give birth. No matter what position she assumed in bed, it was difficult for her to sleep. Her back ached and often she felt irritable.

One Shabbat afternoon, Meir was giving a *drasha*, a homiletical interpretation of Scripture, in a *Beit Midrash* in Tiberias. In the midst of his discourse, a student approached him. Meir listened intently to what the student whispered. Abruptly, Meir motioned to Symmachus bar Yosef, his best and brightest student, to come forward. Symmachus continued to expound on the Torah portion as Meir, accompanied by the student, walked out.

On the front steps, Meir asked: "Where did you see him?"

"Over there," the student said, pointing southward towards Hammat. "He rode a horse in that direction."

"Go back inside," Meir commanded, "but don't mention this to anyone."

Meir ran in the direction the student had shown him. A few minutes later, he caught sight of the rider in the distance. Meir ran with all his strength. Finally, he halted and doubled over. He could scarcely breathe. When he caught his breath, he shouted, "Rabbi Elisha ben Avuya! Can you hear me?"

There was no response. Meir cried out once again: "Rabbi Elisha ben Avuya! It's me, your student, Meir."

The horse stopped. Meir rose and pushed on toward the horse and rider. He had not seen Elisha ben Avuya in a long time.

Meir loved Rabbi Elisha ben Avuya dearly; the man was truly one of the great minds of his day. It was said that on Elisha's birth, his father Avuya, one of the most prominent men in Jerusalem, invited all the persons of renown to celebrate his son's circumcision. No expense was spared. The guests enjoyed themselves with food and drink; there was laughter and dancing. Two of the rabbis, Rabbi Eliezer and Rabbi Joshua, rather than partake in the levity, immersed themselves in study, and intertwined the three components of the Bible: the Torah, the Prophets and Writings. Inadvertently, they brought down the sacred fires of heaven, which encompassed them. Terrified by the phenomenon, the guests pushed and shoved their way out of the room, screaming in panic. The two rabbis sat where they were, deep in thought, encircled by flames, and oblivious to what had happened. Suddenly, Avuya entered the room; his eyes opened wide in amazement. The fire raged, but did not consume. When Avuya called two names, "Rabbi Eliezer, Rabbi Joshua," and the rabbis looked up, the fire vanished. "What have you done?" Avuya asked. "Do you want to burn down my house? Is this how you celebrate with me?"

"Not at all," replied Rabbi Eliezer. "The fire that you beheld was the kind of fire that came down on Mt. Sinai when the Torah was given to Moses. It is the flame of celebration, not destruction."

Avuya had never witnessed anything like it. He had little use for religion and respected only power and money. But now he felt awe. More than all else, he craved the secret of the mysterious flame. "Rabbis," he blurted out, "I had no idea that such was the power of Torah! I therefore swear here and now that my son's life will be dedicated to its study!"

Avuya kept his promise. He raised his son, Elisha, to be a scholar. However, Avuya wanted his son to study Torah not for its own sake, but in order to learn the secret of the fire.

Elisha was blessed with an amazing intellect. Even as a child, he comprehended with ease what aged sages mastered only after arduous study. But Elisha also carried within him the seeds of his own destruction, for, like his father before him, he lacked belief. Knowingly and deliberately, he violated Jewish law.

Torn between two worlds, he knew technically what it meant to be Jewish, but he never felt what it was like to be a Jew.

Elisha was an heretic, by his own account. His brilliant reputation had attracted students from all over. But now, as an old man, no one would talk to him; neither colleagues, nor students. Only Rabbi Meir, who had been his most promising student, refused to turn away from his teacher.

Meir finally reached him. "Rabbi Elisha ben Avuya! One of my students told me –" Meir paused until he could finish the sentence, "that they had seen you riding away."

Elisha rode on, but at a slower pace.

"Rabbi Elisha, please come to my house! Stay with us for a while."

Elisha was silent. Then, finally, he spoke: "Meir," he said, "what were you teaching in the *Beit Midrash*?"

Meir was astonished. Elisha asked the question as though he was continuing with a conversation that had only briefly been interrupted.

"I was expounding the verse in Ecclesiastes: 'God has made the one, as well as the other....'"

"And what did you say?"

"I explained that for everything God created in this world, God also created something adjunctive. Thus, God created mountains, as well as hills; seas as well as streams. In this sense, God has made one thing, as well as the other."

"Meir," said Elisha, "I'm quite sure that your teacher, Rabbi Akiva, would have explained the verse differently. He would have interpreted it to mean that God created the righteous, as well as the wicked; that God created the Garden of Eden, or Paradise, as well as *Gehinnom*, a place of punishment for the wicked in the Hereafter; that everything can be perceived as a duality; that in each resides a Heaven and a Hell. In this sense, God has made one thing, as well as the other."

The interpretation intrigued Meir. He began to consider its ramifications, when Elisha suddenly shouted, "Stop!"

Meir stopped on the spot.

Elisha gestured. "Meir," he said, "I've been calculating the distance we've gone, and I've found that we've reached the point past which one cannot go without desecrating the Sabbath."

Elisha was right. Meir had been so absorbed in the conversation that he had failed to realize how far they had traveled beyond the boundaries of the city.

"Please come back with me," Meir pleaded.

Elisha hesitated.

Meir reached up and took Elisha's arm: "Please, I beg of you –"

Then Elisha dismounted and walked back in silence with Meir.

Meir was very fond of Elisha ben Avuya. That was one of the reasons why, when Rabbi Jacob ben Korshai told Rabban Shimeon ben Gamaliel about the plot to embarrass him, Meir did not rebuke him; Rabbi Jacob ben Korshai was Elisha ben Avuya's grandson.

Meir and Elisha entered the house. Berurya, who had not expected Meir until after sundown, heard her husband's voice and that of a stranger.

"Meir," she called out, "is that you?"

"Yes, Berurya."

As Berurya rose slowly from her chair, Meir and Elisha came into the room.

"Berurya, I'd like you to meet my teacher, Rabbi Elisha ben Avuya. I studied with him for many years."

Berurya glanced at Elisha. "I know much about Rabbi Elisha ben Avuya," she said.

"Berurya, I've got to return to the *Beit Midrash*. I'll be home as soon as the Sabbath is over."

Meir left, leaving Elisha and Berurya alone. Berurya remembered that her father, who rarely spoke ill of anyone, had said with contempt: "This man is rightly call *Aher*, meaning 'other', because even the mention of his name would defile one's lips!"

"Do I refer to you as Rabbi ... or *Aher*?" asked Berurya sharply.

"Apparently, you've already made up your mind. Call me whatever name you wish."

Berurya seated herself again. "My father died the death of a martyr," she said. "He gave his life for the Torah."

"I'm well aware of that," said Alisha. "Your father died like many great sages, who dedicated their lives to one purpose alone: to bring God's kingdom to this world. They were good people, courageous, kind and compassionate." He lifted a hand wearily. "And what was their reward?" he said mournfully.

He was silent for a time, and then went on: "I was there when the Romans put Hutzpit HaMeturgeman on trial in Caesarea. Here was an old, old man – a venerated scholar. Despite his advanced age, he stood erect and unflinching; his fine, smooth skin and white hair gave him the appearance of an angelic being. We begged for mercy. What possible harm could an old man be to Rome? What threat could he pose? But our words fell on deaf ears.

"The Roman said to Hutzpit, 'How old are you?' Hutzpit replied: 'I'm one day short of one hundred and thirty years. If you intend to take my life, allow me one more day.' 'What difference does a day make?' the Roman officer asked. Hutzpit replied: 'So that I may say the prayer *Sh'ma* this evening and tomorrow morning, acknowledging the Divine Name.' The officer screamed: 'You insolent creature! How do you still believe in your God? Your God is helpless; He can't even save the life of a worthless, old man like you!' Hutzpit began to weep. Not for himself, but because God's name had been blasphemed. Staring straight into the Roman's eyes, he said: 'One day, God will exact retribution. Mark my words. One day.'

"The Roman officer, who had wearied of the conversation, condemned Hutzpit to death by stoning and then they hung him. Afterwards, we searched for his body. They had thrown it into a garbage dump. When we finally arrived, we found that a pig had bitten out his tongue and was dragging it in the dirt! The same tongue that eloquently praised God's glory! At that instant, I realized the Roman was right. There was no retribution! Hutzpit's God was powerless. He could not even save an old man!"

Berurya's face flushed. She could no longer contain the anger that had been building inside her. Enraged, she rose to her feet and cried out: "Who appointed you judge of the Almighty! What gives you the right to condemn God? You say that God is powerless because of what happened to Hutzpit! Those are the criteria of your test?! Your faith is based on whether Hutzpit lived or died! You are no better than the Roman!"

Berurya's body trembled, but her voice was firm: "Hutzpit cried not because he feared death; he cried because God's name had been profaned! Had he known that his death would make you an apostate, he would have wept a second time: once for the Almighty, and once for you!

"The Romans can take a person's life; they cannot touch his soul. Tossing a body into the garbage desecrates the body, but the soul is untainted. It returns to God."

Berurya shook her head sadly. "Yes, there is great suffering in this world," she said. "Yet all suffering, no matter how excruciating, comes to an end. Not for you, though, Rabbi Elisha ben Avuya, your suffering is different. It is not the pain of your body but a fire that sears your soul."

Berurya grimaced and placed a hand on her belly.

"Are you all right?" Elisha asked with concern.

"Yes," said Berurya. She sat down again in the chair and then began to regret that she had spoken so harshly. "I must apologize for raising my voice. Meir brought you into our house as a guest – I had no right to speak to you like that. I'm sorry."

Elisha stared at her in silence for a moment, then he said: "Meir has married quite a woman."

"What do you mean?"

"I mean to compliment you. You are beautiful, intelligent, articulate, and ... different from any woman I've ever met."

"Don't patronize me," said Berurya.

"Heaven forbid!" said Elisha. He rubbed his forehead. "Who knows, had I met ..."

Berurya heard Meir come in. "Apparently," she said, "I've lost track of the hour. The Sabbath must be over. After Meir says the blessing of *Havdalah*, you're welcome to eat with us."

Meir greeted Berurya and Elisha. The three of them went out into the courtyard. Three stars shone brightly above – the three stars needed so that one can recite the *Havdalah*.

Berurya especially loved the fact that Havdalah meant separation or distinction. Havdalah distinguished between the holiness of the

Sabbath which had just ended, and the secular nature of the weekdays ahead. Just as the Kiddush, the sanctification over wine, was said at the start of the Sabbath, so Havdalah included a blessing over wine at the close of the Sabbath. Berurya enjoyed the fact that Havdalah included blessings over light and spices, and together with the wine, incorporated the senses of sight, smell and taste.

When Meir finished reciting *Havdalah*, they reentered the house. Berurya again asked Elisha to join them in their meal.

"No, thank you. I must be going."

Meir tried to persuade his teacher to remain, but Elisha was adamant about leaving. Berurya and Meir accompanied Elisha to his horse. Elisha paused before mounting, and said: "I hope our conversation before did not upset you, Berurya."

Berurya found something intriguing about this man. No matter how much you disagreed with what he stood for, there was still a part of him that you couldn't help liking. Without planning it, Berurya said: "Perhaps one day you'll return...."

Elisha smiled. Her words could be understood in two ways. He chose to respond to the hidden meaning. His smile was grim. "I'm already too old to return, Berurya. A fire burns in my soul... I don't know how to put it out."

Before she actually met Elisha ben Avuya, Berurya had disliked him. Now, as she watched him riding away, she did not know what to feel. Perhaps she admired his honesty, for he didn't pretend to be other than what he truly was. She also felt sorry for him. He was a man without a friend. It was a great burden to live life and be shunned by colleagues: it was a far greater burden to be entirely alone. Elisha was utterly alone – he couldn't even speak with God.

Berurya cried out suddenly: "Rabbi, go in peace!"

But Elisha was already too far away and could not hear the words.

11

Of Birth and Childlessness

A week after Elisha ben Avuya's visit, Berurya went into labor. Meir hurried off to fetch the midwife, while Bilha stayed with his wife. Berurya lay in bed; Bilha hovered over her and wiped the perspiration from her forehead.

"Bilha —"

"I'm here."

"The pain! Where is Meir? What's talking him so long?"

"He just left, Berurya. Take it easy. Everything will be all right."

"How would you know? You never gave birth." As soon as she had spoken the words, Berurya regretted her insensitivity. "I'm sorry, Bilha, I didn't mean it," she apologized.

"I know," Bilha murmured, "I know."

Suddenly Berurya moaned. She clutched Bilha's arm.

"If it helps, scream!" Bilha urged.

Berurya stared at her in disbelief.

Bilha knew what she was thinking. "For once in your life," she admonished, "it's all right to be like other women. No one will think less of you for expressing your pain."

Berurya clenched her teeth and tightened her grip. Bilha wiped her forehead and gently caressed her hair.

"I hear Meir!" Bilha exclaimed suddenly: "Wait here and I'll bring the midwife."

"And I was planning to take a walk!" Berurya muttered.

"Good, very good!" said Bilha. "Obviously, your labor hasn't affected your sarcasm!"

Bilha went downstairs, where Meir was talking to the midwife.

"I'll show you the way upstairs," Bilha said.

"Can I help?" Meir asked.

"It won't be necessary," answered the midwife.

Meir sat. Then he got up and paced to and fro. For a disciplined man, the behavior was highly unusual.

"Maybe I should go up and see if they need me?" Meir thought. "No, the woman told me to stay down here! I'd only be in the way. Maybe I'll study? Whom am I kidding? How can I concentrate!?"

Meir walked to the window and stared out. He saw children in the street. "Imagine me... a father! So-and-so, the son of Meir! What name should I give him? Ya'akov...? Ya'akov ben Meir. No. Maybe, Sh'muel, after the prophet. No, not Sh'muel! Maybe I should name him ..."

At that moment, Bilha came down the stairs.

"Has she given birth?" Meir asked anxiously.

Bilha shook her head.

"No," she said, "the midwife says it could still be quite a while."

Meir's eyes filled with an expression of mingled anxiety and disappointment. The two of them sat down at the table. Bilha began drumming on the table-top. Meir was annoyed, but said nothing. Suddenly, there was a piercing scream. Meir jumped to his feet.

"Berurya!" he cried anxiously. "Something is wrong!"

"Nothing is wrong," Bilha said calmly. "Your wife's behaving like a woman in labor and that's all."

But Meir did not understand. "Maybe you should go upstairs and see how she's doing?"

"If it'll make you less nervous, I'll do it."

Bilha left the room. There was utter silence. The minutes and then the hours passed. Meir rose for the afternoon prayer. Then, in the midst of the *Shemoneh Esreh*, just after reciting the words, "Hear our voice," Meir heard the cry of an infant. His heart pounded as if it would burst.

"That's my son," he thought. He concluded his prayers rapidly and raced up the stairs. Berurya lay in bed. Next to her, swaddled in a blanket, was a tiny creature with huge brown eyes and black hair over the crown of its head. Meir stepped over to the bed. He glanced questioningly at the midwife. "May I?"

"Of course."

Gently, Meir touched the smooth skin of the baby's tiny arm. Berurya smiled with a radiance that her husband had never before seen. "Meir," she said softly, "I'd like to introduce you to... Hananiah ben Meir."

Meir was dumbfounded. "Hananiah," he thought. "Of course! A perfect name after Berurya's father. Why didn't I think of it before? Hananiah ben Meir!"

Meir lifted the baby tenderly in his arms. Little Hananiah began to cry. "There, there, Hananiah," Meir comforted. "There's no reason to cry. Nobody will harm you." Meir rocked the infant back and forth, but his son kept on crying. "Here, Berurya," Meir said, handing him back. "I think he prefers his mother."

The midwife was preparing to leave. "I suggest you feed your son," she said. "That is probably why he's crying."

Berurya looked embarrassed. "How ... do I ...?"

"It's easy. Just put the baby's mouth on your nipple and let nature take its course. You'll be surprised how easy it all is."

Berurya sat up and Bilha put a pillow behind her back. With one arm supporting the baby's body and the other under the back of his head, Berurya positioned little Hananiah just as the midwife instructed. Hananiah stopped crying and began nursing.

Berurya looked down at her baby and smiled with deep satisfaction. "A little while ago," she thought, "I felt pain that I did not believe I could endure. Now, when I see this infant, so precious, so fragile, the memory of the pain is blurred by the joy of this moment! I wonder whether the butterfly remembers the caterpillar's struggle to escape the cocoon. And if it knew about the pain beforehand, would it choose to remain a caterpillar, creeping in the dirt like other insects, or would it choose to suffer to sprout colorful wings and soar in the sky? How wonderful to be a woman! At the very least, I am equal to any man, which is to say neither good nor bad. Just human. But God has also given me an understanding of what it means to create, to bring forth life into this world! That is something neither Meir, nor any man, will ever know. He heard the scream of pain, but not the silence of joy. The two are inseparable. And that is why no butterfly ever chooses to remain a caterpillar!"

Penina and Menahem and a few close friends from Sikhnin, came for Hananiah's circumcision. Penina stayed on with Berurya for another week. Bilha kept teasing Penina, telling her that she'd be an old woman by the time she started a family. Penina took the teasing in good spirits. "We've only been married a few months, Bilha. I think you're rushing things a bit."

"Who's rushing? Take your time. Take ten months!"

Penina laughed.

One month after Berurya had given birth, she and Meir observed Hananiah's Pidyon ha-Ben, the redemption of the first-born male. Both parents cherished the custom that dated back to ancient times when all first-born males had the responsibility of assisting the priests. After the Exodus from Egypt, this duty was transferred to the tribe of Levi. Consequently, the Torah specified that all first-born males, except for those born by Caesarean section, were to be redeemed from a Kohen, a descendent of Aaron, for the monetary equivalent of five Shekels.

Hananiah changed Berurya's life. The old routine was no longer the order of the day. Now, instead of rising each morning with the first rays of the sun to pray and to study, Hananiah determined when his mother slept and when she rose. The first two months were very difficult. Although the sages had exempted women from performing

certain *mitzvot*, and   exhaustion, Berurya still managed
to observe all the co⟩   ⟨ she had always fulfilled.

Being a mother ha   d effect on her; it brought to the
surface emotions she h⟨   ⟩ized were inside her. Sometimes,
when nursing her son a⟨   ⟩e warmth of his tiny body next
to hers, she experienced   elming sense of serenity and
contentment. She fed him   body; he nourished her by his
being. It was at these time⟨   ere closest. Hananiah gazed
into his mother's eyes, rec⟨   these were the eyes of the
person who cared for him. E   d into her baby's eyes and
in the reflection could see h⟨   clearly than ever before.
"Precious little Hananiah! Do   ⟩y idea how happy I am
because of you? I'm sure you   But it doesn't matter.
Sweet Hananiah, your mother⟨   ⟩ love you." Berurya
thought she detected a tiny smi⟨   robably imagination.
Hananiah closed his eyes and slep⟨

As the months passed, Berurya's   ⟩g of serenity began
to fade. While she still enjoyed   er son grow and
experiencing the wonder of life with ⟨   ⟩w realized that her
own life was incomplete. Thus, she r⟨ ⟩rned to her studies as one
who has long fasted tastes his first morsel of bread! She decided to
take on the most ambitious goal: she would study *Sefer Y'husin* or,
as it was also known, *Sefer Megilat Y'husin*. The text was a midrash,
an interpretation, on the Book of Chronicles.

Berurya valued midrash because it was a response to Scripture.
The study of God's word required elaboration and the explication
of its textual and its practical meaning. Midrash developed out of
careful scrutiny of the text. Perhaps the verse in question was
problematic or a word required clarification. Even single letters
might be examined to reveal hidden nuances. The relationship of
Scripture to homily was akin to that of dream and interpretation.
The dream was the essence, while it was the interpretation that
revealed its deeper, not readily apparent meanings. Berurya knew to
the Rabbinic mind, the Biblical word and its interpretation

coexisted, midrash was not an addition, but an intrinsic element of the text.

The text Berurya chose to master was extremely complex. She was aware that between First Chronicles, chapter eight, verse 31 and chapter nine, verse 44, there were over four hundred arrangements of midrashim! The compilation revealed the mysteries of Scripture, and also contained the genealogy of numerous families. It recorded the lineage of sages, the wealthy and prominent, as well as the ancestry of individuals of lesser reputations.

Berurya read that Hillel was a descendant of King David; that Rabbi Akiva's father-in-law, the prominent and wealthy Ben Kalba Savu'a, was a descendent of Caleb of the tribe of Judah. She read that Caleb and Joshua were the only two, of the twelve spies, who had brought back a good report of Canaan to Moses and the Israelites. A wealthy man, Ben Tzitzit HaKesset, provided for the inhabitants of Jerusalem when the city was under siege; his genealogy traced back to Abner, the captain of King Saul's army. When Abner died, Saul's son, King David, said of him: "A prince and a great man has fallen this day in Israel."

The lists of genealogy also included Rabbi Meir's colleagues, Rabbi Yose ben Halafta and Rabbi Nehemiah. Both had studied with Rabbi Akiva and had been ordained by Judah ben Bava when the latter was killed by the Romans.

Rabbi Nehemiah was a descendant of Nehemiah, the governor of Judah. Unlike his ancestor, Rabbi Nehemiah lived in great poverty. He used to say: "A single individual is as important as the whole of creation."

So voluminous was *Sefer Y'husin* that Berurya, while committing to memory approximately three hundred different teachings every day over a period of three years, was still unable to complete the task.

During these three years, Berurya gave birth to her second son, whom she named Elhanan after her brother. Meir was delighted. He had two sons to continue in his footsteps.

On the other hand, Penina had not yet given birth and was troubled by the prospect that, for some reason, she might never be able to conceive. Menahem, however, was supportive and reassuring. Again and again, he would tell her how much he loved her and that whether they had children or not, his feelings for her would never change.

Bilha stopped asking Penina when she and Menahem were planning to have children. Occasionally she passed on the old wives' tales she had heard from other women. For example, that salt, hunger, weeping, blood-letting, and certain pungent spices diminished one's sexual potency, while eggs, fish and garlic had the opposite effect. There were differences of opinion about which hours of the night were most conducive to conception. The night was divided into three watches: the first from 6 pm to 10 pm; the second from 10 pm to 2 am; and the third from 2 am to 6 am. Opinion varied on whether the second or the third watch was most propitious.

Penina wished so desperately to become pregnant that she tried every possible remedy. Each disappointment only made her more resolute. She would ask other women, especially those who, like herself, could not conceive. She prayed each day, hoping that God would answer her prayers. Slowly, her hope began to diminish and her frustration turned to anguish. She found it difficult to be in the company of women who did have children. Why should some women have eight, nine, and even ten children – and she not be allowed to have even one?

After Elhanan was born, Penina went to stay with Berurya again. This time her feelings were not quite the same as when Hananiah was born. While she loved her sister, she was embarrassed to admit even to herself that she envied Berurya.

One afternoon, both sisters were sitting in Berurya's bedroom. Penina watched as Berurya rocked little Elhanan in her arms. "Would you like to hold him for a while?" Berurya asked.

"No," answered Penina tersely.

Berurya was surprised by the answer and even more so by the tone.

"Penina, is something the matter?"

"Why should anything be the matter?" snapped Penina. "Can't I just sit here – or would you prefer that I left the room?"

"I'm sorry, Penina. I just asked."

Both of them sat in silence for the next few minutes. Then, without warning, Penina burst into tears. "Why!? Why me?" she sobbed.

Berurya put Elhanan in his crib and went over to her sister. She put her arms around Penina. "Penina," she said softly, "sometimes these things take time. I know women who gave birth only after ten years of marriage. You've got to have patience and believe that your prayers will be answered someday."

Penina wiped the tears from her cheeks. "Berurya," she sniffled, "I'm so ashamed of myself. You've always been so good to me... and I was jealous of you, my own sister!"

Berurya went back to the crib and sat down next to Elhanan. The infant had succeeded in rolling over on his stomach and she was afraid he might fall. She sat facing Penina; behind her, one hand rested on Elhanan. "Penina, why didn't you ever say anything to me? Why did you wait so long?"

"I don't know ..." Once again, Penina burst into tears. "I've been so unhappy."

Berurya went to Penina again and hugged her. After she had calmed down, Penina said quietly: "Berurya, it is hard for me to understand. God created women to bear children. God gave me an overwhelming desire to be a mother – I want it more than life itself! And now, God denies me the fulfillment. What've I done to be punished in this way? If I knew my sin at least, I could bear the punishment. Even a criminal standing before a judge is informed about the nature of his crime. Why should the Supreme Judge deny me this? It is not fair! It is not fair, I tell you!"

Berurya pulled Penina to her feet. "Come on, let's go outside. I'll leave Elhanan with Bilha."

They ambled down to the shores of the Kinneret. Penina unstrapped her sandals and went barefoot. She liked walking on the fine, moist grains of sand. As she looked down, Penina observed: "Strange, how with each step, the imprint of my foot leaves a message for all to see and then, in no time at all, a wave washes it away as though it had never been there. Is that what life is all about, Berurya? Leaving a little print in the sand, which is soon forgotten after we die?" She asked: "Do you think anyone will remember us after we're gone? Do you think anyone will know a hundred years from now, or will care, if we lived? I don't think so. At least, if I had a child, maybe he or she would one day tell his children, and they their children, that Penina and Berurya, the daughters of Rabbi Hananiah ben Teradyon, walked here along the shores of the Galilee one afternoon." She frowned. "Or am I foolish?"

"You're not foolish, Penina. I think that everyone wonders about life. A few years ago, Meir's teacher, Rabbi Elisha ben Avuya, explained why he had become an apostate. My first reaction was anger. I was actually furious! But then I began to wonder why I had reacted so vehemently. Perhaps, I then thought, Elisha had touched on something that I wanted to deny the existence of in myself? In all of us, perhaps? I mean... the voice of doubt. The voice that questions – questions everything. It was the voice that Eve thought came from the serpent. But think of it: did the serpent really speak? I wonder...." Berurya rubbed her chin. "At any rate, Elisha ben Avuya heard that voice, and succumbed. Knowledge necessarily promises nothing. As King Solomon said, 'For with more wisdom comes more worry, and he who adds to his knowledge adds to his pain.'"

They walked along in silence and then Berurya went on: "You know, Penina, I've thought often about the horrible way in which our father died. Time eases nothing. I will never, as long as I live, forget the last moments of his life! Sometimes, when I'm deeply absorbed in prayer, the sound of father saying the *Sh'ma* that last time drowns out my words! 'Why?' the voice asks. 'Why such a tortuous death? For what purpose?' then I answer myself: 'Because of his devotion to God and his reverence for the Torah.' Then the voice nags: 'What about the others? Those who transgress every commandment imaginable daily, yet live out their lives in peace.' I can't answer that question, nor can I answer why other women, far less deserving than you, should bear children while you can't. I don't know the answer; no one does!" Berurya shrugged. "Maybe we ask the wrong question? Remember when we were little, and we'd play make-believe? You pretended to be the heroine, dear Elhanan was the hero, and I would make up the story and tell both of you what happened next. We were only pretending. But in real life, we're also actors. We are given scripts, and it's our duty to play the roles we're given in life as convincingly as possible; to do the best with the parts we've been handed. To be the actor in life is not to pretend, but to be your true self; to be true to that self is ultimately to be the best actor. Yes, Penina, we're all actors, with one Director. The stage is set and the Director calls out: 'Choose life that you may live!' and we act. You must have faith, my dear Penina, in the Director. Listen to His voice; follow His directions, and then choose the kind of life which permits you to understand what it really means to live! Only the Director knows why. And only the actor has the choice of how to live. Working together the actor, with the Director's guidance, can create the story called life."

The winds off the lake had picked up by now and it was beginning to get cool.

"Berurya," Penina said as she halted and turned to face her sister, "what would I do without you?"

"You've done very well without me," Berurya said. "You have a husband who loves you dearly – and, as much as I would love for you to stay with us forever, your place is with him. Don't turn away from him. Go back to Sikhnin. He needs you ... as much as you need him."

Penina smiled wistfully. They turned and began to walk back. They had lost all track of the time and did not realize that evening was fast approaching. In the setting sun, the mountains surrounding the Kinneret were lit with mystical beauty. Berurya reflected that what she saw was, after all, only dirt and stone. Something people trod on daily without giving the matter a second thought. However, if enough were gathered that it became a mountain, when the light of the setting sun accentuated its colors and created shadows, that prosaic dirt was transformed – just as God had transformed earth into Man.

12
Flora

Penina returned to Menahem and Meir journeyed away from Berurya. This time Meir, Rabbi Yosi, and Rabbi Yehuda traveled south, to Lydda. Meir went first to the west, to Sepphoris, a distance of about twenty kilometers, where Rabbi Yosi lived. There he also met Rabbi Yehuda, who had spent the previous Shabbat with Rabbi Yosi. The three of them traveled to 'Ardaskus, about twelve kilometers west of Sepphoris. They then turned southward, stopping briefly in Tiv'on and Bet She'arim which were nearby.

If one traveled on a straight line from Bet She'arim to Lydda, the distance was 100 kilometers. Roads, however, were rarely built in straight lines, but rather conformed to the contours of the terrain. Consequently, the way to Lydda was considerably longer, and the rabbis knew they would have to spend a few nights in a poondak, *an inn. Traveling was always dangerous. They also knew it was unwise to go anywhere alone – the roads were treacherous, and even the* poondak *was unsafe.*

Once, on a journey, Meir met an innkeeper who proved to be dishonest. He had devised a plan with *listim*, or cutthroats, to inform them when a vulnerable traveler was leaving in the morning. A short distance from the inn, the bandits would pounce upon the unsuspecting man, murder him and divide his possessions among themselves and the innkeeper. Meir had sensed disaster in the nick of time and managed to outwit the innkeeper and escape.

Remembering her brother, Berurya would worry each time Meir had to be away overnight. He had now been gone for over a week. As usual, Berurya taught in the *Beit Midrash*, whenever she could leave Elhanan and Hananiah with Bilha. With Meir gone, the days and especially the nights, seemed longer.

One night, the children and Bilha were fast asleep. Berurya, sitting in the triclinium, was just about to join them when a knock at the door startled her. Cautiously, she called out: "Who's there?"

"I'm looking for Rabbi Meir," a woman's voice said.

Berurya unlocked the door. In the dark, it was impossible to discern the woman's features. "I'm Rabbi Meir's wife," she said. "Please come inside."

The woman entered and Berurya closed the door.

"Please sit down," Berurya said. "Maybe I can help?"

Berurya watched as the tall, slender, mysterious woman went over to a chair. When she removed her hood, Berurya was struck by the woman's beauty; indeed, she was the most beautiful woman Berurya had ever seen! There was actually an aura of splendor about her. It was as though God had created a perfect feminine form and endowed it with life. Her eyes were the palest shade of blue, almost the color of a clear sky; her blemishless, white complexion shone; her long, blond hair seemed spun of gold thread.

The woman seated herself and glanced around the room. "When will Rabbi Meir return?" she asked.

"I don't know for sure. He left for Lydda for at least two weeks. That was ten days ago. Sometimes he returns on time, but usually he's delayed an additional day or two. If you want to come back in a week's time, I'm sure he'll be here."

"I cannot go back," the woman muttered.

"Excuse me," said Berurya. "I didn't hear what you said."

"Nothing," said the woman. "It doesn't matter." She took out a piece of parchment and handed it to Berurya, who saw that the words Tiberias, Rabbi Meir and Yaddua, one of Meir's students, were scrawled on it.

"But what do you want?" Berurya insisted.

"I want to be Jewish!" the woman said emphatically.

Berurya was dumbfounded. Here was a woman, exquisitely beautiful, and – given the expensive jewelry she wore – obviously quite wealthy, expressing a desire to be Jewish.

"But why?" Berurya questioned. "What is there about Judaism that makes you want to convert, especially in these times? Surely you know that we are persecuted terribly by the Romans! Countless thousands have died only because they were born Jewish! And yet you actually say... you want to convert!?"

The woman cleared her throat, turned her body slightly, looked Berurya directly in the eyes and said: "I am a prostitute!"

Again, Berurya was thunderstruck.

The woman rose. "Maybe you're right," she said slowly. "Maybe it's best that I return in a week when Rabbi Meir is back."

Berurya got up herself and reached for the woman's arm. "Please sit down. It's too late for you to leave. It's unsafe. You must stay the night; we've plenty of room."

The woman reflected. "That is ... very kind of you. I will accept your offer."

Berurya and the woman sat down again. "What's your name?" asked Berurya.

"I'm called Flora – after the goddess of flowers."

"My name is Berurya. I'm very curious about the note you showed me. Beside my husband's name and the name, Tiberias, there was the name of a student, Yaddua. Is he in any trouble?"

"Trouble?" asked Flora. "No, he's not in any trouble. As a matter of fact, he's the reason I'm here!"

Berurya gestured. "Yaddua learned recently that his mother died,
and so he has gone back to Nehardea, a town in Babylonia, to be
with his family."

"Will he be coming back?"

"Yes, definitely"

Flora seemed reassured by Berurya's words. "Berurya," she said
firmly, "I said I wanted to convert to Judaism and I definitely intend
to do so. But I know little about the religion."

"Tell me first why you want to convert? I surmise that it has
something to do with Yaddua."

"I don't want to get him into trouble," said Flora.

"You won't. You have my word."

Flora sighed and leaned forward in the chair. "I think I should
begin by telling you about myself. I suppose that my story really
starts with my grandmother. She was, from what my mother told
me, a very intelligent and beautiful woman. She was brought to
Rome as a slave and purchased by a wealthy Roman aristocrat. Her
job was to tend to the needs of his wife, a distinguished matron.
Apparently, the Roman nobleman also had his own needs in mind,
if you know what I mean. In any event, his wife found the two out;
instead of blaming her husband, who was truly at fault, she vented
her anger on my grandmother. She worked the poor woman until
she literally collapsed. The husband was not aware of what was
happening and let my grandmother suffer. To make things worse,
my grandmother became pregnant. As soon as the matron found out,
the beatings began: she would hit my grandmother, and punish her
for no reason. At length, the husband got wind of it, took pity on my
grandmother, and sold her into a brothel, where my mother was
born."

Flora closed her eyes, as if remembering; then she opened them
and went on: "My grandmother was not a strong woman and soon
succumbed to an illness. Mother was only five years old at the time.
Imagine how it was to be a child raised in a whorehouse! But my
mother said that most of the prostitutes were good to her. Not all of

them, mind you – but most. My mother grew up very quickly; she was determined to get out of the place and not end up like her mother. One day her dreams were realized. A young Roman soldier took a fancy to her and she seized the opportunity. He paid the manager a bribe, and the soldier took her. He wanted to marry her, and she agreed – anything was better than the life she had known.

"Her marriage was short-lived – or I should say, the soldier was short-lived. One night, five months after they had been married, he simply failed to return home. My mother never knew for certain, but she suspected that he had been robbed and subsequently murdered. Although she had never truly loved him, she felt pity for him.

"She also felt sorry for herself because she, like her mother before her, was pregnant. It was then that she made the fateful decision that ultimately changed her life. She decided to leave Rome and journey to Tyre. Tyre had been under Roman rule since the time of Marc Anthony and had become one of the Empire's richest centers of commerce. My mother realized that money meant power, which was just as important as freedom – maybe even more so. People often relinquish freedom but power, once it is tasted, is never readily surrendered."

An expression of mingled regret and helplessness came into Flora's eyes. "Even after I was born, my mother continued to earn her living as a prostitute. Slowly but steadily she accumulated money; she began to dress in finer clothes and pampered herself. She also restricted her clientele, which prompted her to raise her prices. To her surprise, she realized that people would pay whatever she asked, as long as they felt they were getting something special – something that was denied to others! The sexual experience was different only in the imagination, which is where the pleasure resides."

Flora leaned forward. "My mother showered me with affection as I grew up. She literally gave me everything that money could buy. When I was old enough, I made my choice. I wanted to be a prostitute, but I decided to take it one step further; I would charge more money than anyone else had ever charged. By doing this, I would create an illusion that no man could resist. Thus my brothel became a lavish fantasy! Instead of wooden furniture, I had silver and gold; the rooms were fitted out with ivory and the finest silks. In one special room, there were three beds, one higher than the next with a ladder connecting one to the other. The top bed was the most opulent, decorated with gold and silk. In my house, each man was made to feel as if he himself were the Emperor of Rome; therefore, it was worth the cost. The fee, by the way, was always paid in advance!

"When a client came to my brothel, a servant-girl would greet him; if for any reason she decided he would not be to my liking, his money was promptly returned and he was asked to leave. The Roman authorities, of course, were 'partners' in my business; the percentage I gave them was considerable. But the tax was worth it; if a problem arose, I knew where to turn.

"About three years ago my mother died. I had loved her deeply, and I missed her very much. To me, she had been everything: parent, friend, confidant. After her death, something went out of my life. I made more money than ever, but I felt empty. At first I attributed the feeling to the fact that my mother had died. I expected that, in time, I'd get back to my former self. But with each passing day, it got worse. I was desperately seeking something. I didn't know what...."

Flora fell silent; she gazed vacantly past Berurya. Then, after a time, her gaze again focused on her hostess and she continued to speak. "About three months ago," she said, "I had an appointment in the early afternoon. The servant-girl walked into my chambers and said that a young man was waiting for me. She turned and ushered him in. Then she lit the incense and closed the door behind her as she left. Usually men talk, but this one didn't say a single word as he undressed. I stared at him. He was young and it was obvious by his appearance that the money he'd paid to be with me was far beyond his means. Also, the clothes he wore were unusual;

for example, there were fringes attached to the four corners of his undergarment."

Flora lifted a hand. "I was lying in the top bed, the one gilded with gold. As he climbed toward me, he suddenly stopped. He was still for a moment and then he said hoarsely: 'It's not right!' You can imagine how astonished I was! And I was hurt and angry. How could anyone reject me!? 'Where are you going?' I asked as I saw him climbing down the ladder. He didn't answer. That only made me angrier! I just couldn't let him leave without an explanation! So I put on a robe and descended. He was dressing. I seized his arm and told him that I wouldn't let go of it until he told me what was wrong with me. He stared at me in amazement. 'You're the most beautiful woman I've ever seen,' he said softly. 'You're absolutely magnificent! The problem is not you... it's me!' He cleared his throat. 'I'm a Jew,' he said, 'and I suddenly realized that, in spite of my overwhelming desire for you, what I was about to do was wrong! I would be breaking one of God's commandments! And that realization was stronger than my passion.'"

Flora shook her head. "I listened to what he said, but it made no sense to me. No man has ever resisted me! No man has ever seen me naked and walked out on me! So before he went, I asked him to write his name, the city from which he came, and the name of someone who could explain the strange beliefs which Jews had. That's how I got your husband's name." Flora sighed. "When he was fully dressed again, I offered to return his money. He didn't want it. That troubled me as well.

"During the next few days, I couldn't get the young man out of my mind. I wanted to know more about his religion and its power to control his behavior. So I went to the Jewish community in Tyre and found an old man in one of the synagogues. I offered to pay him handsomely to reveal the secrets of his religion. He said he'd teach me, but refused to accept any money.

"Many of the things he explained seemed strange at first. He told me about God, who created the universe and redeemed a nation of slaves from Egypt. Yet this God was invisible! No one could see Him! Then the old man explained the importance of the commandments. These, too, seemed contrary to logic. There was a commandment to care for strangers, orphans and widows! A commandment to rest for an entire day! Never before had I heard of such things.

"The more I learned, the more fascinated I became with this peculiar religion. I studied with the old man for seven weeks. By then, I'd made up my mind to become Jewish! I also wanted to meet the young man, Yaddua, again. There was something about him that intrigued me! The more I learned about Judaism, the more I thought about him."

Flora folded her arms across her chest. She smiled gently and rather sadly. "Well," she said, "that's just about my story. I decided to leave. I gave one third of my wealth to the Roman authorities – a bribe to insure my leaving the city without any questions being asked. I gave another third of the money to the poor – partly to make amends for my previous life. The remainer of my money I kept for myself."

Berurya nodded slowly. "That's an amazing story," she said. "As I told you, Rabbi Meir will probably return in a week or so. Yaddua will be away for at least a month. But you're welcome to stay with us."

"Are you certain?"

"Yes, I am! We have plenty of room; and besides, I can be of help in answering more of your questions about Judaism."

"You're very kind."

Then Berurya rose and took Flora to a guest room.

"It may not be as comfortable as what you're used to...."

"It's fine!" said Flora. "Thank you for everything."

13
Lentil Soup

During the following days, Bilha gave Flora her own special tour of Hammat and Tiberias. Berurya began teaching Flora Hebrew; she explained to Flora that it was one thing to learn about Judaism – to intellectually understand it – and quite another to actually live Judaism. If Flora really wanted to become Jewish, then she had to acquaint herself with its customs and rituals, as well as to learn its language.

Berurya also received word that Elisha ben Avuya had become seriously ill and had requested that Meir be at his side. The messenger did not have much information; he only knew that Elisha's health had been seriously deteriorating over the last few weeks and that there was not much chance for his recovery. Berurya hoped that Meir would have a chance to see his teacher one last time before Elisha died. Berurya felt sorrow for this bitter, tormented man who was about to die.

In the meantime, the three rabbis were on their way home. They had accomplished what they had set out to do, although not without problems. The worst, however, was yet to come. It began in the late afternoon, on Friday. They spotted a *poondak* in the distance and all three of them agreed to stop there. The innkeeper greeted them as though they were long-lost friends. Meir was at once suspicious. Furthermore, the innkeeper's name, Meir learned, was Kidor. This too troubled Meir, for Deuteronomy 32, verse 20 contained the phrase, "*ki dor tahpookhot haymah*", "for they are a treacherous generation". Surely, it was a forbidding omen. But Rabbi Yehuda and Rabbi Yosi made light of Meir's concerns and left their valuables and money with the innkeeper for safekeeping until after the Sabbath.

Meir, on the other hand, kept his money with him, which irritated the innkeeper. Meir found a small jar in the room and placed all his money in it. With the jar hidden under his garments, he asked the innkeeper where the cemetery was located. Kidor could not understand why the rabbi would possibly wish to visit a graveyard, especially before the Sabbath. Nonetheless, he gave him directions.

Once at the cemetery, Meir found the burial site of Kidor's father and buried the jar at the head of the grave. He returned to the inn only minutes before the onset of the Sabbath.

Saturday night, when three stars appeared in the sky indicating that the Sabbath was over, Meir went back to the grave and retrieved his money. At the same time, Rabbi Yosi and Rabbi Yehuda approached Kidor and asked that their possessions be returned to them. Kidor first appeared surprised. "Possessions!" he growled. "What possessions!? Didn't you tell me that you'd changed your minds and preferred to keep the money in your room?"

"No," said Rabbi Yehuda, "that was Rabbi Meir! Rabbi Yosi and I gave our money to you."

"I'll check, if you insist," Kidor said, "but you're wrong. I distinctly remember our discussion."

Kidor left the room and returned shortly. "Just as I told you," he said. "I have other guests' possessions, but definitely not yours."

"Do you mind if we check too?" asked Rabbi Yehuda.

Kidor's tone was hostile; he spoke in a raised voice: "But, of course, I mind! Furthermore, I don't like your insinuation! You have until morning to get out of my inn and I don't ever want to see you here again! Understand?"

Rabbi Yosi and Rabbi Yehuda stared at each other in disbelief and dismay. But what could they do? They returned to their room.

An hour or so later, Meir returned. He took the jar out from under his garments, brushed off the dirt and extracted the money.

"You were right," Yosi said.

"Right about what?" asked Meir.

"About the innkeeper, Kidor. He denies that we gave him our money and valuables."

"Yes," said Meir, "I was right. My instincts didn't fail me."

"What should we do?" asked Yehuda. "We can't leave without our money. How will we get it back? We've no way of knowing where he's hidden it!"

"I have a plan," Meir said, "but it might be dangerous."

Meir outlined his plan and the others agreed to it. The three of them went downstairs and found Kidor. "We owe you an apology," Yosi said to Kidor. "The oddest thing happened; we found our money under our beds!"

"You did?" Kidor asked incredulously.

"Yes," said Yehuda, "it was there all the time. And to think that we accused you of being dishonest!" He clucked his tongue. "Let us buy you some wine – at least we'll be able to make up for our discourtesy."

"That's very nice of you," Kidor said, still puzzled, but never willing to pass up a free drink.

The four of them sat at a table. Yosi and Yehuda poured the innkeeper one drink after the other. Kidor could barely keep his head up.

"Meir," Yosi whispered, "what'll we do now? He's about ready to pass out and we still don't know where he's hidden the money."

"Shhh!" Meir said. "Be patient."

Meir lifted Kidor's head. "Look closely at his beard," he said to Yosi and Yehuda. "What do you see?"

The other two stared. "Lentils," Yehuda murmured. "That merely shows that Kidor is a slob, as well as a thief!"

Meir shook Kidor. "Kidor," he said loudly. "is it true that you had lentils for dinner?"

"Lentils?" Kidor muttered thickly: "Yes ... there were lentils in the soup."

Kidor's head dropped heavily to the table.

"Come with me," Meir said to the other two, "I know where Kidor lives. But you two say nothing: let me do the talking."

In a short time, they arrived at Kidor's house. Meir knocked on the door.

"Who's there?" a woman's voice called out.

"We're friends of your husband," Meir replied.

The door opened a crack, so that the woman inside could see the strangers.

"Kidor sent us over," said Meir. "He said you should give us the money he took from those two rabbis."

"How do I know you're telling the truth?"

"Kidor told us that you served him lentil soup for dinner! No one else but you would know that. He gave us this information as a sign for you to give us the money."

The woman hesitated.

"How else would we know what he ate," persisted Meir, "if he hadn't told us?"

"Wait here," the woman said.

After several moments, the woman returned and handed Meir the purses that Kidor had taken from Yosi and Yehuda.

"Thanks," said Meir.

The door closed.

"Now," urged Meir, "we must leave before Kidor snaps out of his stupor and discovers we've tricked him! It won't be safe here once he's sober!"

Meir, Yosi, and Yehuda hurried back to the inn, took their belongings and rushed downstairs.

Meir left a note at Kidor's side.

"What did you say?" asked Yosi.

"Not much," Meir answered. "I simply wrote that lentil soup might be good for his hangover."

Yosi and Yehuda laughed.

As they rode away, Yosi remarked: "In a way, I'm sorry for Kidor's wife. When he finds out what happened, he'll beat her mercilessly!"

"You're probably right, Yosi," said Meir. "But somehow, I feel they're two of a kind."

14

The Death of Elisha Ben Avuya

Meir returned to Hammat four days later than he had initially planned. Berurya was overjoyed to have him home. She informed Meir that Elisha ben Avuya was dying, which saddened him greatly. He decided to leave first thing in the morning to be at his teacher's bedside. Berurya also told her husband about Flora and Yaddua. Flora was not actually there in the house – she was staying with a widow, whose husband had been slain in the war with the Romans. Meir scarcely spoke; he was preoccupied with his dying teacher.

The next morning Meir departed. He was exhausted by his journey to Lydda and had his teacher not been mortally ill, would have welcomed a rest and then a return to his studies. However, there were things in life that could not be postponed; people found excuses for not attending various celebrations, but death was different. There was no excuse for being absent. Meir felt the death of a friend should remind one of his own mortality. No one can know the years allotted to him. "Yet," Meir thought, "people acted as if there would always be another tomorrow ..."

Meir found Elisha in a very frail condition. The sick man's eyes were closed; Meir stood silently beside the bed gazing down at the teacher whose knowledge he so respected. Elisha lay on his back; a blanket was pulled up to his neck. He still had a full head of hair, although it had thinned and was now almost completely white.

Meir remembered how Elisha had stood tall and erect; his hair had been jet black. He had always been clean-shaven, meticulous in his appearance. He had always refused to grow a beard, but now, lying helplessly there, the stubble on his face made him look unkempt.

How Elisha had aged! So quickly! Only three years had passed since they had last seen each other. Meir recalled the Sabbath when he walked alongside Elisha on his horse. How strange that Elisha, unconcerned as he was with Jewish law, should have kept track of the distance they traveled so that Meir should not inadvertently transgress the Sabbath!

Without warning, Elisha's eyes opened.

"It's me, Rabbi, your student, Meir."

Elisha turned his head in Meir's direction. Meir got a chair and sat down close to the sick man. Elisha just stared.

"May I get you something?"

"I knew you'd come," Elisha said in a gruff voice.

"Yes, I came as soon as I heard...."

Elisha turned his head away; he gazed up at the ceiling. His mouth was slightly open; his breathing was labored and uneven.

Meir bent forward. "Rabbi," he said, "repent now, before it is too late."

"It is... already too late," Elisha said weakly.

"No, Elisha, it's not! There's still time! Repent!"

It was the first time Meir had ever called his teacher by his first name. He reached out and took Elisha's hand. "Please."

Elisha turned to Meir again. His lips were parched; he could scarcely utter a word. "Meir," he whispered. Tears filled his eyes. "Meir ..."

And then he was silent.

Rabbi Elisha ben Avuya was dead. Meir began to weep; it felt as if his own father had died. No, it was worse! Elisha was more than a parent!

Meir rose and gently set Elisha's hand down. Tears flowed from Meir's eyes. "Blessed be the righteous Judge," proclaimed Meir. "The Lord hath given. The Lord hath taken away. Blessed be the name of the Lord."

The next morning Meir buried his teacher. The sky was dark, packed with thick gray-black clouds. A strong wind had sprung up. Lightning lit up the horizon, followed by a deafening crash of thunder.

Meir stood at Elisha's grave, the wind whipping his face. While his heart ached with the pain of his loss, there was also a tiny spark of joy. Deep within himself, Meir believed that Elisha ben Avuya's tears in the final moments of life were his way of asking God's forgiveness. Though he had not used words, Elisha ben Avuya had expressed his remorse.

At length, Meir turned and left. There was nothing more to do. Suddenly, there was another bolt of lightning and a clap of thunder. Meir looked back. "It struck ... his grave," Meir murmured hoarsely. Indeed, the shaft of lightning had struck Elisha's grave and set it afire! Meir raced back. He removed his cloak and flung it over the burning grave. The fire went out; only a plume of black smoke rose up.

Meir knelt down and froze. The words that Boaz spoke to Ruth ran through his mind, only this time with a different meaning: "Tarry this night, for it shall be in the morning, that if he will perform to thee the part of a kinsman well; let him do the kinsman's part; but if he will not do the part of the kinsman to thee, then will I do the part of a kinsman to thee, as the Lord live: lie down until the morning." Meir thought: "The world we live in is night, and only the World to Come can truly be called morning. If God, in His goodness, will redeem you, Elisha, fine; but if not – then let me redeem you! As the Lord lives, lie in peace, Elisha, until the morning." As Meir spoke, the winds quieted down. The world was still dark, still anticipating another morning. Meir set out for Hammat.

Berurya was saddened by the news of Elisha's death, even though she had expected it. Meir was sullen. Not a single rabbi had come to visit Elisha ben Avuya as he lay dying. Not one sage had attended his funeral. No one had made an allowance for him – not even his daughter, nor his grandchild. Meir felt that to be ostracized was one thing; to be condemned to die alone was by far the gravest punishment of all. "An infant is born," Meir thought, "and immediately cries. The response to his cry is love and attention from his parents. A person dies and there is another cry, the cry of the bereaved, of family and friends who really weep for themselves. Then, there is a third cry: not the cry of the infant, nor the cry of mourning. It is a cry unlike any other and its sound races from one end of the world to the other, yet cannot be heard by human ears; it is the cry of the soul as it leaves the body."

15
A Change of Name

Berurya continued to instruct Flora. The teacher was astonished to discover when she taught her pupil the prayer *Sh'ma*, "Hear O Israel, the Lord is our God, the Lord is One!" that Flora already knew it!

"Who taught it to you?" Berurya asked.

"My mother," replied Flora.

"Your mother!? How would your mother know it – and why would she teach it to you?"

"I don't know," Flora answered. "The only thing she ever said was that she remembered learning it from her mother. She didn't know what the words meant but my grandmother would always say the words to her before putting her to sleep."

Berurya was intrigued. "What was ... your grandmother's name?"

Flora reflected. "I'm not sure, but I think it was something like Damar, or Damir."

"Could it have been Tamar?"

"Yes! That's it! It was Tamar bat Yehudit! I remember the name: Tamar bat Yehudit." Flora drew a deep breath. "Why, that's a Hebrew name! My grandmother was Jewish!"

To Berurya, it seemed to make sense. Flora's grandmother, as best as she could determine, had been taken to Rome around 70 C.E., the year in which the Temple in Jerusalem was destroyed and thousands of Jews were sold into slavery!

Berurya did considerable checking and it did indeed appear to be true that Flora's grandmother was Jewish. Flora was also amazed to learn that, while her grandmother had been enslaved, her grandmother's older brother had managed to escape and that his descendents were now living in Susita, a town opposite Tiberias, on the far side of the Kinneret.

In a brief time, Flora's world had been totally transformed. When Yaddua at length returned from Nehardia, he was astonished to find Flora in the *Beit Midrash* with Berurya! His shock soon turned to joy.

After several additional months of study, Flora was married to Yaddua. Before the wedding, Flora changed her name to Tamar, after her grandmother.

16
Bathsheva

Berurya's third pregnancy proceeded without incident and was easier than the first two. She gave birth just prior to the holiday of Shavuot, the Festival of Weeks, commemorating the giving of the Torah. Berurya called her daughter Bathsheva, the name of King David's wife; it was a name she had always liked. One of Berurya's childhood friends had been called Bathsheva and the girl had died at a young age; calling her daughter Bathsheva was a memorial.

One afternoon, when they were children, they were playing outside. Bathsheva told Berurya that she felt like she was burning up and Berurya brought her friend home to her parents, who put her to bed immediately and called the doctor.

The doctor prescribed that she drink water in order to reduce the burning sensation. But the fever only increased. The doctor then tried bloodletting, but this did not produce the desired results either. She was also given red meat with diluted wine – a common treatment for fever. Bathsheva's condition steadily deteriorated, and at length she died. Later it was determined that the water Bathsheva drank while playing outside had probably been contaminated; it was not uncommon, for instance, for the corpse of an animal to pollute the drinking water.

Berurya was terribly saddened by her friend's death; at the same time, she felt other, troubling emotions. Noticing a change in her behavior, Berurya's father asked if something was wrong. At first, his daughter denied she had a problem, but later on she admitted that she had felt relief because she had not drunk from the same well as Bathsheva. She remembered having waited for Bathsheva to finish drinking. And how many times had she herself drunk water from a well or a stream without giving it a second thought? For whatever reason, this time Berurya had decided not to drink and so she was alive and her friend dead. All this disturbed Berurya greatly.

"Why," Berurya had asked her father, "was my life spared and Bathsheva's life taken? Was she being punished for something she did wrong? But how could that be? Bathsheva was such a good person! Why did she die and not me!?"

Berurya's father tried to find an appropriate response to this difficult question. "First, I have to tell you that any answer I give you probably won't be satisfactory. There are things in life we simply don't understand. The question, 'why did she die and not me?' can be understood as two separate questions: one is, why did your friend, who was such a good person, have to die? The other is, why was your life spared?

"Let's take the second question first: why was your life spared? Berurya, you became aware that your life was spared only because Bathsheva drank from the water and died. Had she not drunk the water, the question would never have arisen. Perhaps everyone is spared many times during his life, but isn't aware of it. While walking in the country, you cross the path of a snake, and yet for some inexplicable reason the snake does not strike! God protects us and most often, we are simply unaware of it....

"Sometimes, people's lives are spared because of small acts of kindness they do for another person. Recently I spoke with Rabbi Akiva and he told me that when his daughter was born, astrologers foretold that on the night of her wedding, she would be bitten by a snake and die. You can imagine what a burden he carried in his heart! Usually, a child's marriage is one of the greatest moments in a parent's life but Akiva feared it would be an occasion of great sorrow and mourning.

"At his own daughter's wedding, Akiva had to pretend that he was happy when his inner pain was all but unbearable. He dreaded that it might be the last day of her life. He did not sleep that night. The next morning, he went to see his daughter, expecting to find her dead. To his joy and surprise, there she was – as healthy as ever! When he commented, Akiva heard a fascinating story.

"On the night of her wedding, as his daughter was getting undressed, she removed her brooch and stuck the pin into a crevice in the wall. When she removed it the next morning, she saw – to her amazement – that the pin had pierced the head of a serpent and killed it! Akiva realized that this was no coincidence. He asked her if anything unusual had happened that evening. At first, nothing came to mind. But then she remembered that during the wedding festivities, a poor man had come to the house and begged for food. Everyone was so busy that the beggar was ignored. 'But I heard him call out,' his daughter said, 'and I took the portion of food that you had given me and gave it to him.' Rabbi Akiva understood from this incident that while certain things appear fated and seemingly out of our control, the truth is that we can control our destinies and even avert Heavenly decrees about death.

"And now as to your first question, 'Why did Bathsheva die?' I don't know. No one can answer that. The answer lies only with God. Animals lose offspring – it is simply a part of nature. Humans lose children and the pain is unbearable. The only question the bereaved parent wants answered is 'Why?' But 'Why' is the only question for which there is no answer. Therefore, when you enter a house of mourning, you are supposed to sit in silence. Words enter the ear; silence touches the heart. Silence is the only language that communicates concern, sorrow, and sympathy. Silence is the only response to 'Why?' It comforts until the question 'Why?' itself fades into silence...."

17
Frustrations

Unlike his responses to the births of Hananiah and Elhanan, Meir displayed few outward signs of enthusiasm when he was informed that his third child was a daughter. He simply inquired about Berurya's health and well-being and after spending some time with his wife, returned to his routine. At first, Berurya rationalized this: she told herself that the novelty of fatherhood had worn off for Meir, so that the birth of this child could be received almost nonchalantly. But as time went on, she noticed that Meir seemed to keep his distance from Bathsheva. "But how could Meir be upset with an infant?" Berurya thought. "Especially one as adorable as Bathsheva!"

Once again, Penina came to stay with Berurya and help out. Berurya sensed that her sister had accepted the fact that she might never give birth; Penina actually seemed happier now.

"Penina," Berurya said, as she rose from the dinner table one evening, "would you help me with the dishes?"

"I can do the dishes," Bilha interrupted.

"Thanks, Bilha," said Berurya, "but I'd like you to take care of Bathsheva. The two of us were awake most of the night and I really don't have the strength to look after her now."

Bilha picked up Bathsheva and gently cradled the baby in her arms.

"There now," Bilha said in a lilting voice, "have you been a naughty girl? Did you keep your mother up last night? Maybe I'll tell you all about how your mother used to keep me up when she was a baby?!"

Berurya smiled. "You still haven't forgiven me, eh?"

"No, I haven't," Bilha shouted back from the stairs.

At that moment, Hananiah and Elhanan came into the house.

"You're home earlier than I expected," said Berurya.

"Yes," said Hananiah. "Father was busy with one of his pupils, and so we decided to come home."

"He'll be upset when he finds out that you left without his permission."

"But we were so hungry! You wouldn't want us to starve to death, would you?" said Elhanan.

"I'll give them something to eat," said Penina. "After all, they're growing boys."

"Growing boys!" exclaimed Berurya. "That's an understatement! If they grow any more, we'll need a bigger house!"

Penina set the plates of food down in front of them. The two boys attacked the food ravenously.

"Mother, we'll be home a little later this evening," said Hananiah between mouthfuls.

"Why?" questioned Berurya. "What's so important that'll keep you out late?"

"Nothing much," replied Hananiah: "We just thought –"

"Who is this 'we'?"

"Elhanan and I," Hananiah answered.

"To begin with, whenever you use the world 'we', the truth is that it's probably your idea, and that you're dragging your brother along!"

"That's not right," protested Elhanan. "I thought it was a great idea."

"Exactly what I meant!" said Berurya.

"Please, Mother ..." said Hananiah.

"How do you expect to master your studies," said Berurya, cutting him off, "if you don't devote enough time to them? Learning doesn't come automatically: it takes effort and diligence! Your father and I have devoted our lives to study. You're the next generation. I want you to understand that learning our traditions, that following our laws and customs as they were transmitted to Moses at Mt. Sinai and handed down to each successive generation – this is your heritage, and nothing in life is more important!"

"Mother, you've told us this many times," protested Hananiah. "Really, I don't mean to be disrespectful, but did it ever occur to you that we're not like you and father. Did it ever occur to you that we might not have the same interests or abilities? Did you ever think that the only similarity between me and my grandfather might be the same name? Even that wasn't my choice! You cannot make me what I'm not! The truth of the matter is ..."

Berurya put up a hand. "Enough," she said. "After supper, I want you both to return to the *Beit Midrash* and get on with your studies!

"But Mother ..." persisted Elhanan.

"You heard what I said! That's the final word!"

Hananiah and Elhanan finished their meal in silence and left the house for the *Beit Midrash*.

"Aren't you being a little harsh on them?" Penina asked.

"Perhaps," said Berurya, "but I know they're capable of learning if they'd apply themselves. Especially Hananiah. If he devoted half the energy he expends on avoiding his studies, he would excel. He definitely has the ability. That's what's so frustrating."

Penina shook her head. "But Berurya," she said, "you can't make them like you. In our own household, there were three children. But only you followed in our father's footsteps. There are things in life we can't control, nor should we even try. Maybe you'll have to face the fact that Elhanan and Hananiah aren't meant to be scholars like you and Meir."

"Penina, if you had children ..." Berurya stopped herself. "I'm sorry, Penina, but sometimes I get frustrated! I want the boys to love the same things I love. I want them to appreciate our heritage as much as I do. I want them to carry on our family traditions."

"But Berurya, just listen to what you're saying: 'I want them to do this; I want them to do that.' The question is: what do they want? I, for one, am very happy with who and what I am. I could never be like you, because I don't have your mind or your ability. Nor do I pretend to be what I'm not. Allow the boys to be themselves! If they aren't scholars, so be it! Maybe your grandchildren will be scholars. Maybe your great-grandchildren will be farmers. Whatever they are, let them be themselves."

Berurya reflected on her sister's words. Rarely had she heard Penina speak so forcefully. She stared at her sister. "Who says you couldn't have been a scholar?"

Penina laughed. "I don't have to be a scholar; my sister is one."

Later that afternoon, Meir returned. Penina greeted Meir but he passed her by, absorbed in his own thoughts. He seated himself. Berurya came downstairs, carrying little Bathsheva in her arms. "Meir," she said, "I thought I heard someone come in but I didn't expect you now. Did you leave Hananiah and Elhanan in the *Beit Midrash*?"

Meir muttered something inaudible.

"What's that?"

Meir looked up. The expression on his face was one she rarely saw. His eyes blazed with anger. He pounded his leg with a fist.

"Those stupid people," Meir shouted at the top of his voice. "Why do I have to put up with their stupidity!? They don't deserve to be called human. They aren't human. They're really animals – cows and bulls – or better yet, jackasses which have learned to walk upright and talk!"

Meir's face was beet red. His shouting made Bathsheva cry. "Do I have to listen to her cry? Can't you shut her up?!"

"I'll take her," Penina ventured, reaching out for Bathsheva. "I'll be upstairs if you need me." Penina patted Bathsheva gently on the back and calmed her. "There, there now, everything's going to be all right. Daddy's not angry with you."

When Penina left the room, Berurya turned to her husband. "Meir, what's happened?"

"You want to know?" said Meir. "Well, I'll tell you what happened. Saturday night three weeks ago, after the Sabbath, I went into the *Beit Keneset*, as I always do, to lecture. For whatever reason, there was a large crowd. I spoke. I was absorbed in my subject matter and talked longer than usual. Apparently, there was a woman who remained until the end of the lecture. When she went home, it was late and her husband was furious. He ranted and raved and accused her of all kinds of ridiculous things. She tried to explain, to tell him that she had attended my lecture and that it had run longer than usual. The husband ordered her to leave the house and not come back until she spat in my face! That was three weeks ago – and the obdurate fool still won't allow his wife back in the house."

Berurya came over to him. "No matter how ludicrous this sounds the man might actually suspect his wife of being unfaithful with you."

Meir looked at Berurya in disbelief. "You can't believe that!" he stammered.

"I'm not at all suggesting that it happened. I'm merely trying to imagine what was going on in the man's mind. Maybe he's just a jealous husband."

"Not very likely."

"But how do you know?"

"If you saw her," said Meir, "you wouldn't even ask the question."

"That's not fair!" Berurya said sharply.

Meir was silent for a moment, then he said slowly: "I've spoken with people who know the husband. He's a boor. He is crude, ill-mannered and vulgar. His wife would be fortunate if he divorced her! Besides, I'm told that he detests rabbis. That's why the provision permitting her to come home is that she spit in my eye!"

"What'll you do?" asked Berurya.

"What will I do?" said Meir. "I don't think anything depends on me. This man hates me and we've never even met! Do you think I could convince him that his wife is faithful and was only attending a lecture? The truth is irrelevant. He simply wants to humiliate me."

"So what are you going to do?"

"Nothing. Absolutely nothing. Eventually, the man will come to his senses and let his wife return."

Berurya rubbed her chin. "You do have an alternative." She said slowly: "You can let the woman spit in your eye."

Meir stared at her in shock. "Never ..." he murmured through clenched teeth. He got to his feet. "It's not only me personally whom he wants to humiliate; he's scoffing at our religion. He wants to spit at Judaism!"

Berurya nodded. "You may very well be right," she pointed out, "but you can turn it around ... so that it becomes an utterly meaningless gesture."

"How could I do that?" asked Meir incredulously.

Berurya touched her husband's arm. "Why don't you let it be known that you're having some difficulty with your eye, and ask that a woman pronounce some incantation to relieve the ailment?"

"Yes," said Meir, "and then what?"

"Tell the woman in question that instead of the incantation, you want her to spit in your eye. Tell her it's the only way you can be cured."

Meir seemed skeptical. "But what if some other woman, some woman with no connection to the problem, shows up?"

"That's no problem," said Berurya. "I'll send Bilha to inform the man's wife about our plan. She'll go home immediately and tell her husband that she intends to spit in your face."

"And if her husband doesn't believe her?"

"You'll go to their home and let her spit in your eye in front of him. You'll ask her to spit not once – but seven times!"

Meir looked doubtful. "There has to be some other way...."

"There is no other way," said Berurya. "But if you take my suggestion, you'll render the act meaningless and show yourself to be above this man. Even more importantly, you'll demonstrate what Judaism teaches: that for the sake of tranquility in a household, you're willing to set aside your pride and your good name. You'll be acting in the name of peace and that can never bring you shame."

Meir had been pacing back and forth; now, he seated himself again. In a restrained voice he said: "You make it all sound so simple."

Berurya smiled, but said nothing. She leaned over and kissed Meir's cheek. "You'll no longer be just a great rabbi," she said. "Up to now, your reputation has been based on knowledge and your brilliance. After tomorrow, your life will reflect the aphorism of Hillel: 'Be of the disciples of Aaron, loving peace and pursuing peace, loving thy fellow-creatures, and drawing them near to the Torah.' You'll demonstrate that it's not enough simply to love peace – one must also pursue peace actively!"

As Berurya stood by her husband, she reflected that peace can be perceived in the serenity of day. At sunrise, the horizon glows with shades of red and violet; so too, it is at sunset. But when the sun moves across the sky, the colors disappear.

In a like manner, Berurya thought, at the moment we enter life and at the moment we exit it, the promise of peace glows brilliantly. But during life itself – especially when the sun is brightest and its warmth encourages us to struggle, build, provide, become – the promise of peace is noticeably absent. People rush about in wrong directions, run after the wrong things. What they grab are only shadows. It is peace which must be one of the prime goals of human existence.

That is why peace is at the very core of Judaism. And the promise of peace is too important to be limited to our immediate selves; it must be sought after for all Israel and for all mankind. Only then will it be real; only then will brilliant colors flood our lives!

Meir reached up for Berurya's hand. "When will you send Bilha?"

"The sooner, the better. Tell me her name and where she lives. Bilha will find out where she's staying now."

At the close of the next Sabbath, Rabbi Meir once again gave a discourse. At the end of the lecture, he announced that his eye was giving him a problem and asked if there was a woman there who might be familiar with some incantation to heal his ailment. A woman in the rear stood up and called out: "Rabbi Meir, I know an incantation that might help you!"

The crowd left and Meir went up to the woman. "I'm sure that Bilha has explained everything...."

The woman was extremely nervous. "Rabbi Meir," she said haltingly, "I don't know if I can carry this off. I don't know a single incantation, and I'm afraid of my husband. What can I do?"

Meir spoke softly: "Please just calm down. Take me home."

They walked together silently. When they arrived, Meir said: "Listen to me carefully, and do exactly as I say." He pointed. "Open the door and say to your husband that Rabbi Meir is here to comply with his wishes."

"But ..."

"Please, just do as I say."

Meir waited several minutes and then knocked. The door opened: there stood the woman's husband. "Rabbi Meir is here," said the woman, "to do your bidding."

"Come in, Meir," the husband said, "I've been expecting you."

Meir entered. The man turned to his wife. "Miriam," he said, "we have an honored guest. The great and learned Rabbi Meir has actually come to my house! I wonder what has brought him here?" He went to the table, on which stood a bowl of food. "I hope you don't mind if I finish my meal," he said to Meir.

Meir shook his head and the man sat down at the table. With his fingers, he scooped moist oats from the bowl. Meir watched him eat. A fly fell in the food. The man picked it up with the food, glared at

Meir defiantly, and stuffed it into his mouth. Deliberately, he chewed the mouthful and then, with an exaggerated gulp, swallowed. Meir watched him without expression.

Then Meir turned to the wife. "I have a problem here," he said, pointing to his left eye. "I've heard that if someone spits in it seven times, it will be healed."

The woman hesitated.

"Please, do it," said Meir in a low, firm voice.

The wife shuddered and then spat in the rabbi's eye. Once... twice... three times... four times –

Meir stood there like a statue, without movement and without expression.

Six times... and the last time!

His left cheek ran with the woman's saliva. In silence, he walked slowly to the door. With a hand on the knob, he turned and said: "Thank you. Thank you very much. I'm sure my eye will be better. May God bless you with peace!"

Meir closed the door behind him. He took out a handkerchief and dried his face. The ordeal was over. When he got home, he told the story to Berurya. She listened intently. When he finished, Meir said: "You know, Berurya, if this hadn't involved a woman, none of it would've happened. There would've been no jealous husband and I wouldn't have been forced to suffer this indignity."

"Meir," said Berurya, "had the woman been a man, she might've been just like her husband! Whom do you prefer? A woman who needed to learn about Judaism – or a man who wanted her to spit on your face!?"

18

Demons and Chickens

Bathsheva was now six years old. Berurya had discovered that raising a daughter was easier than raising a son. From the time the boys were Bathsheva's age, they managed, with little difficulty, to cover themselves with scrapes and bruises. No matter how many times Berurya lectured them, it didn't help. Once, Elhanan fell from a tree which his mother had expressly forbidden him to climb. While the pain from his broken arm was severe, Elhanan was more concerned about what awaited him at home.

As Hananiah grew older, he proved to be the more difficult of the two to control. He would sneak out of the house while everyone slept and return in the early hours of the morning. Berurya suspected him, but she could never catch him; actually, it became a kind of game between the two of them.

Once, she spread soot around his bed and in front of the door, so if he left, she could find footsteps. Hananiah went to the butcher and got a chicken's foot. That same night, he made prints in the soot with the chicken's foot and cleverly managed to leave without leaving any of his own. The next morning, Berurya said: "I saw the strangest thing."

"What's that, Mother?"

"Peculiar looking prints about your bed ... and downstairs. It looked to me as if a one-legged chicken had gotten into the house! How could that have happened?"

"I've no idea," said Hananiah.

"Wait a minute!" Hananiah exclaimed suddenly. "Did you say it looked like a chicken-foot!? I remember hearing – maybe in the *Beit Midrash* – that demons leave tracks that look like those of a chicken or rooster! Maybe some evil spirit was in my room last night, no!?"

"I don't doubt it for a minute," Berurya said, struggling to keep from laughing.

Elhanan, who didn't know what was going on, was frightened. "Evil spirits – demons – in our house!" he said hoarsely. "What are we going to do? How'll we protect ourselves? Can they harm us?"

"Harm us?" Hananiah echoed. "It's worse than that! You know, there are three types of demons: *mazikim*, *shaydim*, and *ruhot*. From the look of the prints, it was probably one of the *shaydim*!"

"What'll we do?" Elhanan asked plaintively. Hananiah stared at his brother. "I'm not sure," he said in a grim tone, "but I think there are two possible methods. One is that just before you're ready to sleep, hold your breath until your face turns colors. If demons come into your room, your face'll definitely frighten them away! The second method might be better. You cut off your hair and put a dead chicken on your head until it begins to stink. Not only will demons stay out of your room, they probably won't bother you again for the rest of your life!"

"Must it be a dead chicken?" Elhanan asked mournfully.

"Enough!" Berurya commanded. "Can't you see that your brother's teasing you!? There aren't any demons in the house!"

When Berurya went out of the room, Hananiah leaned over to his brother, "Elhanan," he whispered. "Mother just said that so you wouldn't worry. If I were you, I'd look for a dead chicken as soon as I could."

"Leave me alone," shouted Elhanan. "You're just poking fun at me!"

19
Therapeutic Waters

Berurya often considered the matter of raising children. She thought that, like a bird teaching fledglings to fly, parents tried to impart what they learned in life to their children. But for most children, the words were heard, not really understood. Sometimes, reflected Berurya, only the passage of years makes us receptive to the wisdom of parents; by then, however, the child finds himself a parent and so is confronted with the same impossible task – that of teaching another generation which knows how to hear, but not yet how to listen....

Berurya pondered the phenomenon of aging. She knew that youth perceived the consequences of old-age; bones become brittle, posture bowed under the burden of the years. Nonetheless, the young took their youth for granted. In the decline of life, the infirmities of age – and not promiscuous strangers – became bed companions! No one looked forward to old age; for many, it was a time of loneliness and isolation. Perhaps that is why when companions left us, we asked God to remain our friend. It was King David who said: 'Cast me not off in the time of old age; forsake me not when my strength faileth.'

Bilha, though she was not old, began to notice the effects of aging. Her hair was turning grey; her eyes saw less clearly; the formidable energy she had enjoyed in her youth gave way to sighs and aches.

Bilha had been with Berurya's family for very many years. Rabbi Hananiah ben Teradyon and his wife had known Bilha's parents when they all lived in Sikhnin. Bilha had a sister, Shulamit, who was some five years older. When Bilha was a child, her parents planned a trip to visit relatives in Egypt and asked Hananiah and his wife if they would watch their little daughter while they were away. They had no children of their own at the time and readily agreed.

Bilha's parents and Shulamit left for Egypt in the year 115 C.E., the year the War of Quietus broke out. Jews throughout the Diaspora – in Libya, Cyrenaica, Egypt, Cyprus, and Mesopotamia – rose up in revolt. Caught in the conflict, Bilha's parents decided it would be safer to travel back to Israel when things quieted down. But their return was not meant to be.

The circumstances of their deaths were not known. Some believed that one night the non-Jews of Alexandria slaughtered anyone they thought to be Jewish. The blood thirsty mob murdered Bilha's parents and her sister while the three slept. When word of their fate reached Sikhnin, Rabbi Hananiah and his wife decided to keep and raise Bilha. The girl was sixteen when Berurya was born.

Bilha loved caring for Berurya; the infant was almost like her own daughter. Bilha very much felt herself part of the family. Her intimate involvement with Berurya, and later with Penina, was probably one of the reasons she never married. Rabbi Hananiah ben Teradyon tried subtly to persuade Bilha to marry and have a family of her own but Bilha answered simply that the family she already had was more than enough.

The death of Berurya's parents had been as devastating to Bilha as it had been to Berurya. After they died, Bilha saw Berurya and Penina as her responsibility.

One afternoon, while bending over to pick up Bathseva, Bilha felt a stabbing pain in her back. She did not pay much attention; she straightened up as best as she could. When Bathsheva began crying,

Bilha again bent over to lift her. If the first pain had been a warning, the second pain was punishment for disobeying. The stab was violent. Bilha shut her eyes and tried to keep from screaming. After what seemed an interminable time, she slowly managed to make her way to a chair and sit down. However, that was little better than standing. At length, Berurya came home and assisted Bilha to her room.

After two weeks of lying prone, Bilha was able to stand up without the searing pain. The winter months had begun and the temperature dropped. As hot as Tiberias and Hammat were in summer, so were the winters harsh. The cold, wet air penetrated to the bone. Bilha had pain in her shoulder, which she attributed to a neighbor who had probably given her the "evil eye." All she had to do was find out who the culprit was, and the matter would be resolved.

Berurya was concerned. "Bilha," she urged, "I think you should go to one of the bathhouses in Tiberias and soak in hot mineral water. It'll do wonders for you."

"Since when are you an expert on health?" Bilha snapped.

"Have you heard of Rabbi Shimeon bar Yohai?"

"Of course I have," said Bilha. "I'm not altogether ignorant, you know."

"I never meant to infer that you're ignorant," said Berurya. "What I meant was, are you familiar with the story of how he was healed?"

"I can't wait to hear."

"Well," began Berurya, "the rabbi ..."

"Is this going to be a long story?"

"If you'd stop interrupting, I'd have finished by now!"

"I doubt that," said Bilha irritably, determined to get in the last word.

"At any rate," Berurya went on, "Rabbi Shimeon bar Yohai, like our Meir, was a student of Rabbi Akiva. In fact, when Rabbi Akiva ordained the two, he showed preference for Rabbi Meir by seating him before Rabbi Shimeon. Rabbi Shimeon was visibly disturbed by this, but Rabbi Akiva admonished: 'It's enough that I ... and your Creator recognize your strength.' What Akiva meant by the remark isn't entirely clear. Rabbi Shimeon, of course, was and is a great scholar. But as great as his knowledge is his hatred for non-Jews, particularly Romans....

"One day," Berurya continued, "Rabbi Shimeon, Rabbi Judah and Rabbi Yosi were with Yehuda ben Gerim. Rabbi Judah observed that the Romans should be credited for setting up market-places, building bridges and bathhouses. Rabbi Yosi remained silent. But Rabbi Shimeon bar Yohai could not restrain himself. He burst out: 'All that the Romans built was in their own interest! They built markets for prostitutes, baths for their own pleasure, and bridges so they could levy tolls.' Judah ben Gerim told the Romans what bar Yohai said. As a result, the Romans praised Rabbi Judah for his words, banished Rabbi Yosi to Sepphoris for remaining silent, and condemned Rabbi Shimeon to death for slander.

"As soon as Rabbi Shimeon learned of the sentence," Berurya related, "he and his son, Eleazer, hid in the *Beit Midrash*. By night, his wife secretly smuggled them food. Rabbi Shimeon knew the Romans would probably interrogate her and that if they tortured her, they would extract any information they wished. Without his wife's knowledge, he and his son crept out of the *Beit Midrash* and hid in a cave for many long years. They ate the fruit of the Carob tree and drank water from a nearby stream. Since their clothes would disintegrate if worn constantly, they cast them off and covered themselves in sand. Each day, they steeped themselves in the study of Torah. They dressed only when it was time to pray – as a measure of respect. In the twelfth year of hiding, they left the cave. Hadrian was dead and his decree annulled. It was safe to return. Nonetheless, they waited another twelve months until their return to normal life.

"When Rabbi Pinhas ben Yair, Rabbi Shimeon's son-in-law, heard of his whereabouts," said Berurya, "he went to see him. He was shocked to see that his father-in-law's skin was covered with blisters. Worse than the cracks in the skin of his chest and his back were the deep cuts on his arms and legs and the abrasions on his neck and face. The pain had to be excruciating. His son-in-law brought him to Tiberias, to the baths, and it was here, in the mineral water, that he was healed.

"Until then, Tiberias had been considered off-limits to priests, Kohanim, since there was still doubt about whether bodies were buried in the city. Grateful for what the city had done for him, Rabbi Shimeon saw to it that Tiberias was declared ritually pure."

Berurya took Bilha's arm.

"Bilha, I tell you all this so you won't neglect the curative powers of the waters. You owe it to yourself to try. How can it possibly hurt? I'll even go with you. In fact, I'll ask Meir to come as well."

"All right, I'll go," Bilha acquiesced. "Besides, I don't have the strength to listen to another lecture!"

Berurya convinced Meir to accompany her and Bilha to the bathhouse. Meir wanted to take Hananiah and Elhanan along with him but, as usual, they were nowhere to be found. After the morning prayers in the *Beit Keneset*, they had disappeared before their father had the opportunity to speak with them. Meir brought along Symmachus bar Yosef and Ephraim Makhs'ah instead.

They all walked to the bathhouse at a brisk pace. Bilha chattered on, complaining about the weather – it was raining lightly – and expressing her opinion that it all seemed a waste of time. When they arrived, Meir and Berurya agreed to meet outside the gate in about an hour. Meir paid the entrance fee and, with his two pupils, walked down the corridor to the left; Berurya and Bilha turned to the women's area on the right.

The bathhouse was rectangular, and divided into several large halls. It contained three pools, each with water at varying temperatures. Their water was brought through pipes from a nearby wadi. The smallest one was filled with cool, fresh water. The second one was somewhat larger, and filled with tepid water. The main pool, situated in the large main hall, was round. The walls of this chamber were ornately decorated and its floor was made of marble. Above the pool was a dome supported by four columns. Five steps ran along the circumference of the pool and led down into the hot mineral water. The water reached up to the chests of those who sat on the fifth and bottom step. The floor of the pool sloped gently toward its deepest point at the center.

There were three smaller rooms, which could be entered from the main pool area: the first was a dressing room; the middle, a room for resting; and the last, a steam-room. The benches in the steam-room, as well as its floor, were made of wood; beneath the floor were hot coals. Every so often, the *balan*, or bath attendant, would pour water into a hole in the floor and steam would rise through the planks.

Meir and his students disrobed in the changing room and went into the pool. The cold marble underfoot was a sharp contrast to the hot waters. Meir made his way down to the third level of the pool and seated himself. "Aaah..." Meir sighed. "It feels so good!" he murmured. He glanced around the pool. At this hour, there were only about nine or ten other bathers. An elderly man with a discolored face caught his attention. A scab ran from the center of the man's hairline down his forehead, between his eyes, and then plunged diagonally down his left cheek; obviously the man hoped that the hot springs would cure his skin ailment.

To the man's left sat a group of young men. They conversed in Latin and were probably soldiers bathing for relaxation. On Meir's other side, a rather distinguished–looking man sat leaning backward, gazing at the dome above.

Symmachus interrupted Meir's thoughts. "Rabbi, take a look at the man over there," he said, turning towards the dressing room. Meir glanced at a man standing on two narrow strips of wood. The man placed one board in front of him, stepped on it, then picked up the second board and set it down before him. He stepped on the board farthest away, picked up the board underfoot and placed it ahead of him. In this somewhat awkward manner, he made his way across the floor of the pool.

"Why is he doing that?" Symmachus asked.

"The marble floor's too cold for him, and he's taking extra care so he won't get sick," said Meir.

Meir sat silently, absorbed in thought.

"Rabbi," asked Ephraim, "is something the matter?"

"No, Ephraim," Meir mused. "I was just thinking about something that happened in this very place to Rabbi Eleazer, Rabbi Joshua and Rabbi Akiva."

He paused for a moment, and then continued: "The three were sitting right here, under this dome, when a *Min*, a sectarian who was versed in magic, uttered an incantation; suddenly, they were unable to budge from the spot. The rabbis were dismayed: the *Min's* spell had rendered them helpless.

"Rabbi Eleazer turned to Rabbi Joshua, who was familiar with the occult, and urged him to put a counter-spell on the *Min*. As the *Min* was about to leave the bathhouse, Rabbi Joshua muttered some words, and the *Min* found himself stuck fast to the gate! He could not move and every time someone entered or left, the gate hit him in the back or chest. Discomfited, the *Min* begged Rabbi Joshua to release him. The rabbi said he would comply, provided the *Min* rescinded his spell first. Both agreed, and were freed from the paralysis."

Meir stroked his beard. "Realizing that the *Min* was dangerous," he went on, "Rabbi Joshua asked him if he could perform other magic. The *Min* smiled. 'Watch this!' he said. He pointed to the water of the lake, uttered another incantation, and in a flash the water parted! Then he turned to the three rabbis and said: 'Isn't that what your great rabbi, Moses, did at the Red Sea?' 'Not exactly,' said Rabbi Eleazer. 'Moses actually walked on a path between the walls of water.' 'That is no problem,' grinned the *Min*. He descended into the lake and calmly strolled between the parted waters. When he reached the center of the lake, Rabbi Joshua commanded the water to return to its normal state and the *Min* drowned!"

"What a fascinating story," exclaimed Symmacus.

"An interesting story, indeed!" said the distinguished-looking stranger. "Excuse me for listening, but I couldn't help being amused by the tale!"

"I didn't relate the incident to amuse anyone," protested Meir.

"Please, I have to apologize once again. I wasn't trying to ridicule your beliefs: I simply thought that Judaism was devoid of witchcraft and magic."

"That's true," said Meir. He stared at the man. "You strike me as someone who is well-versed in Judaism," he said. "Have you ever studied in a *Beit Midrash*?"

The other smiled. "You flatter me," he said. "No, I didn't study in a *Beit Midrash* but I had excellent teachers who instructed me in many subjects. I studied Torah, Greek philosophy, poetry, and music."

"You certainly aren't implying that Judaism can be relegated to the level of art or music are you!? Judaism is so much more! It's a way of life," said Meir.

"True," said the other: "It's a way of life for some; however, music and art can also be a way of life. A musician who thinks about music all the time, who hears it in his sleep, who listens to its enchantments in the sounds of nature – who can deny that this is also a way of life? As for me," the stranger continued, "I'm devoted to many subjects. I study life, including Torah, as well as music. One could say that I enjoy the music of Torah as one of the subjects of life...."

"But," rejoined Meir, "music, art and philosophy – these are products of the human mind; how much more fulfilling it is to be involved in that which stems directly from God!"

The stranger nodded. "But don't we also say that Man was created in the image of God? What is the 'image of God?' Obviously, it's not something physical! I believe that the spiritual and intellectual capacities of Man in some measure reflect God. Music, in its pristine form, for example, is an indirect reflection of something that emanates from God."

"An interesting observation," mused Meir. "But you have used the words 'reflect' and 'reflection'. Why settle for reflections of God when you can have the real thing?"

The stranger was silent for a moment; then he said. "Thanks very much. I enjoyed our discussion, but I must be going."

"We're leaving as well," said Meir.

The stranger, Meir, and his two disciples entered the changing room and dressed. As they left the bathhouse, Meir turned to the stranger. "My name is Rabbi Meir. May I ask you yours?"

"Nathan ... Nathan ben Barak."

"Nathan, I'd like to invite you to my *Beit Midrash*, so we can continue our discussion. I, too, enjoyed speaking with you."

"Thanks for the invitation, Rabbi Meir, but I must decline. I'm extremely busy, and don't really have the time...."

As Nathan was about to depart, Berurya and Bilha walked through the gate. Berurya called out to Meir, and Nathan turned. "Who is that woman?" he asked.

"She's Berurya, my wife."

"Your wife..." Nathan mused. "Why, she's absolutely stunning! Forgive my forwardness, but she's absolutely the most beautiful woman I've ever laid eyes on!"

"Not only is she beautiful," said Meir, "but she's also one of the most intelligent of women!"

"Then you are a fortunate man, indeed."

Berurya and Bilha came up. "Berurya," said Meir, "I'd like to introduce you to Nathan. He has just told me how beautiful he finds you."

Berurya flushed.

Meir smiled. "That's the first time in years I've seen you blush," he said.

"It's probably the hot baths," said Bilha. "I feel like I've been cooked alive!"

"Nathan," Meir said, gesturing, "this is Bilha. She runs our entire family."

"If I really ran the family," Bilha said crisply, "I wouldn't have come to these baths for an hour of torture!"

"You don't feel any better at all?" Meir asked.

"Oh, yes, I feel a great improvement! My skin has shriveled!"

"That's quite an improvement," Berurya quipped. "You should have seen her before."

"Your wife has a keen sense of humor," commented Nathan.

"Yes," said Meir. "She is special."

"I don't know whether that's a compliment or an insult."

"A compliment, my dear," said Meir. "What else could it be?"

"I believe all women are special," said Nathan. "Your husband meant that you are special among the special...."

Berurya smiled broadly.

"I've invited Nathan to the *Beit Midrash*, Berurya, but he's declined," said Meir.

Nathan massaged his chin. "Perhaps I was too hasty in deciding," he said. "Where exactly is your *Beit Midrash*?"

"It's in Hammat. Ask anyone there, and they'll give you directions." He faced his wife. "Berurya, I think it's time to go home. We have a busy day ahead."

As they spoke, the drizzle stopped, and the sun came out.

"I hope to see you again soon," said Nathan. "May you go in peace!"

Meir's party headed for Hammat. Nathan beckoned to two men who had been watching from a distance. They hurried over to him and bowed.

20
In the Name of Yeshua

Berurya had been flattered by Nathan's words. He seemed different from other men; there was something about him which intrigued her, though she wasn't certain what it was. It was obvious that he was cultured and refined: his speech, his manners, the way he carried himself ... Berurya daydreamed. Suddenly, she awoke. "Strange," she mused, "that I should think about him."

There was a knock at the door. Berurya opened it. It was Yaddua. "Is Rabbi Meir in?" he asked.

"No," said Berurya. "He should be in the *Beit Midrash*."

"He's not there," Yaddua said, a little breathlessly.

"Is there a problem?"

"It's Tamar," said Yaddua anxiously. "She's terribly sick. I don't know what to do."

"Did you call a physician?"

"I did. But he hasn't come yet." Yaddua clenched his fists. "What if she dies?" he blurted out. "I don't know what I'd do without her!"

"Don't think of the worst, Yaddua," Berurya said calmly. "Who's staying with her now?"

"A neighbor," said Yaddua. "She also brought someone who knows about healing, but he's not one of us. He follows some messiah. It's probably wrong, but ... I don't want Tamar to die!"

"Take me to your home right away," Berurya ordered.

They hurried to Yaddua's house, which stood near the wall encircling Tiberias. A number of cities in Israel were surrounded by walls for protection. Tiberias was not completely walled in since the water on one side formed a natural boundary.

When they arrived, Yaddua asked his neighbor how Tamar was doing.

"She's about the same – still in a stupor. I don't know if she can hear us at all."

"How long has she been that way?" asked Berurya.

"Since last night," replied Yaddua. He shivered. "I prayed all nightlong. I didn't know what else to do."

"When did you send for the physician?"

"Over an hour ago," Yaddua said, "perhaps longer. He must be with another patient."

"Is Tamar alone now?" Berurya asked.

The neighbor shook her head. "No," she said. "Someone is with her, praying for her recovery."

"Yaddua," Berurya commanded, "go and find the doctor yourself! I'll stay with Tamar."

Berurya entered the bedroom. There were two men there. The older man knelt by Tamar's bed; the younger man stood in a corner. Berurya's sudden entrance startled the old man; he rose hurriedly to his feet. "I was ... praying for her recovery," he mumbled.

"Who are you?" asked Berurya.

"I'm a Jew."

"That's not what I meant."

"I am Jacob, of K'far Sama," said the old man. "I've come here to heal this woman, in the name of our Messiah, Yeshua ben Pandira."

"I know exactly who you are," said Berurya, recognizing his name. "You are the same person, who, many years ago, came to heal Rabbi Eleazar ben Dama after he'd been bitten by a snake."

"Yes," said Jacob. "I am that man."

Berurya thought for a moment. "I remember," she said, "Eleazar's uncle, Rabbi Ishmael, wouldn't allow you to heal him. But his nephew, the sick man, argued that, according to Jewish law, the healing was permissible."

"You're well informed," said Jacob. "And so you must also know that Rabbi Eleazar ben Dama died."

"I know," Berurya said softly. "But how do you know he would have lived even if you had said your prayers?"

"I don't know," said Jacob. "But neither do you."

Suddenly, Tamar moaned. Jacob turned and was about to continue his prayers.

But Berurya raised a hand. "No," she said resolutely. "She's not one of yours!" She strode to Tamar's side.

"Not one of ours?" said the younger man from the corner. "But Jacob's prayers heal! Even a woman like you should recognize his power! Now, back off, or you'll cause your friend's death!"

He started toward Berurya, but Jacob interceded with an authoritative wave of his hand. "You must excuse Marcellus, he's brash, but he means well."

"Marcellus," Berurya murmured. "That's a Latin name."

"So it is," said Marcellus. "I was a Roman soldier. But I have rejected my former life and embraced our Saviour. I admonish you: let Jacob pray so that this woman will live and return to health!"

At that moment, Yaddua and the physician entered. Berurya said to Jacob: "I think we can both leave now. Tamar will be cared for."

Jacob turned to Yaddua. But Yaddua indicated that he concurred with Berurya's point of view.

At once, Jacob and Marcellus departed. Berurya spoke to Yaddua for a few minutes, and then left.

Jacob and Marcellus were waiting outside.

"Apparently," said Jacob to Berurya, "you know little about me." He cleared his throat. "I was born a Jew ... and I still consider myself a Jew. I observe the commandments of Judaism now, just as I observed them when I was young. I keep the Sabbath and observe the Festivals, my children are circumcised; and I accept the Torah, the Prophets, and the Writings as Holy Scripture. I do this because our Messiah has taught: 'Whoever then relaxes one of the least of these commandments and teaches men so, shall be called least in the Kingdom of Heaven; but he who does them and teaches them shall be called great in the Kingdom of Heaven.'

"Since the time of my youth, I have believed that the Kingdom of Heaven is imminent and this I have taught to my Jewish brethren. And I believe that, as it was told to the woman of Samaria: 'Salvation is from the Jews.'

"Our Messiah," he went on, "whom I accept as my personal Redeemer, was a prophet and saintly man – a man who kept the whole Torah in every possible way. I attempt to do likewise."

Berurya had listened to Jacob, but watched Marcellus. She folded her arms across her chest. "This is what you believe, Jacob," she said. "But I don't believe that your friend, Marcellus, is of a like mind. Correct me if I'm wrong Marcellus, but do you indeed agree with Jacob?"

"I agree," replied Marcellus, "with part of what he said." He stiffened. "But I don't see why I am in the least obliged to defend my religious beliefs."

"I'm not asking you to defend your beliefs," said Berurya in a level voice. "I'd simply like to understand them. I sense that you believe very differently from Jacob."

Marcellus was silent for several moments; his eyes clouded and his brow furrowed. At length, with a grimace, he glanced over at Jacob and said, not without bitterness: "The Law of Torah that you so lovingly refer to... I regard as a stumbling block! Yeshua was sent to earth by God; his death was meant to atone for the Original Sin, the sin which has burdened Mankind from the time of Adam and Eve. Our Saviour is the end of the Law." His eyes burned with anger. "You Jews," he said with acrimony, "are being punished for your transgressions! You are no longer the Chosen People! God has chosen ... a new Israel!"

The last statement shocked Jacob and enraged Berurya. She turned to the old man. "You see, Jacob," she warned, "people like this man are your spiritual descendents! You have taken a terrible step away from our traditions; those who come after you will slam the door shut! Generations from now, they will neither recognize nor respect the religion you cherish."

Marcellus seized Jacob's arm. "Let's go," he growled. "This is an utter waste of time!"

"A waste of time!?" echoed Berurya. "What is a waste of time, discussing Judaism – or speaking to a woman!?"

Marcellus flushed. "You are a stubborn, stiff-necked people," he said through gritted teeth. "You don't recognize our Messiah and so you'll continue to suffer! Israel is like a barren woman: she has no future. She has only a past!" His lips curled in disdain. "You ask for proof? Consider the words of the prophet Isaiah, 'Sing, O barren, thou that didst not bear...' Israel is that sterile woman. And what is she bidden? She is bidden to sing? Maybe you'd care to sing for me?" he concluded with a sneer.

In a controlled voice, Berurya said: "You are truly a fool, Marcellus. If you quote from Scripture, you should remember to cite the end of the verse. Perhaps you've forgotten? The verse finishes: "... for more are the children of the desolate than the children of the married wife, saith the Lord." And the verse means that happy is the household of Israel, which has not given birth to children destined for Gehenna, such as are yours ..."

"I'd rather go to hell with my beliefs," shouted Marcellus, "than inherit your 'World to Come' and never know the truth!"

Berurya stared directly into Marcellus' eyes. "They have eyes," she said in a fierce tone, "but they do not see. They have ears, but they do not hear. They have a mouth, but it is full of lies."

Marcellus trembled. "Damned Jew!" he hissed. Then he spat at the ground and strode away. Jacob lowered his eyes and slowly shook his head, partly in disgust, partly in disbelief. "You seem to be a kind, sincere person, Jacob," Berurya said. "If you listened to what Marcellus said, you could understand why we, as Jews, are unable to accept your beliefs. One day, the Messiah will come, and I believe there will be peace. But until that time, the Messiah waits and watches; he waits for God to say to him, 'your time has come.' Perhaps he hesitates because those who claim to speak in God's name go on fighting and shedding blood in His name! With all our achievements, mankind hasn't really progressed very much."

Berurya fell silent. Jacob walked off without a word. Then Berurya, walking in the opposite direction, returned to Yaddua's house.

21

Attitudes Towards Women

Berurya remained with Yaddua for several hours. They prayed together that Tamar would recover. When the physician left, he gave Yaddua some encouraging news and told him precisely what needed to be done.

Yaddua and Berurya went into the sick-room. Tamar lay in bed, with her eyes open. Yaddua kissed her on the forehead. Berurya stood at the door and smiled.

Yaddua caressed Tamar's face and whispered"Rest, my darling."

As he walked away, Berurya saw tears in his eyes. "Poor, Yaddua," she thought. "Not long ago he lost his mother and now he has almost lost his beloved wife."

Berurya was weary. On her way home, she recalled her confrontation with Marcellus and Jacob. Had she said the right things? Perhaps it would have been wiser not to have argued? But if she had ignored them, they might have construed it as complacency.

Berurya knew that Judaism was being threatened from without, as well as from within. The years under Roman rule had decimated the Jewish population and the internal schisms were just as devastating. The only hope, she felt, was to strengthen the Jewish remnant and to build the future on them. Israel's hope in the years to come was not in the literal promise made to Abraham that his descendents would be as numerous as the stars in heaven and the sand by the sea: it lay rather in the cryptic message contained in God's words.

Berurya reflected that Israel was a people likened to stars and sand. In the worst of times, Jews were sand, of which it might be said that there was nothing lower in the world. The boots of foreign soldiers trampled on the grains and crushed them! There had been and would be much tears and suffering. But one day, Berurya believed, Israel would be likened to the stars in the heavens. When the time came, Jews would ascend to the stars and nothing would be higher or more glorious! The ascent of Israel to the heavens would not be because of numbers, but because of a promise made to a man that his people would become a great nation. A promise that they would be blessed and also become a blessing! Abraham's descendents, led by scholars and sages, would make such a journey; they would light up the heavens and shed light on an otherwise darkened world. Berurya had faith that such was the destiny of Israel – a people of sand and stars....

Before going home, Berurya went into the *Beit Midrash*. The hour was late – there was only one student there. He sat silently in the rear. "How many times have I said," Berurya thought, "that in order to learn, they must repeat the words aloud to themselves!? I say it over and over: if they don't actually hear the words, they won't commit them to memory. Why can't they grasp that?" Agitated, she walked up to the student and, in her frustration, slapped him on the back.

Startled, the student turned. It was Hananiah!

Twice that week, Berurya went to visit Tamar. Each time, she found Yaddua's wife looking stronger and healthier. By Friday morning, Tamar had recovered completely and was able to get out of bed. Yaddua insisted on cleaning the house and happily made all the preparations for the Sabbath.

Whatever Tamar's ailment, it passed as quickly and mysteriously as it had come. The doctor prescribed continued bed-rest for another three or four days.

Winter came. The winters in Tiberias were harsh. There were days of continuous rain. The damp, driving cold penetrated deep into the bones. Berurya walked back to Hammat along the shore of the Kinneret. She bent her head, and pulled the corners of the shawl tightly against the freezing wind. As she walked, she gazed out over the water. "What is it about water that calms people so?" Berurya wondered. She halted, picked up several smooth pebbles and flung them into the lake. The water was choppy; as the stones struck its surface, they made a plunking noise, and quickly disappeared. In still water, pebbles created widening concentric circles, which gradually dissolved into nothingness.

Berurya's thoughts skipped from subject to subject. First, she tried to concentrate on her studies, but her thoughts went back to Tamar and the incident involving Jacob, of K'far Sama. She remembered the words in the prayer, *Shemoneh Esreh*, directed against apostates and those who sought to destroy Judaism: "May the apostates have no hope, unless they return to Thy Torah, and the *Minim* disappear in a moment. May they be erased from the Book of Life, and not be inscribed with the Righteous." Then she thought of Marcellus. "May he be erased from the Book of Life!" she murmured aloud. Even those words didn't seem forceful enough to express her anger! But Jacob was another matter. She had been touched by his gentle character; perhaps one day he would return....

Berurya stared at the fishing boats out in the Kinneret. The fishermen set out routinely before sunrise and returned in the late afternoon. Today, on Friday, they would return shortly, in order to sell their catch well before the onset of the Sabbath. Fish, of course, were more readily available to people who lived close to the Kinneret, but even for them it was a luxury. Not everyone in Israel had the means to purchase fish or meat, but most people saved what they could during the week so that the Sabbath meal would be special.

Berurya thought that by now, for certain, Bilha would have purchased fish from the market-place and would be busy preparing it for dinner. She bent yet again. As she picked up a stone and was about to throw it, someone waved to her from one of the boats. Instinctively, she waved back. "That's odd," she thought. "Who could it be?" Berurya hurled the stone and continued on her way.

Looking down at the water as it lapped the shore, Berurya recalled the time she and Penina had strolled here. "Poor Penina" she mused: "Life has not been good to her – she has suffered terribly."

Berurya could not even begin to imagine what her sister had endured in Rome. If Berurya ever pitied herself for the loss of father, mother, and brother, at least she had been blessed with children! Penina would have been overjoyed to have given birth to a single child.

Then Berurya's thoughts turned to Meir. She had been troubled for some time by his behavior toward his daughter. It was increasingly apparent that Meir wanted as little to do with the girl as possible. He spent time with her only when he had no choice. It was far different with his sons. Berurya remembered how Meir would watch little Hananiah sleep in the middle of the night.

Meir was no less attentive to his younger son. He greatly enjoyed spending time with Elhanan. Lying in bed on his back, Meir would playfully push Elhanan into the air and then lower him slowly to his chest. Elhanan gurgled gleefully, making his father laugh.

When Elhanan was a year old, Meir would throw the baby into the air and catch him. Elhanan loved it; Bilha was appalled. "What if he falls?" she exclaimed.

"Bilha, you worry too much," Meir responded. Berurya was always happy when Meir spent time with his sons. On the rare occasions when he held Bathsheva, it was at Berurya's request.

Berurya worried that Meir's lack of affection was affecting Bathsheva. Once, Bathsheva asked her mother why her father didn't love her. Berurya told Bathsheva that her father did, indeed, love her; she said that if he didn't have much time for her, it was because people made such great demands on him. It was the only excuse she could provide. Berurya could hardly tell her daughter the truth: that Meir had only wanted sons.

"Why does Meir resent the fact that he has a daughter?" she wondered. "Is it something from his past?" Berurya didn't know but she was determined to confront him.

Berurya arrived home much later than anticipated. However, Bilha had everything ready for the Sabbath. "How's Tamar?" Bilha asked.

"Very well, considering how sick she was." Berurya looked around. "Where is everyone?"

"Bathsheva is upstairs. Meir hasn't returned from the *Beit Midrash* yet. As to Hananiah and Elhanan, your guess is as good as mine. I warned them to be home before Shabbat!"

"They'd better be home soon," said Berurya, "or they won't hear the last of it." She gestured. "Bilha, do you need any help?"

"No, thanks."

"In that case, I'm going up to look after Bathsheva."

Berurya went upstairs. About fifteen minutes later, Meir came in with Hananiah and Elhanan. Bilha greeted them with a stern expression on her face. "Don't you know how late it is?" she admonished.

"Bilha," said Meir, with a smile of amusement, "I've never seen anyone worry as much as you do! We've plenty of time before Shabbat."

He glanced over at the two boys.

"For the first time, Bilha," he explained, "I caught Elhanan and Hananiah red-handed as they were trying to sneak out of the *Beit Midrash*! They thought I was unaware of their tricks, but this time I caught them in the act! They tried to slip out the side entrance, but

I ran around and confronted them. You should've seen their faces! I made them stay with me until everyone else had gone home."

Hananiah quickly managed to change the subject. "That smells delicious, Bilha!" he exclaimed. "What are you cooking?"

"It's the bread I baked this morning, you smell. But you're not getting a morsel until dinner!"

The two of them bounded up the stairs to change into their best clothes for Shabbat.

"Has Berurya returned?" asked Meir.

"She's upstairs with Bathsheva."

"I think I'll rest a bit before Shabbat."

Meir left the room. Bilha was tired, but she had to finish preparing the food. During the winter months, Fridays were particularly difficult as the days were shorter and there was less time to prepare everything.

The dinner that evening was delicious. Meir was in an unusually good mood. He told Berurya how he had outsmarted Hananiah and Elhanan as they were attempting to sneak away. Berurya did not consider it as amusing as did Meir, but she let the story pass without comment.

After dinner, Bilha put Bathsheva to sleep and cleared the dishes from the table. There was still an hour left until the flame in the oil-lamp would burn down and the house would go dark. Meir asked Elhanan and Hananiah if they would like to study the Scriptural portion to be read the next morning from the Torah with him. They declined, claiming they were tired and preferred to go to sleep early. Meir simply nodded. Every Friday night, they made the same excuse.

After they had gone upstairs, Berurya went over to Meir and put her hands on his shoulders and gently messaged them. "That feels good," Meir smiled. "Please don't stop ..."

"Meir," said Berurya soberly, "I want to talk to you about a serious matter." She moved around to confront him. "What's troubling you?" she asked.

Meir looked surprised. "Troubling me? Why, nothing. Why do you ask?"

"You avoid Bathsheva as though she were infected with a contagious disease! You talk to her only when necessary and even then it is absolutely to the point." Berurya drew a deep breath: "What in the world do you have against her?"

"Nothing," Meir said forcefully, "nothing at all! I must tell you that I'm surprised by the question."

"Do you deny that you wish she'd been born a boy?"

"That's silly! You're talking just like a woman! Whether I wanted a boy or not is irrelevant. God wanted you to bear a girl: it would have been wrong for me to wish otherwise."

"That," said Berurya slowly, "confirms my suspicions."

Meir stared at his wife. "I prefer not to discuss the matter further," he said resolutely.

"I know what you prefer, Meir, but your attitude toward Bathsheva is inevitably going to raise the issue again."

Meir said nothing.

"I think I'm going to sleep," said Berurya. "I'm more tired than I realized."

Meir sat alone. He began his review of the Torah portion, but to no avail. He was upset because he couldn't get Berurya's accusations out of his mind. He knew very well there was a measure of truth in what she had said. Meir had indeed wanted only sons. But why? He had never bothered to consider the reasons. Did his attitude toward women in some way derive from his religious beliefs? Women were exempt from certain commandments, which had to be performed at a specific time, therefore giving to men a higher degree of responsibility. Did that, he wondered, give men a more respected status in Judaism? He did not believe that. Berurya, his wife, fulfilled as many *mitzvot*, if not more, than anyone he knew. And if the religion were responsible, then why were the attitudes of many non-observant Jews, as well as many non-Jews, toward women no better – and often worse?

Perhaps, thought Meir, his opinion of women had been influenced by what he had heard throughout his life. Men so often referred to women as simple-minded and irrational creatures, subject to their own emotions. If you had a son and he were strong, he would assist in his father's livelihood, be it farmer or merchant, or whatever. On the other hand, a daughter was a source of constant concern. She had to be protected: she might be seduced or, worse yet, raped. One worried about her welfare until the day she married and even then, there was no guarantee that her husband would properly care for her. Meir personally knew so many men who abused their wives and treated them with utter contempt!

Meir reflected on Pappas ben Yehuda. Here was a man who had never permitted his wife contact with the outside world! Rumor had it that for the last three years, she had not even been allowed to visit her mother, her sister, or any of her relatives! Nor did Pappas permit them to come to his house! To ensure that his wife didn't disobey him, when Pappas left he locked all the doors and the window shutters. What sort of life was that? What had made this man so jealous that he would not allow anyone to speak to his spouse, not even other women? Had she wronged him? Even if she had, could the wrong have been so great that she was denied contact with all other human beings? Poor woman! She was literally a prisoner in her very own home!

Of course, that case was extreme. Meir could just as readily think of women who had made their husbands' lives miserable. The famous rabbi, Yosi the Galilean, married his niece. What a shrew she was! She ridiculed the rabbi in front of his own students! They were shocked by the way she derided him. Several summoned up the courage to tell Rabbi Yosi that he might be better off if he divorced her. He replied that this wasn't possible, since the payment stipulated in the marriage-contract in the event of divorce was far more money than he had, or for that matter, ever hoped to earn. His wife knew this and despised him even more so because of it!

One day, Rabbi Yosi was studying with Rabbi Eleazar ben Azariah. When they finished, Rabbi Yosi invited his colleague to come home with him for lunch. Rabbi Eleazar agreed. As they entered the house, his wife looked at her husband with an expression of utter contempt and then proceeded to leave, passing him by as though he did not exist. Rabbi Yosi attempted to make the best of a bad situation. He saw that his wife had been preparing food and asked her, while she was still within hearing distance, what it was. She replied that it was relish. When he lifted the lid of the pot, he found poultry. Neither rabbi said anything. Rabbi Yosi was embarrassed; Rabbi Eleazer did not know what to say. At length, Rabbi Eleazer said: "Your wife told you there was relish in the pot, but you found poultry! That sounds to me like a miracle!" That comment broke the ice. Rabbi Eleazer went on: "Please forgive me," he said, "for being so presumptuous, but she doesn't seem the right woman for you. Have you ever considered divorce?" Rabbi Yosi sighed deeply; he explained that he was in no financial position to divorce the woman, whereupon Rabbi Eleazer volunteered to raise the necessary funds.

In time, the two were divorced. Each subsequently remarried: Rabbi Yosi to a woman who was kind; his former-wife to a guard. Unfortunately, the guard soon went blind and lost his only means of support. His wife now had to lead him through the streets he had once protected, so he could beg for charity.

Since the woman wanted to conceal the fact that she had formerly been married to Rabbi Yosi, she avoided his area of town. After a while, her husband, being familiar with the city, realized what she was doing. He confronted her and demanded to know why they were skirting that particular neighborhood. She had no choice but to tell him the truth. The husband was furious. Outraged because of her deception, as well as at his own disability, he turned her world into a nightmare. He began to beat her mercilessly. Ultimately, word got back to Rabbi Yosi. Since he was a compassionate person, the rabbi arranged for them to be taken care of for the rest of their lives.

Meir wondered how Rabbi Yosi had ever entered such a marriage. Didn't he see what kind of woman he was marrying? A man, Meir believed, should always marry a woman whom he considers his equal. Unfortunately, most men did not.

Meir pressed his fingers to his temples and rubbed them. Why was his attitude toward Bathsheva different from that to his sons? He didn't know. Suddenly, the flame of the oil-lamp flickered and died. Meir sat in darkness.

At length, he rose slowly from his chair and made his way upstairs. He wondered if Berurya was still awake, if she would still be angry? But he decided not to approach her. He undressed in the dark and climbed into bed with his back toward his wife.

Berurya did not move or speak. She lay there facing the window, and staring out into the night. She saw the sky, but there were no stars....

22
Tragedy

In the morning, the air was crisp and the sky clear. Meir had gone to the *Beit Keneset* with Hananiah and Elhanan. Berurya was helping Bathsheva to dress. When they finished, she would give Bathsheva breakfast and then they would go to the *Beit Keneset*. Bilha knocked gently on the door. "Do you need help?" she called out.

"No, thanks, I'm almost finished. Why don't you go back to sleep?"

"I was hoping you'd say that," Bilha remarked. "After lunch, I'll take Bathsheva with me to visit some friends. That'll give you time to rest."

"Thanks." Berurya heard Bilha's footsteps echoing down the hallway. She stepped back and viewed her daughter.

"Bathsheva, you look so beautiful all dressed up!"

Bathsheva stared at her mother. "Do you like Bilha, Mommy?" she asked suddenly.

"Do I like Bilha?" Berurya repeated with astonishment. "Very much, my dear! Beside you, father, your brothers, and Penina, I love Bilha more than anyone else in the world! Why do you ask?"

"Because when you told Bilha that people were coming to the house and she'd have to make more food, she said, 'You'll be the death of me yet!'"

Berurya laughed. "Bathsheva, my sweet, that's only an expression! It doesn't mean I want Bilha to die at all! God forbid such a thing."

"Is Bilha going to die?" asked Bathsheva.

"Eventually. All people die. Someday I'll die, and your father will die. That's how life is. We grow old and then we die...."

"Does it hurt to die, Mommy?"

"That depends on how people die. Some are ill for a long time and they and their families suffer a lot. Others die quickly and feel no pain."

"What happens to you when you die?"

"Your soul returns to God."

"Is that where your mother's and father's souls are?"

"Yes, Bathsheva," Berurya said, "their souls are with God."

She touched her daughter's head. "My, but you have a lot of questions today! But if we don't hurry now, we are going to be late."

After morning prayers in the *Beit Keneset*, the family sat down at home for the Sabbath meal. Meir first said *Kiddush*, the blessing over the wine and they washed their hands, having recited the appropriate benediction. Following the blessing over the *Challah*, the meal commenced.

During Sabbath meals, the family avoided topics of conversation that were normal throughout the week. They never discussed business or financial matters. Meir and Berurya always stressed that the Shabbat meal should be special. Not only was the food superior, but talk itself reflected the holiness of the day. Their discussions almost always included that week's Torah portion.

When the meal was over and they had finished chanting the final prayers, Meir announced that he would take a short nap. Elhanan and Hananiah asked to be excused and Meir warned them not to be late for afternoon prayers.

Bilha took Bathsheva to visit friends. She informed Berurya that they'd probably return at night and told her not to worry. Berurya wasn't in the least concerned: no one was more responsible than

Bilha. With everyone gone, Berurya cleared the dishes. She stacked them to the side – they would only be cleaned after the Sabbath was over.

Berurya had considered reopening the discussion about Bathsheva with Meir, but changed her mind. Meir looked very tired. He needed his rest. There would be another occasion.

Berurya sighed, seated herself, closed her eyes, and put her head on the table. Suddenly, she felt a hand on her shoulder. She looked up. It was Meir. "You must have dozed off," he said.

Berurya was puzzled. "Where's Bathsheva?" she mumbled.

"Don't you remember? She went off with Bilha."

"Of course. Now, I remember ..."

"Are you all right?" asked Meir. "You don't look well."

"I ... had a dream," Berurya said.

"What dream?"

"I don't remember! Really, I can't remember a single thing about the dream. But I have ... a terrible feeling." Berurya looked down. "Just see my hands are covered with sweat."

"You don't remember anything at all?" asked Meir. "Not one little detail?"

"No." Berurya reflected. "Wait! Yes! Now, I remember. I remember that people were screaming ... horrendous screams!"

"Who were these people?"

Berurya shook her head. "I don't know! I can't remember another thing ..."

Meir stroked her shoulders. "Berurya," he said, "don't take your dreams so seriously. Most dreams are silly; they have no significance." He squeezed her. "Get the dream out of your mind. Come with me to the *Beit Keneset.*"

"No, no, Meir. Go without me, please. I'll have dinner ready when you return."

"As you wish."

The dream had shaken Berurya. She felt that something was amiss, but didn't know what. All she recalled was that people were in dreadful pain. There had been weeping and wailing. She tried to overcome her sense of dread. Meir must be right: most dreams could not be taken seriously.

She sat at the table for several minutes. Suddenly, there was a knock at the door. "Strange," she thought. "Who could it be? No one comes to the house without an invitation on Shabbat. Was it Bilha? But why would she knock?"

Berurya went to the door. A man stood outside it. "You don't know me," he said. "I'm an innkeeper at the *poondak* down the road." He swallowed and took a deep breath. "There's been... a terrible tragedy."

Berurya felt light-headed and dizzy. She leaned against the door-frame.

"There was a fire," continued the innkeeper. "I'm ... sorry," he said haltingly, "to have to tell you this but your two sons ... your two boys ... perished in it."

Berurya felt herself reeling. The innkeeper grabbed hold of her. He helped her back into the house and sat her down in a chair. "They were ... supposed to be out walking," she muttered in a thick voice. "What were they doing ... in a *poondak* on the Sabbath!"

The innkeeper brought her water; she pushed it away. "How? Tell me ... how it happened."

The innkeeper cleared his throat. "When the fire first broke out, people panicked. Most of them ... managed to get out." He paused and then went on: "I heard ... that your boys went up to the second floor and tried to help others get out; apparently, they were overcome by smoke. They died ... trying to save other people."

Berurya shook her head dazedly. "Why ... were they in a *poondak*?" she mumbled hoarsely. "They said ... they were going for a walk ... and then to the *Beit Keneset*. They promised ... they'd come home before the afternoon prayers."

The innkeeper pulled at his beard. "I asked a couple of men to bring the bodies here," he said in a flat voice. "They're waiting outside. Do you want them to bring your sons into the house?"

"My ... sons. Yes, my sons. Their names are Hananiah and Elhanan. They're going ... to the *Beit Keneset* to pray."

The innkeeper stared at her. "Your sons' bodies are waiting outside. Do you want them brought in?"

"Bring them in..." whispered Berurya.

The innkeeper opened the door and gestured. A tall man walked in carrying Elhanan in his arms. Elhanan's head hung down, his mouth ajar. Berurya set a hand on Elhanan's forehead and caressed it. A second, shorter man brought in Hananiah. Berurya bit her lip until it bled. If this were a dream, the pain would waken her! But ... she knew the nightmare was real.

"Where should we put them?" asked the tall man.

"What?"

"Your sons' bodies. Where should we put them?"

"Follow me." Berurya moved stiffly up the stairs to the boys' bedroom. "Put them there," she said, pointing to the bed.

The men put the bodies down side by side.

The innkeeper watched Berurya as she stood motionless, gazing fixedly at the bed. He had expected hysteria. In the *poondak* he had heard men shrieking, women sobbing bitterly and beating themselves. How could this woman stand there that way?

"Do you ... smell the smoke ..." she intoned dully. "The quaestionarius ... started the fire ... with his torch."

"The quaestionarius?" said the innkeeper, puzzled.

"Yes," Berurya muttered. "No more water. Please, no more water ..." she breathed with difficulty. "I won't cry. I promised myself: I will not cry!"

The innkeeper grasped Berurya's shoulder.

Startled, her eyes opened wide and she drew back.

"I must be going," said the innkeeper. "There are others to care for. Is there anything more I can do before I leave?"

Berurya's eyes were clouded. "No."

The three men departed. Moving slowly and methodically, Berurya covered her sons' faces with a sheet. She hesitated; she felt that she wanted to look at their faces once again. She folded the sheet back. It seemed as if the boys were sleeping: they looked so calm and peaceful. Berurya leaned over and kissed them. "Sleep," she whispered, "sleep ..." She shivered and pulled the sheet over their faces again.

"How do I tell Meir?" she murmured aloud. "What ... do I say? 'Meir, our sons profaned the Sabbath ... and died in a fire.' 'Meir, Hananiah and Elhanan lost their lives while trying to rescue others.' 'Meir, our sons are no more!'"

She went downstairs and began to prepare food. Numbly, she gazed out the window. "The sun is setting," she muttered. "Meir will be home. How will I tell him? I must be strong."

When Meir returned, Berurya saw that he looked annoyed.

"Well, where are they?" he demanded.

"Hananiah and Elhanan?"

"Of course, Hananiah and Elhanan! Who else?"

"Didn't they say that they'd meet you in the *Beit Keneset* after their walk?"

"That's what they said! Apparently, they aren't to be believed." He waved a hand. "I looked all over for them, but I couldn't find them anywhere! After yesterday, you would assume they'd know better!"

"It's not the right time," she thought, with mingled panic and determination. "I must pretend a little longer – just a little longer."

Berurya passed a cup of wine to him. "Meir, the Sabbath is over. You must recite *Havdalah*."

Meir's brow furrowed. "I don't understand why Hananiah and Elhanan can't be at the *Beit Keneset* on the Sabbath! It's inexcusable!"

"Meir," Berurya said quietly, "it's possible that you missed them in the *Beit Keneset*, and they went off somewhere. That's happened before remember? Sit down. I've made your meal."

Meir sat down and ate silently, but he was still agitated. Berurya observed him closely. "Meir," she said at length,"I have a question. Something's been troubling me: maybe you can advise me."

Meir looked up. "What is it?"

"Some time ago, someone gave me something for safekeeping. I forgot about it completely, and then one day he showed up unexpectedly and asked me to return it to him. Do I have to give it back?"

Meir looked askance. "Berurya, I'm surprised that you'd even ask such a question! Jewish law is explicit. You haven't a choice: return it immediately!"

"I thought you'd say that ..."

Berurya slowly rose from the table and reached for Meir's hand. "Follow me," she said abruptly.

Meir followed her, somewhat perplexed, as she led him up the stairs. She opened the door to her sons' room and entered. Meir came behind.

"What – !?" he began.

But before he could continue, Berurya went over to the bed and pulled the sheet back. A convulsive shudder ran through Meir's entire frame. Tears flooded his eyes and streamed down his cheeks. He swayed and dropped to his knees at the side of the bed. "My sons," he wailed, "my sons!" He buried his face in his hands and sobbed. "Hananiah, Elhanan," he howled. "Hananiah, Elhanan..."

Berurya waited, and then helped him to his feet. He stood, arms hugging his chest, and swayed. "They were my sons!" he sobbed. "They were ... like teachers to me; they taught me ... as much as I taught them...."

"Listen to me carefully, Meir," said Berurya huskily. "Sometimes we're entrusted with precious objects for safekeeping. We take care of them; in the course of time, we become attached to them. Then one day, the owner comes to us unexpectedly and asks that his possessions be returned to him." She paused and then said: "God gave us two lovely sons, two wonderful sons. But God has asked for them back. Now, their souls are with Him ..."

Meir was only half-attentive. He trembled.

"How...?" he said. "When...? Why...?"

Berurya gave him the only answer she could: "The Lord hath given, and the Lord hath taken away. Blessed be the name of the Lord."

23

Mourning

Both Hammat and Tiberias had their cemeteries. In Tiberias, the cemetery was located in the northwestern part of the city; the one in Hammat was situated near the *Beit Keneset*.

The boys were buried twice. Initially, the bodies were interred deep in the earth. After time passed and the flesh decomposed, the remains were carefully and respectfully disinterred and placed in ornately-designed ossuaries. These ossuaries were made usually of cedar, although some sarcophagi were made of marble. Rabbi Meir had the names "Hananiah ben Meir" and "Elhanan ben Meir" inscribed on the sarcophagi, along with the words "May his soul rest" and below them the word "Shalom".

During the mourning period, a great outpouring of townspeople, as well as students from the *Beit Midrash*, came to the cemetery. Friends of the family came from Usha, Sikhnin, Gadera, Sepphoris, and from the upper and lower Galilee. Penina and Menahem came. Menahem spent the week; Penina remained for the entire month.

Among those who came to express their condolences, Meir and Berurya were surprised and pleased to find Nathan. Meir recalled that he had asked Nathan to visit so he might have the opportunity to meet his two sons. That opportunity was now lost and gone forever....

Bilha took the deaths of Hananiah and Elhanan very hard. She blamed herself for all the times she'd rebuked them, or even raised her voice. If only she hadn't shouted at them so much! And there were her sarcastic comments. Most of the time they were meant in jest, but how could she now be certain that Hananiah and Elhanan had really understood her remarks? Had she ever bothered to tell them how much she loved them? Perhaps when they had been younger, but not recently! During the last few years, her love had been taken for granted. If only she had another chance to tell them how special they were to her! But that would never be.

Bilha often thought back to the day the boys died. She wondered what would have been had she done or said things differently. If she had stayed home and asked the boys to help her, perhaps Hananiah and Elhanan would still be alive....

Bilha knew that some things in life were irreversible. While a part of her understood that she couldn't change the past, another part refused to let the past go. She persisted in asking the unanswerable question: "What if...?"

Bilha hurried around the house, looking for things to do – anything that would keep her occupied. Most of the time, however, she was upstairs, behind the locked door of her room. Occasionally, she would go to the boys' room, stand there as if she wished to enter, and then turn and walk away. Most of her days were passed in silence.

Meir's reaction to the death of his sons was peculiar. When Berurya had first brought her husband to the bodies of Elhanan and Hananiah, he had broken down completely. For most of that night, he had wept without control. After the funeral, he had lapsed into silence. His students gathered and discussed the laws relating to mourners in his presence. If they erred, he corrected them in a faint, all but inaudible voice. Not once did he question them.

Some sages had ruled that a mourner should gradually return to the normal routine of his everyday life. For example, during the first week of mourning, the bereaved was not allowed to enter the *Beit*

Keneset to pray. During the second week, he might do so, but he should not sit in his usual place. During the third week, he was permitted to sit in his usual place, but not to speak to anyone. By the fourth week, his life in the *Beit Keneset* could return to normal.

Meir disagreed with this ruling. For the first two weeks, he would not enter the *Beit Keneset* at all. The third week, he returned, and took his normal seat and on the fourth week, he returned to a normal routine. While Meir was away from the *Beit Keneset*, he nevertheless continued to study in the *Beit Midrash*.

Berurya never really wept. She mourned inside herself, privately. In part, she was preoccupied with worrying about everyone else; she had to be the strength and mainstay of the family. Meir needed her support desperately during this period. Following her brothers' deaths, Bathsheva wept and could not be consoled. Berurya tried to comfort them all.

Berurya also controlled her emotions because of a vow she made after her father's death. She had never forgotten it: "I will never cry again. I will never hurt... as I hurt at this moment. I will be strong. I will be as strong as my father, and ever more so!" And the vow that had been born in fire was now confirmed in fire!

Penina worried about her sister. It wasn't natural for a mother to lose her children and not cry! But Berurya said to Penina that she'd be all right, and that everyone grieved in his own way. She, Berurya, had to be strong for everyone else.

The day designated for "the gathering of bones" was particularly difficult. Berurya and Meir went to the burial site accompanied by a few students. The group arrived in the late afternoon, an hour or two before dusk. The bones of the two boys were exhumed and carefully placed on sheets. Then they were taken to and laid each in its respective ossuary in preparation for transferral to a cave, which was the final resting place.

Two students, groaning as they exerted themselves, opened the heavy basalt doors which sealed the cave. The entrance was quite large: it was reminiscent to Meir of walking into the belly of Sheol.

As the group slowly moved down into the catacomb, the temperature suddenly dropped: the air was cool and dry. A chill seemed to enter Meir's body – not from the cold, but from the dark mystery of the cave itself.

As the cave wound farther back, its ceiling drooped lower and there were passages that struck off to the right and the left. Holding a lamp, Meir led the way. At the very end of the cave, they went left and down into a smaller passage.

Berurya noticed that their shadows, which loomed larger than life, accompanied them along the jagged rocks. At last, they reached the end of the passage. Directly opposite were two empty niches, large enough to receive the ossuaries of Hananiah and Elhanan. The students inserted the ossuaries into the niches. Meir stepped forward and placed a hand on each of the ossuaries; he felt the smooth marble on the tips of his fingers. In a low voice, he intoned the words of the Prophet Isaiah: "He that walks in his uprightness, shall enter in peace to them that rest in their graves." His hands dropped. He turned and moved away.

Berurya stood there a moment longer in the light of a flickering lamp. "How much pain must a person suffer in one lifetime?" she thought. "First my brother; then my father and mother; and now my two sons! Is this your test, God? As you did to Job, will you now afflict me with sores on my body? What will be next, God? Perhaps my daughter, or my husband? If you're planning another tragedy, I beg of You to let it happen now! I haven't the strength to wait! Enough, God! Enough!" A tear welled in her eye, but before it moistened the cheek, she wiped it away.

Meir came back and took Berurya's arm. "Let's go, Berurya," he said. "There's nothing more for us to do here." His wife did not answer. She followed him silently back to the entrance of the cave. As they exited, the sun dropped behind the mountains on the other side of the Kinneret. The students swung the heavy black doors shut. Berurya looked back and repeated her plea: "Enough, God – please..."

A few weeks later, Berurya returned to her teaching in the *Beit Midrash*. The day she came back, the students were studying the Torah portion *Sh'mini*, from the book of Leviticus, which described the death of Aaron's two sons. Berurya perused the text: "And Nadav and Avihu, the sons of Aaron, took each of them his censer, and put fire therein, and laid incense thereon, and offered strange fire before the Lord, which He had not commanded them. And there came forth fire from before the Lord, and devoured them, and they died before the Lord. Then Moses said unto Aaron: 'This is it that the Lord spoke, saying: Through them that are nigh unto Me I will be sanctified, and before all the people I will be glorified.' And Aaron held his peace."

Berurya listened as one of the students spoke. "From what Moses tells Aaron," he said, "it seems that the severity of the punishment... was a consequence of their priestly status. Since they were Aaron's sons, more was expected of them than of others. But my question is: 'Why wasn't Aaron ever given the reason for his sons' deaths?'"

"That's an excellent question," Berurya observed. "Does anyone want to respond?"

The students looked at each other, but no one answered.

"Well," said Berurya, "there are several explanations but the one which seems most plausible to me is that they were drunk! How do I infer this? Well, if you read ahead just a few verses in the Torah, the very next pronouncement of God to Aaron is: 'Drink no wine nor strong drink, thou, nor thy sons with thee, when ye go into the Tent of Meeting, that ye die not...' Aaron and his two younger sons, you see, were warned not to enter the Tent of Meeting intoxicated; to do so would mean death. Apparently, that's what happened to Nadav and Avihu."

As Berurya spoke, the irony of what she was saying suddenly struck her. Aaron's sons had died because they were intoxicated in a holy place; Elhanan and Hananiah had died in an unholy place, a tavern, where people went to drink. Aaron's sons had died serving God; Elhanan and Hananiah had died desecrating the Sabbath and disobeying God. The fire that had devoured Aaron's sons came from God: in this sense, their deaths were significant, special. Elhanan's and Hananiah's deaths were anything but sanctified! Her heart convulsed with bitter pain. They were so young, her boys: if only they had listened!

Suddenly, Berurya realized that she had drifted off. "That'll be enough for now," she murmured. "We'll continue in the afternoon."

The students left the room; Berurya remained alone.

24
Nathan

Several weeks later, Nathan came to see Rabbi Meir in the *Beit Midrash*; Meir invited his guest to return with him to the house for a meal, and Nathan accepted the invitation.

"I enjoyed your lecture," Nathan said to Meir as they walked home together, "at least, the part that I understood."

"You're too modest, my friend," said Meir.

"No, I'm not being modest. As I once mentioned, my father saw to it that I had an excellent education. From my early childhood on, he employed tutors to instruct me in Greek and Latin, philosophy and the arts. My father, though he wasn't an educated man himself, was nevertheless determined that his son would be cultured and learned. Thus, he spared no expense in my education. He sent me to Athens and Alexandria so that I'd be under the tutelage of some of the world's greatest teachers." Nathan smiled. "I consider myself to be very fortunate. However, the one area my father didn't deem important enough for me to study in great depth was Torah. I must confess that I sometimes think he was suspicious and mistrustful of rabbis." He raised a hand. "Please don't take offence, Meir."

"I do not," said Meir.

"While father saw to it that I learned Hebrew as a language," Nathan went on, "my studies didn't extend much beyond the basics. What my father's reasons were for this, I can only surmise. But interestingly enough, he contributed generously to the construction of synagogues in Tiberias, Hammat and other places. He once joked to me he was 'playing it safe.' 'Just in case,' he said, with a wink of the eye, 'I'll pay for my name to be inscribed in the synagogue for life.'" Nathan stared at his host. "I really hope you don't find this offensive."

"No," Meir said evenly. "You'd be surprised how many people behave exactly like your father. I wish that all *Tzedakah* was donated for the noblest of reasons but people give money for all kinds of reasons. It does good, and that's something!"

"Nathan," said Meir, "I gather that your father is no longer alive."

"He died about five years ago."

"And your mother?"

"She died... giving birth to me." Nathan's eyes clouded. "My father never really got over her death," he said, "and that was probably the reason he never remarried."

When they arrived at Meir's home, the meal was ready. Meir and Nathan sat down in the salon. "Nathan," said Meir, "what's your occupation?"

"What I do is rather hard to explain," said Nathan. "You might say that I do a little bit of everything."

Meir nodded.

"I'm involved in business. I go fishing. Some people consider me a farmer."

Meir glanced at Nathan's hands. "Excuse me for saying so, but you don't have the hands of a fisherman or a farmer."

Nathan stared at his hands. "That's true," he said.

Meir was about to ask another question when Berurya and Bathsheva came downstairs. "It's good to see you again, Nathan," said Berurya. "Have the two of you been here long?"

"No," said Meir. "We arrived a few moments ago. Nathan was just telling me about what he does for a living."

"The food's ready," said Berurya. "We can sit down to eat and continue the discussion at the table."

After the blessings, they began to eat. Meir turned to Nathan. "I don't mean to pry, but what you said before aroused my curiosity."

Nathan smiled. "Perhaps it's my fault for being so mysterious. I was intentionally being evasive because I felt that what I do would be of no interest to a scholar such as yourself."

"Quite the contrary."

Nathan gathered his thoughts. "I inherited a great deal of money from my father," he said. "As you've probably surmised, he was a man who amassed a fortune. But life wasn't always easy for him. As a young man, he earned only meager wages as a fisherman. After denying himself everything but the necessities he needed to survive, he scraped together enough money to become half-owner of a boat. He was an ambitious man, an extremely ambitious man. When the war broke out with Rome, he saw opportunity for himself in other peoples' misfortunes. If he found out, for example, that someone had been killed, he would buy the man's property from his widow. He allowed the widow and the children to remain on the land – not out of the goodness of his heart but for the potential profit to be made: they became tenants. Whatever they raised my father took as payment, leaving them with just enough for themselves. If they prospered, my father benefited. If there were lean years, my father took less – that ingratiated my father to them, but in reality it was just smart business.

"My father began with a small piece of property just beyond Tiberias. In time, he purchased property in Tiberias itself."

Nathan cleared his throat.

"His tenants grew olive trees, mostly; several tenants also had livestock. Soon, my father bought out his partner and began building up a fleet of his own fishing boats. This brought him much greater wealth.

"I remember that as a child, once, we passed a factory where glass utensils were manufactured. Outside, a vendor was selling glass vases. I asked my father to buy one for me. He asked me if I really liked the vases; I said they were very pretty. There and then, my father apparently made up his mind to acquire the factory! The owner had his own ideas. My father offered him a substantial amount of money but he turned it down. This only made my father more determined. He raised his offer; still the owner doggedly refused to sell. But the man's obstinacy only increased my father's resolve. At length, my father – and keep in mind that he knew absolutely nothing about the glass business – bought a building and set up a glass factory of his own! At first, things didn't go at all well. His competitor's glassware was of a finer quality, and my father knew it. He was losing money. He didn't want to admit defeat, but he wasn't foolish enough to hold on to a losing proposition. One night, however, my father's luck turned. A fire broke out in his competitor's shop and everything in the place was destroyed. The owner angrily accused my father of deliberately starting the fire but my father was away at the time and nothing could be proved."

Meir interrupted: "Did you ever feel that your father had ordered someone else to start the fire?"

Nathan shook his head slowly. "I don't know. I don't really know. One time, when I asked him outright, he said: 'Nathan, you'll learn that things in life happen – some to your benefit, some to your disadvantage. The intelligent person doesn't ponder on the question "Why?", but simply seizes his opportunity! Life, my son, is filled with limitless opportunities but most people just let them slip by, endlessly asking the question why?'"

Nathan rubbed his forehead. "I know what you must be thinking, Rabbi Meir, that the response incriminates my father. But if you knew my father, you would know that was truly his attitude toward life. 'Never look back,' he would say. 'If you do, you'll run the risk of losing the here-and-now!'"

Nathan shifted his weight in his chair. "Well," he said, "after the fire, my father hired his former competitor's glass-maker and his business soon became the most successful in all of Galilee! All of his days, my father had an uncanny ability to take a good business and turn it into something better. He succeeded in almost everything."

"You say, 'almost everything.' Was there a business venture in which he failed?"

"Yes, Rabbi Meir," Nathan replied, "but I wouldn't exactly call it a business. As much as my father succeeded in business, he failed in his family life." Nathan reflected and then went on: "I have an older brother and sister," he said. "My older brother is very much like father, perhaps too much so. They constantly argued and were at each other's throats. Yohanan, that's my brother's name, was born when my father was still struggling hard to make a living. My father had no time for him. Father worked seven days a week, without rest. He never played with Yohanan. In my father's mind, there was a clear choice: he could increase his wealth or devote himself to his family. He didn't believe he could do both. Consequently, Yohanan was always getting into trouble. From what I learned later, my mother would inevitably excuse Yohanan's behavior: she felt that he tried to get his father to notice him. Perhaps she was right. Of course, Father did notice him: whenever Yohanan made trouble, Father punished him. The punishments grew increasingly more severe and more regular. Eventually, a day didn't go by without my father raising his hand against Yohanan."

Nathan paused for some time and then, in a more subdued voice, went on: "It got so bad, I learned, that Father often took a cane with which to beat Yohanan. The louder Yohanan screamed, the harder Father struck. When Yohanan was too old to be taken across the knee, Father slapped his face. Yohanan was shocked by the slap at first – apparently, the shock hurt him more than the slap. After a while, it became a contest-of-wills between the two of them. Yohanan actually seemed to derive some sort of pleasure out of the relationship, as strange as that sounds. He got into trouble knowing what awaited him, but didn't seem to care. One day, Father took a swing at Yohanan; Yohanan put up his hand and deflected Father's arm. Father was stunned. He tried to swing at Yohanan with his other hand, but again Yohanan deflected the blow. Yohanan stood and laughed in his face. The harder he laughed, the redder Father's face became. At length, in his savage anger, Father swung at his son with a fist. Yohanan stepped nimbly out of the way, Father lost his footing and fell to the ground. Yohanan roared. 'You stupid old man,' he shouted. 'You control the lives of all of those helpless people out there! I wish they all could see you now, lying there in the dirt like a cur! You think you're a success because you have money. But you're really poor! You're just a poor excuse for a father and a man!' Yohanan repeated his last words over and over. After a time, Father got to his feet, brushed himself off, and looked Yohanan straight in the eye. In a controlled voice, he said: 'Get out, and don't ever come back.' 'With pleasure,' said Yohanan. So Yohanan left and no one has ever seen him since that day."

There was a brittle silence that was broken at length by Berurya. "You said that you had a sister," she remarked.

"Yes, a sister named Yokheved," said Nathan. "She is seven years younger than my brother, and eight years older than I."

"That's an unusual age difference," said Berurya.

"So it is," Nathan agreed. "I don't know why my parents waited so many years between each child...." He stared intently at his hostess. "Unfortunately, my sister Yokheved didn't fare much better than my brother. The very little time my father gave to Yohanan was still more than he gave to his daughter. Vaguely, he hoped that she would marry someone to manage some of his business, and that she'd give him grandsons who would carry on after him. Father always thought about who would take over after him, since he had disowned his firstborn."

Nathan grimaced. "Well," he continued, "my sister did give birth to a grandchild. The problem was ... she had never married! She wouldn't say who the father was. And so she and the child were packed off to relatives in some remote village. Once again, fate laughed in Father's face!"

Nathan ran his long, tapered fingers through his thick hair. "I was the last child born and my father's only chance. He was determined not to repeat his mistakes. He reckoned that if he could succeed in business, he could succeed in raising a child. You might say that he saw me as an investment. Therefore, he provided me with my excellent education. Whatever he perceived as refining my character, he did or acquired for me. Did he succeed this time? If you had asked him, he probably would've said no. He had really given so little of himself to his family! I once told him that I loved him. He didn't know how to react. What a shame!"

Bilha brought more food to the table.

"Tell me about yourself," Nathan said.

"Myself?" said Meir. "I don't know what there is to tell."

"What about your parents?"

"I never knew... my father."

Berurya was astonished. In all the years she had known her husband, he had never mentioned anything about his past to anyone but her!

"When I was young," Meir said in a voice that was all but hushed, "I once overheard someone say that my father was a convert to Judaism, and that he was a descendent of the Emperor Nero! But the truth is that I know nothing of my past. As a child, they called me Maisha. It is the Aramaic equivalent of Meir: it means, 'giving off light.'"

"For a moment," observed Nathan, "I thought you might say that it's like the Hebrew name, Moshe."

"Moses?" asked Bilha.

"Yes," said Nathan. "If I'm correct, I believe that when Moses was born his room was illuminated with light. And like Moses, you, too, Rabbi, are a scribe."

Meir smiled. "Nathan, you amaze me! For someone who professes to know little about Rabbinic literature, you know a great deal."

"Not really," laughed Nathan, "but I accept the compliment!"

Bilha cleared away the dishes, brought a deep bowl, and placed it in the center of the table.

"Would you care for some wine?" asked Meir.

"Why, thank you," said Nathan, "I would ..."

Meir left the room to get a jug of wine.

Nathan turned to Berurya. "Are you always so quiet?"

"I'm not good at small-talk. When I have something worth saying, I speak."

"I imagine that anything you'd say would be worth listening to."

"May I ask you why you've never married, Nathan?"

"It's simple: I haven't found a woman who possesses the qualities I'm looking for in a wife."

"What qualities?"

"Well, she'd have to be intelligent, wise, compassionate and loving. I hope that she'd be pretty, but that certainly wouldn't be the most important factor. She'd have to be someone with whom I could share my innermost feelings. At the risk of sounding immodest, I'd want a wife whom I could respect as my equal."

"Meir says the same thing: 'A man should marry a woman who befits him in character and intelligence.'"

"It's clear that Meir has found an ideal companion."

Meir returned, carrying a jug of wine. After removing its lid, Meir reached for the device to remove the drink. The implement was hallow and its bottom tapered gently to a point; the sides were perforated by holes which enabled the wine to enter. Once the wine was in the tube, Meir placed his thumb over the top; he then took the container, set it over an empty glass, and removed his thumb. The wine flowed out of the perforations into the glass. "What'll they think of next!" Meir said. "Would you like some wine, Berurya?"

"No, thanks."

"What about you, Bilha? You enjoy wine."

Bilha, preoccupied with Bathsheva, had not been listening.

"I'm sorry, Meir, were you speaking to me?"

"I asked if you'd like some wine."

"No, thank you."

"In that case, Nathan, it looks like only you and I will enjoy ourselves."

When the meal was over, Nathan thanked his hosts for their hospitality. "Everything was delicious. I'd like to return your kindness and invite you to join me on my boat."

Meir obviously liked the idea. "We'd be happy to accept your invitation," he said.

"I'm not sure," Berurya said. "Perhaps the two of you should be by yourselves."

"I wouldn't think of it! Please, Meir, convince your wife to come along."

"She'll change her mind, I'm sure," said Meir.

"Then it's settled," said Nathan. "Come to my house two weeks from today."

"Where do you live?" Meir asked.

"It's a bit complicated to explain. I'll send one of my servants to guide you."

Nathan rose and headed towards the door.

Meir got up to accompany him.

"Please," Nathan said, "I'll see myself out." He smiled and waved. "Again, let me thank you for your hospitality. Until we meet again, Shalom!"

When Nathan had departed, Meir said: "He's quite intriguing, don't you agree?"

Berurya said nothing.

"Berurya," Meir persisted, "is something wrong? You seem uneasy."

"Nothing's the matter. I've been preoccupied with my thoughts."

"Which are?"

"I've been thinking about all the married couples we know ... and which of them have truly good marriages."

"How would you define a 'good marriage'?"

Berurya hesitated. "I'm not quite sure," she said. "From a man's point of view, it's far less complicated. A husband wants a wife to bear and raise his children, to cook and prepare his meals, to mend his clothes, and do all the other necessary daily tasks."

"And you think it should be different, is that it?"

"Don't misunderstand, Meir. I'm not implying those things are unimportant. But something ... is missing. Unfortunately, I don't know what it is."

"If you'd been born a man, do you think you'd have been happier?"

"Not at all! I enjoy being a woman. I wouldn't want it any other way. It's just that something is missing from life. I've had the feeling for many years. Do you know what I'm talking about, Meir?"

"No, Berurya," said Meir. "Honestly, I don't have the faintest notion of what you mean. God created woman to bear children, to raise and to nurture them. That's a full-time occupation. What else is there? Your problem is that you question everything. Some things should be left unquestioned. God created Woman to help Man: it's as simple as that! Don't look further."

Berurya sighed. "Maybe you're right," she murmured.

25

Sorrow of Sorrows

The next week went by quickly. Unfortunately, Meir got word that he was needed in Lydda; he would have to be away for at least two weeks. As usual, Berurya would take over as head of the *Beit Midrash*. She told Meir that when Nathan's servant came for them, she would explain the situation and extend their apologies. However, Meir insisted that Berurya not decline the invitation; he wanted her to take Bilha and Bathsheva to Nathan's, as planned. He felt a change of scenery would be good for them and that they would enjoy the experience of sailing on the Kinneret. Berurya disagreed. She said that there were far too many things which had to be attended to, and that sailing could wait. But Meir was adamant; and he finally persuaded Berurya that a day away from home would not make that much of a difference.

Immediately after morning prayers, Meir left for Lydda with two of his students. Two hours later, Nathan's servant arrived. Berurya explained that Meir would not be joining them; the servant simply nodded and they started off.

The trip to Nathan's house proved longer than Berurya had anticipated. His home was built on the slope of one of the mountains surrounding the Kinneret. The dirt road leading up to the house was very steep and the climb for the horses was slow and arduous.

As they neared their destination, two servants emerged from the house. They dismounted and the servants led the horses off to the stables. Bathsheva was amazed; she had never seen such an enormous house! "Mother," she cried out, "how many people live here?"

"I don't know," said Berurya with a smile.

"Mother, when are we going on the boat?"

"That depends on Nathan, Bathsheva. I don't exactly know his plans."

"Mother, is Nathan very rich?"

"Bathsheva, what's gotten into you today!? I've never heard you ask so many questions."

"Rich," muttered Bilha, "isn't the word for it! By the look of this house, the man must be very wealthy, so wealthy it makes my head swim!"

"Bathsheva," said Berurya, "we mustn't judge people by their money. There's a famous passage which asks the question: 'Who is wealthy? The person who is satisfied with whatever he possesses.' Do you understand what that means?"

"I understand very well," said Bilha. "It means that if you're poor, don't complain because it won't help one bit!"

"I'm surprised at you, Bilha! What kind of example do you want to set for Bathsheva?"

"You're not going to make me feel the least bit guilty," Bilha retorted. "Who made up that saying anyway?"

"Meir did."

"Oh," said Bilha, "really? And I suppose he's the only one ever to define wealth?"

"No, there were others."

"For example ..."

"Well, Rabbi Tarfon defined a wealthy man as 'He who has a hundred vineyards, a hundred fields and a hundred servants to till them.'"

"One last question," said Bilha. "Was Rabbi Tarfon, by any chance, wealthy?"

"Yes. As a matter of fact, he had considerable wealth."

"That just goes to prove my point! The wealthy have no problem defining who is rich."

"Bilha," said Berurya acidly, "perhaps our host, Nathan, has need for an extra servant? Would you like to apply for the job?"

"Very amusing!"

"I never knew that money preoccupied your thoughts, Bilha."

"Do you think I lie in bed all night counting my wealth?"

"Then you must be happy."

"Forget the hundred vineyards," exclaimed Bilha. "If I just had a house like this, I'd never complain again as long as I lived!"

"I seriously doubt that, Bilha, you love to complain. You may never be rich, but as long as you are poor, you'll always have something to complain about, and that should make you happy."

"Maybe you should tell Meir to formulate another saying: 'Who is happy? Someone who has something to complain about!'"

"Not bad, Bilha! You may be a great sage yet."

Bilha laughed.

One of the servants led them through the house to a large room where Nathan awaited them. "Welcome to my home," said Nathan politely, "and where is Rabbi Meir?"

"Meir got word," said Berurya, "that he was needed in Lydda. He sends his apology. I hope you don't mind that I've brought Bilha and my daughter with me."

"Mind?" Nathan boomed. "I am absolutely delighted that you're all here! We'll make another date for Rabbi Meir."

"Does that mean we're not going on the boat?" Bathsheva asked.

Berurya glanced over at her. "Bathsheva, where are your manners?"

"That's all right," Nathan said. He smiled warmly. "Today, my dear, we're all going on a big boat right to the middle of the lake! How's that?"

Bathsheva's face beamed with excitement. "Mommy! Mommy! Can we?"

"Yes, of course."

"Before we go sailing," said Nathan, "I'd like very much to show you one of the rooms in which I enjoy spending time." He turned and started up a flight of stairs. Berurya walked behind; Bilha followed, holding Bathsheva by the hand. Nathan moved up the spiral staircase; abruptly, he stopped. "Tabi," he said, nodding at a servant, "attend to the matter I discussed with you earlier." The servant bowed slightly from the waist and left the room. Nathan continued to climb the stairs.

Upstairs, the four of them entered a spacious room whose entire east wall was made of glass. From there they could see Lake Kinneret. The view was spectacular: blue skies, with clouds racing across it; mountains in the background, with the radiant sun hovering above; fishing boats casting off from shore to seek the morning catch – all of this could be seen from the immense, glass window!

"It's ... magnificent!" Bilha said breathlessly.

"I thought you'd enjoy it," said Nathan. "Sometimes, when life becomes a little too much of a burden, I come up here and view the world as it was meant to be seen. The time of day never matters. At night, I watch the moon bathe solitarily in the lake." Nathan paused. "But enough about me and the room. I just wanted to show you the view." He smiled. "Few have seen it."

"We're honored," said Berurya.

"We'd better start now," said Nathan. "When you're out on the lake, with a breeze blowing, you forget how dangerous the mid-day sun is."

As Nathan spoke, Bathsheva went over to a table in the far corner. "Mother, look at this pretty coin!" she exclaimed.

"Bathsheva, put it down at once."

"That's all right," said Nathan. "She didn't do anything wrong." He glanced at Berurya. "Do you mind if I show her some of my coins? They're really interesting."

Berurya nodded. Nathan went to the table and drew out a box from beneath the top. He unlocked the box and opened its cover.

"Mother!" Bathsheva blurted out. "Come see all the beautiful coins!"

"Now you must promise me, Bathsheva, not to tell anyone where I keep this box. Do you know how to keep a secret?" asked Nathan.

"Oh, yes! I'm very good at keeping secrets. I promise I won't tell anyone in the world!"

Nathan arranged the coins on the table; Bilha and Berurya came over to see them.

"These," said Nathan, pointing to a number of silver coins, "were minted during the third and fourth year of the Bar Kokhba rebellion. You can even read the inscription, 'Shimon, the son of Koziba.' Bathsheva, you're too young to know who he was, but some day your mother and father will tell you all about him. Now, if you look carefully at these coins, Bathsheva, you'll see many interesting pictures. Some have simple designs, and others, like this one, have real pictures on them."

"What's that building?" asked Bathsheva.

"It's a picture of a temple," answered Nathan. "The people who made this coin," he explained, "worshiped many gods. The temple was the place where they came to offer sacrifices." He held up a coin so that Bathsheva could inspect it at close range. "This is Belus, the deity representing the river of the city. In his hand is a reed; beneath his feet is a crocodile. This coin comes from the city of Akko. And these five coins were minted here in Tiberias. You can see the figure of Poseidon, standing on a galley."

"What's that in Poseidon's hand?"

"That's a trident. And the animal in the picture is a dolphin." Nathan smiled and held up another coin. "Can you tell me what you see on this one, Bathsheva?"

"It's a woman sitting on a rock and there ... is a snake."

"That's excellent, Bathsheva!" Nathan pointed a finger. "Now, the woman is Hygieia, the goddess of health, and she's seated on a rock and feeding a serpent from a bowl. Now, down here, water gushes from the rock: that shows the hot springs in Tiberias." Nathan gestured. "These were minted in the reign of Trajan – it was a way of inviting people to come here and enjoy the healthful waters of the hot baths. Now, on this coin, you see the same woman, Hygieia but this time she's facing her father, Asklepios." Nathan's eyes sparkled. "I suppose this is all very confusing to you, Bathsheva. But tell me, which coin do you think is the prettiest?"

"That's easy," said Bathsheva at once. She pointed to the gleaming stack of coins. "Those –"

"Bathsheva, you have splendid taste for such a young girl! Those coins are made of gold. The largest one is the Roman Aureues of Domitian. Alone, it's worth almost as much as all of the other coins together!"

Berurya nodded. "Domitian was the son of Vespasian and the brother of Titus," she explained. "While he was Emperor of Rome, he forbade conversion to Judaism, and rigidly enforced the Fiscus Judaicus, the humiliating tax which Jews alone had to pay to Rome."

"That's true," Nathan added. "Domitian was murdered and I find it ironic that some of the money Jews were compelled to put into Rome's coffers probably found its way back home." Nathan glanced at Bathsheva. Then he picked up a bright silver coin and handed it to her. "This is for you," he said jovially.

Bathsheva looked up at her mother for approval.

"You are very generous, Nathan," said Berurya.

"Not at all," said Nathan, waving a hand. "Next time you come here, Bathsheva, you can have one of the gold coins."

"Don't forget to invite me, too!" interjected Bilha.

"Bilha, who would forget such a witty and spirited lady? My house is always open to you."

"I knew I liked you from the first moment I met you," Bilha laughed.

"Well, let's be on our way," said Nathan. "It's getting late."

It took them almost half an hour to reach the shore of the Kinneret, where Nathan's boat was moored.

"Mother," Bathsheva cried out, "the boat's so beautiful and so big!"

"It is."

"Do we have to row ourselves?" asked Bilha.

Nathan grinned. "Only if you enjoy calluses and an aching back." He pointed. "My men will take us out."

Tabi, Nathan's chief-servant, issued orders to the crew. Within a few minutes, all was ready. Nathan helped Berurya, Bilha, and Bathsheva board the vessel. The day was perfect. The warmth of the sun and the smell of the water made Berurya understand why men chose to spend their days at sea. The last hawser was freed. Slowly, the boat moved away from the dock and headed out toward the far shore.

"Would anyone like to eat or drink?" asked Nathan.

"I would, Mother," Bathsheva said eagerly.

"Tabi," Nathan called out, "bring refreshments for our guests."

Tabi descended a ladder to the boat's lower deck.

"Has Tabi been with you long, Nathan?" asked Berurya.

"As long as I can remember. His father, whose name was also Tabi, was a servant before him. My father spotted the elder Tabi in one of the wealthier households of Tiberias. As I've told you, my father was uncannily shrewd. He knew this Tabi's worth immediately, and waited patiently for the right moment to offer Tabi's master considerably more than the going rate for a servant at that time. So my father bought him for what initially appeared to be a poor investment. Of course, the investment paid off a hundred-fold.

"Instead of giving Tabi menial tasks," Nathan continued, "my father, who perceived the servant's innate intelligence, taught him to run the household and placed him in charge of all the other servants. Then my father arranged for Tabi to marry an equally capable woman. Soon afterwards, she became pregnant. There were complications and the baby had to be delivered by Caesarean section. The infant survived; unfortunately, the mother did not."

Nathan stared out over the glittering, blue surface of the water.

"Once again, my father did something which appeared to reflect poor business judgment. He raised Tabi not as the son of a slave but rather as an adopted child. He provided an education for him, which many envied. In return, he demanded complete loyalty. His plan succeeded. When Tabi's father died, Tabi took over. As chief-servant, he surpassed his own father! His master knew he could confidently leave Tabi in charge of everything. I can't even begin to speculate on the wealth my father accrued because of the faithful service of father and son."

Nathan's gaze turned again to his guests. "When my father died, I offered Tabi his freedom. I thought it was only fair. To my utter surprise, Tabi refused to go. He said that he felt obliged to serve our family as long as he lived and that he would always remain with me. The subject has never come up again."

"Who are his people?" asked Bilha.

"It's hard to say. Tabi's father told me that his ancestors were Jebusites, the descendents of the Canaanites."

Nathan's story brought to Berurya's mind the Scriptural verse from the story of Noah: "And Canaan begot Zidon his firstborn, and Heth, and the Jebusite..." Later Noah says: "Blessed be the Lord, the God of Shem; and let Canaan be their servant."

"Mother," said Bathsheva, "is it all right to go to the front of the boat?"

Berurya looked to Nathan and he nodded.

"Please take Bathsheva, Bilha."

"All right." Bilha turned to Bathsheva. "If we stand way up front, we'll have a terrific view!"

"Be careful," Berurya called after them. "Don't lean over the side! And, Bathsheva, hold onto Bilha's hand!"

Nathan lifted a hand. "Don't be anxious," he said. "The water's calm today. And Tabi'll keep an eye on them when he comes up."

A wind sprang up and blew against their faces.

"Why don't you take off your scarf?" Nathan suggested to Berurya. "You'll be more comfortable."

Normally, Berurya would have declined but for some inexplicable reason she removed her head covering. Then she unfastened the pin in her hair, ran her fingers through it, and let the long locks fall. Berurya rarely left her house without her covering: covering the hair was a sign of modesty in a married woman. But now she felt differently. It wasn't as if she were in public. And the breeze on her hair was refreshing.

"I ... see why you like being out on the water," she said.

"I like it immensely," said Nathan, staring at her. "Don't consider me ill-mannered, but I must say you look magnificent with the wind in your hair...."

Berurya averted her eyes.

"I'm sorry, Berurya. Really, I am. I didn't mean to embarrass you." He sighed. "I remember so clearly the first time we met. I've been fascinated by you ever since. And the time I waved to you from the lake when you were walking on the shore and you waved back: it made me so happy!"

Berurya remembered the incident, but did not comment.

Nathan smiled wistfully. "Berurya," he said hesitantly, "there's been something ... I've been wanting to say to you ... but I haven't found the appropriate words ... or the right time." He wet his dry lips with his tongue. "I suppose now ... is as good a time as any."

At that moment, Tabi approached with a lavish assortment of fruit on a tray.

"Some fruit?"

Nathan was clearly frustrated by the interruption. He turned to Berurya agitatedly. "Would you like something, Berurya?"

Berurya pointed to a pomegranate. "Thanks."

Tabi set the tray down; with a sharp knife, he sliced the pomegranate in half and offered a half to Berurya. She took several of the brilliant red seeds and put them in her mouth. Their juice was deliciously tart.

"Do you know what the sages observe about the pomegranate, Nathan?"

"No," Nathan said, with an expression of amusement on his face. "What do they say?"

"That even the most empty of Jews is as full of good deeds as the pomegranate."

"I thought ... that you would quote from the Song of Songs. How does it go? 'Thy lips are like a thread of scarlet, and thy mouth is comely, thy cheek is like a piece of pomegranate....'"

Berurya flushed. "I didn't know you were so well-versed in Scripture."

"I'm not, but I adore the Song of Songs! Especially, the words of the last chapter: 'Set me as a seal upon thy heart, as a seal upon thine arm; for love is strong as death, jealousy is cruel as the grave; the flashes thereof are flashes of fire; a very flame of the Lord. Many waters cannot quench love, neither can the floods drown it....'"

"Some fruit, Master?" said Tabi.

"No, Tabi. But see to it, please, that Bilha and Bathsheva have some."

Tabi bowed and withdrew.

"I wonder how Bathsheva is?" wondered Berurya.

"Undoubtedly, she's enjoying every minute."

"You're right, I'm sure."

"And what about you, Berurya? Are you enjoying yourself?"

"Initially," said Berurya, "I didn't want to come without Meir."

"What made you change your mind?"

"Meir. He insisted that I not change our plans and that I take Bilha and Bathsheva in his stead."

"I'm glad you listened to him."

Berurya clasped her hands together. "I must admit ... that I looked forward to seeing you again...." She paused, and then added: "As a friend, I mean."

"Of course ... as a friend."

"I'm glad to be here, Nathan."

"I'm very glad you're here, Berurya." He cleared his throat. "If you don't mind my asking," he said, "I'd like to know more about Meir."

"What do you mean?"

"Obviously, he's a brilliant scholar; his mind is unlike any I've ever encountered. But I'm curious about his personality. What sort of man is he? They say that extremely intelligent people are sometimes difficult to live with. Is that true?"

"Not at all," said Berurya, without hesitation.

"I'm sorry," murmured Nathan. "Obviously my question was somewhat indelicate. I didn't mean to infer ... anything by it. Please accept my apology."

"I didn't take offense," said Berurya. "Meir is an exceptional man. I respect him not only as a scholar, but for his honesty and integrity as well. His colleagues use the words 'holy and modest' to describe him – and they're right. When he finishes his compendium of Jewish law, his Mishna, he will be compared to Rabbi Akiva." She smiled. "I hope I've answered your question."

"No," he objected. "I know very well that Meir is an outstanding scholar. I know very well that you have the utmost respect for his knowledge and his erudition. But I'm sorry, that wasn't my question. I am curious about Meir, the man. What kind of father is he to Bathsheva? What sort of husband is he to you?" Nathan's eyes shone. "I'm certain of one thing: if I were fortunate enough to have a wife like you – intelligent, beautiful, full of life, and loving, in short the ideal woman – and if I had a daughter like Bathsheva, I'd fall on my knees and thank Heaven every single day for my good fortune!" He sighed deeply. "Actually, my question was harmless, Berurya. I just wanted to know if Meir appreciates the two of you?"

"I'm sure he does," said Berurya shortly.

"Can I offer you something else? Perhaps you're thirsty?"

"No, thanks, I'm fine."

Nathan rose. "Please excuse me for a moment, I must speak with Tabi."

Nathan moved away; he sensed that Berurya needed time alone. Perhaps he'd been too probing in his questions? He had spoken from his heart, more than from his mind. At the same time, he was painfully aware that the woman he yearned desperately for was another man's wife! "Why," he asked himself, "must the one thing I desire most in my life be the one thing I can't get?" He reflected. "What draws me to her so? We're so different... we're worlds apart! Her world revolves around the Torah; mine dances around golden calves! What irony! I'm not permitted to love from close by – so I must adore from a distance! '...for love is as strong as death, jealousy is cruel as the grave ... Many waters cannot quench love, neither can floods drown it...' For everyone else, it is the Song of Songs; for me it will always be the Sorrow of Sorrows...."

Nathan spoke to Tabi and then walked forward to Bilha and Bathsheva in the prow. Berurya saw him point at the mountains. Apparently, he was explaining something.

Berurya felt perplexed. "Here is a man," she reflected, "who has more wealth than most men could wish for in ten lifetimes. He is good-looking, intelligent ... and yet, in spite of it all, he seems unhappy. Why? Why is he so curious about Meir? Why does he question me about our marriage? What possible difference can the sort of husband and father Meir is make to Nathan?"

Berurya gazed at him. At that instant, he turned to look at her. Berurya quickly turned her head and looked off in another direction. "He is very handsome," she thought. "Why hasn't he ever married? Many women must have wished to be his wife."

Berurya felt intrigued by Nathan. With all his wealth, one could easily assume that he'd be more demanding, but he wasn't. Actually, she'd never met anyone as gentle and as considerate as he. She pondered. He was a complex person. Superficially, he appeared to be calm. But who could really say? Berurya watched intently as Nathan caressed Bathsheva's hair. There was no doubt that he'd make a wonderful husband and father.

Nathan returned. "The water's getting choppy," he said. "I've seldom seen such a drastic change. Tabi thinks – and I agree with him – that we should head back to shore."

"That's a shame," said Berurya.

Nathan shrugged. "There'll always be another time."

Berurya stared out at the choppy, white–fringed waves. "How long will it take to get in?"

"It's difficult to say. If it doesn't get more turbulent, we should be on dry land within an hour."

"And if it gets worse...?" Berurya did not finish the sentence.

"The boat's sturdy; it can take plenty of abuse."

"Are Bilha and Bathsheva all right?"

"They're probably in the safest place there is. Don't worry; I've been in far worse situations. Everything'll be fine."

Berurya wanted to believe him but the boat was rolling heavily; she gripped the gunwale tightly. Once again, Nathan spoke to Tabi, who shouted orders to the crew. Berurya couldn't hear the orders, but the expression on Nathan's face was grave. Nathan now moved forward to calm Bilha and Bathsheva. "The water's a bit rough now," he said.

"Well, I'd hate to think this is calm!" She clucked her tongue. "And just when I considered fishing for my livelihood!" Bilha snorted.

Nathan handed Bilha two lengths of rope. "This is only a precaution and probably won't be necessary at all, but take these and tie one around Bathsheva's waist and the other around your own. I'll tie the ends to the mast."

"Is the boat going to sink?" asked Bathsheva in a quavering voice.

"Of course not!" Nathan said firmly. "We're just going to have a bit of fun, that's all."

"You might want to check below," suggested Bilha.

"Check for what?" Nathan asked with surprise.

"Maybe there's a passenger down there who's sleeping. Wake him up and if he says his name is Jonah, don't ask anything more! Just chuck him overboard!"

Nathan laughed. "I'm sorry, but I really don't think you'll find a fish in this lake big enough to swallow a man!"

"Even a small man?"

"Not even a small woman!"

As they spoke, the crew rowed, their backs straining, their brows covered with sweat. Nathan made his way aft to Berurya. At that moment, one of the men stood up and, shouting, pointed in Berurya's direction. Berurya whirled. She could scarcely believe her eyes! A fishing-boat was actually being swallowed up by the seething water! The lake had opened up like a tremendous tub of water whose plug had been pulled!

"Nathan!" Berurya cried out. "Can we help them?"

"If we get too close, we'll be swept under too!"

"What's happening, Nathan?"

"I think we're caught ... in an earthquake."

"An earthquake!?"

"I hope I'm wrong," shouted Nathan. "Tabi," he called out, "change the ship's course! Head out – there! If it's really an earthquake, there'll be a giant wave at any moment."

"What about Bathsheva and Bilha?" asked Berurya anxiously.

"I've tied them to the mast. They'll be fine. Find something to hold onto yourself, and ..."

Berurya held fast to a gunwale and began to pray. She closed her eyes, moved her lips silently, and pleaded for God's help. As she prayed, she suddenly felt the vessel being pulled in the opposite direction. She opened her eyes in alarm. A tremendous wave was speeding directly toward them! It looked as if the boat would be engulfed at any instant! Berurya braced herself. Her glance darted toward Bathsheva. Bilha was hugging the girl in her arms. Berurya wanted to be with the child, but she would never get there in time.

"If this be the will of God and we are about to die," she thought, "then may God forgive me for the sins and transgressions I may have committed. May my death be an atonement ..." At that second, the wave smashed into the vessel with awesome force; the boat listed far to one side. Berurya was flung into the air....

When she regained consciousness, she was looking up at Nathan; he was craddling her in his arms. "What ... happened...?" she muttered weakly.

"You hit your head when you went flying! I'm afraid you've got a nasty bump."

"Bathsheva, is she ...?"

"Bathsheva and Bilha are perfectly fine. Don't try to stand, please."

Berurya relaxed. She raised a hand to her forehead and touched her right temple at the hairline. "That hurts," she said softly.

"You really have a bad bruise."

"Please ... help me up...."

"Slowly," cautioned Nathan.

Berurya felt Nathan's strong arms lift her as if she were weightless. She stood for a moment in Nathan's embrace.

"I think ... I can stand by myself now."

"Are you sure?"

"Yes."

But as soon as Nathan let go, Berurya's knees buckled. He caught her before she fell.

"You're not as strong as you think you are, Berurya."

"I guess you're right. My head ..."

Berurya lost consciousness again. Nathan held her firmly and brushed back her hair with his fingertips. "How ironic," he thought bitterly. "She will never be closer to me ... than at this moment."

His eyes scrutinized her every feature. He gazed at her full lips. For an instant, he wished desperately that he could kiss her and that her eyes would open and that she would be his for all time!

Just then, Tabi came up. "Will she be all right, master?" he asked.

"Yes," answered Nathan. He glanced around the boat. "How much damage did we sustain?"

"I'm afraid, sir, that we have two badly hurt men. Three others were injured slightly. I don't ever remember a wave like that one."

"Imagine the damage it did on shore!" Nathan mused.

"We'll find out when we dock, sir."

Berurya made a barely audible sound. Her fingers moved. Nathan bent his head and kissed her forehead.

"Shall I bring her daughter, sir?" said Tabi.

"Yes," replied Nathan. "But wait just a few minutes."

Berurya opened her eyes. She tried to speak but Nathan checked her. "Don't talk now. You passed out when you tried to stand. We don't want you to faint again."

Berurya heard Bathsheva call out to her; she turned her head in the direction of the child's voice. Bathsheva ran up. "Mommy, Mommy," she cried out, "I was so very scared!" She fell to her knees and hugged her mother's legs.

Berurya raised a hand and set it on her daughter's head. "There's nothing to be frightened about, Bathsheva. Everything's fine."

Berurya glanced at Nathan, as if seeking reassurance. His gentle smile comforted her.

When Bilha saw Berurya, she went pale.

"This must be the first time in my life I've ever seen you speechless!" Berurya teased.

Bilha wasn't at all amused. "Should she see a doctor when we land?"

"I don't think it's necessary," said Nathan. He beckoned Bilha closer. "Switch places with me," he said, "so I can attend to the crew."

Bilha squatted and cradled Berurya's head in her lap. Nathan left to assess the damage. He shook his head. Still, it could have been much worse: they all could have perished.

As the boat neared shore, Nathan glimpsed the earthquake's damage. Even from a distance, he could see how many buildings had been demolished. When the vessel docked, Tabi jumped out. "Get a doctor for the injured!" he called out to the waiting servants.

Bilha helped Berurya up. Berurya leaned against a mast for support, uncertain as to whether she could stand on her own. She still felt lightheaded and weak. Her eyes surveyed the landscape: Tiberias looked as if it had been ravaged by a hostile army! Parts of the city's great wall had been reduced to debris. It had all happened in a flash, without warning. Bilha helped Berurya disembark. Bathsheva gripped her mother's hand tightly. Berurya leaned on Bilha.

Nathan saw to it that the boat was secured and that his injured crewmen got proper attention. Then he turned to Berurya. "How are you feeling?" he asked.

"I'm doing a little better. Don't worry about me, I'll recover."

"I'm sure you will."

Nathan glanced at Bilha. "Tabi will escort you home. Normally, I'd do it myself, but I'm needed here." He waved a hand. "The damage, as far as I can see, is in Tiberias. You'll be much safer in Hammat."

"Do you think there'll be another earthquake?" asked Bilha.

"I don't know. But I think we've got to assume that the worst isn't over. But even if we don't have more tremors, the damage done by this one is extensive." He nodded his head. "But I must go. Tabi will look after you."

As he glanced at Berurya, Nathan thought: "It took literally the violence of an earthquake to throw Berurya into my arms! When everything's quiet, the memory of that moment and my unrequited longing will continue to rage inside me!" He bit his lip and thought further: "I reached out for something that wasn't really there." Then he glanced at Bathsheva and at Bilha and forced a smile. "Shalom!" was the single word he uttered. He walked off without looking back.

Tabi indicated that they had to leave. As they walked on, Berurya looked around; she could scarcely believe her eyes. Hours ago, the city had been peaceful; now, it was in utter turmoil. People ran frantically through the streets. She heard the shrieks of parents and smelled the acrid smoke rising from countless fires. The Angel of Death had slaughtered men and women indiscriminately; the Romans and the Jews alike would mourn their dead.

Bathsheva tugged at Berurya's arm. "Look!" she cried out, pointing to a side street, where several houses had collapsed and people were frantically trying to clear the debris.

"Perhaps people are trapped underneath?" said Berurya to Tabi. "We've got to help out."

"Are you well enough, Madam?" asked the servant.

Without answering, Berurya hurried down a narrow path. She halted and began clearing stones.

"Our child," a man wailed. "She was ... in the house when it collapsed! God, please let her be all right!"

Tabi, Bilha and Bathsheva helped remove the debris. The child's father worked feverishly; his wife, overcome with exhaustion, stared vacantly at the spot where her house had once stood. Every so often, she whimpered like an animal.

A putrid smell hung in the air. The odor was familiar to Berurya but she couldn't place it.

They dug with their bare hands. Suddenly, Tabi shouted: "I think I see her!" Everyone crowded around Tabi. A dozen pairs of hands tossed aside the rubble. At length, the little girl's body was uncovered. Her father gently lifted her – but the body was lifeless.

The girl was Bathsheva's age, perhaps younger. Dazedly, the man handed his dead daughter over to his wife, who sobbed wildly. Bilha wiped her tear-filled eyes. Nothing more could be done. Berurya took Bathsheva's hand and turned away. She held her breath; the sight of the dead child in her father's arms brought to her mind the memory of the innkeeper's men carrying the corpses of Hananiah and Elhanan.

They walked in utter silence to the stables where Tabi helped them mount; then they rode to Hammat, which, as Nathan surmised, had sustained only minor damage. When they reached home, Tabi politely took his leave and set out on his journey back to Tiberias.

26
Reflections on Miracles

That night, after Bathsheva was asleep, Berurya and Bilha sat and talked. "As we walked through Tiberias and saw the suffering the earthquake caused, especially the tragic death of that little girl," said Berurya, "I thought about Korach's rebellion. The Torah tells us that Korach, like Moses and Aaron, was a descendent of Levi. He was joined by Dathan and Abiram, descendents of Reuben, the eldest of the twelve tribes, along with two hundred and fifty princes of the assembly, men of great renown. All of them conspired against Moses' and Aaron's authority but their rebellion ended in their own deaths. They died in an unusual manner: the ground split open and swallowed them – them and their houses and possessions. They plunged into the pit and the earth closed over them! And then a fire from the Lord consumed the two hundred and fifty men who had joined forces with Korach, Dathan and Abiram. Those people and their families died in an earthquake, just like the people did today. But what's the difference in the two cases?"

Bilha shrugged.

"The difference," said Berurya, "is that the first example proved that Moses was indeed sent by God. Moses had explicitly stated that if his opponents died an ordinary death, it would prove that the Lord hadn't sent him; but if the earth opened up and swallowed them, it would prove that they had provoked the Lord!"

"I don't know what you're getting at," said Bilha.

"It's really very simple: the earth opened up precisely when Moses prayed; wasn't that a miracle?"

"I suppose it was."

"And what happened today though it was a similar phenomenon, wouldn't be called a miracle, would it?"

"No, it wouldn't."

"But that creates a problem. Tradition teaches that ten things were preordained from the time of the Creation – one of which was the splitting of the earth which swallowed Korach. If it was indeed preordained, then it wasn't a suspension of the natural laws of the universe and therefore wasn't a miracle. It was something destined to happen at a precise moment. Korach and his followers were standing precisely on the spot where it had been preordained that the earth would open."

"So then it wasn't a miracle," asserted Bilha.

"Right," said Berurya. "But the fact that Moses asked God for the earth to open up exactly when it was destined to do so takes us beyond what we would normally call coincidence. Let's imagine that Moses, for one reason or another, had awakened later than usual that morning. Then the earth would have opened up before Korach and the others ever arrived! Or consider the result if Moses had stipulated something different – what, for example, if he'd predicted that scorpions or snakes would suddenly appear and instead of that happening the earth opened up? And what if Korach never rebelled, but it was predestined that the earth would open up and so people died anyway? You wouldn't call that a miracle, would you?"

Bilha looked puzzled. "Are you saying that it really was a miracle?"

"No, I'm not saying that at all."

"Now I don't know if it was or wasn't a miracle," said Bilha in exasperation, "I'm completely mixed up!"

"Actually, Bilha, it doesn't matter. In the final analysis, so-called 'miracles' prove nothing. There is something in human nature that while desiring to believe in miracles and being utterly fascinated by them nevertheless resists them. The consequences of miracles are always negligible. For example, what more spectacular miracle than the splitting of the Red Sea could there have been? But in the final analysis, it didn't change the character of the Israelites. What greater scene than thunder and lightning at the foot of Mt. Sinai as Moses was to receive the Ten Commandments? Yet forty days later, the Israelites fashioned a golden calf! And the day after the earth swallowed up Korach, the Israelites rejected Moses and Aaron once again! What do miracles change?" Berurya paused. "Nothing at all, I'm afraid."

"Are you telling me that God's miracles are of no consequence?"

"Not exactly. What I mean is that comprehending the mystery of life is far more important. Life is essentially a mystery. We take so much for granted, we seldom appreciate the awe and wonder of it all. From the moment we enter this world until the moment we leave it we are surrounded by miracles! Even when we sleep, the miracles don't cease. Our problem is that we lose the ability to appreciate. We've seen sunrises and rainbows, but we've forgotten that in order to see a rainbow, it has to rain; that before each sunrise there must be darkness." Berurya's eyes glowed. "Life is ... a succession of earthquakes and tears, followed by sunrises and miracles. Each of us walks through life, not knowing when the earth will open up under his feet and swallow him up! The true miracle is when all is quiet and there are no earthquakes; it's the moment we open our eyes and appreciate the mystery, the wonder, and the awe."

Bilha shook her head vigorously. "I don't know, Berurya. I haven't your intelligence or learning. Some things in life I understand; most, I do not. I often imagine it would have been easier living long ago in history, when things were less complicated than they are in our world." She sighed and went on: "Maybe every Garden of Eden has its serpents? As I grow older I think less about miracles and wonders. I just thank God for each day that passes without pain. Today, I grieved for the people in Tiberias who

suffered so terribly. I really did. But there wasn't anything I could
do about it. I also thanked God that it didn't happen to us. You see,
Berurya, God, in His infinite wisdom, made me a simple woman.
That's what I am. I don't grasp the intricacies of *Halacha*; Jewish
law is beyond me. And I don't understand why a lot of things in life
happen. I am a simple woman whom God has created according to
His will."

"Don't say that, Bilha. You're anything but simple!"

Bilha smiled. She looked worn out. The day had exhausted her.
"I'll see you in the morning," she said to Berurya as she rose and
left the room. "Don't you stay up too late."

Berurya was silent. She rose and went out of the house.
"Everything is so peaceful," she thought. The air was fresh; the night
sky was clear. It seemed as if nothing had happened. Overhead, the
glittering stars seemed utterly unaware that for many it was a night
for weeping....

For several weeks, the people of Tiberias dug themselves out of the
ruins. They buried their dead. They mourned and they prayed. They
wept and consoled each other. At length, they rebuilt the stone wall
around the city. Then they felt safe.

27

Of One's Reputation

Meir's trips to various communities around the country became more frequent and of longer duration. His reputation as a scholar was now without parallel. People said that his dialectic ingenuity was such that seeing him in the *Beit Midrash* was like seeing a man of extraordinary strength overturning the mightiest of mountains and then grinding them effortlessly to powder! Often, when colleagues disagreed with him, it was simply because they weren't able to follow the intricacies of his mind. He would logically demonstrate that something regarded as impure was actually pure, while something known to be pure was, in fact, impure. And he could arrive at his conclusion by using several different arguments!

His memory was phenomenal. Once, while traveling in Asia Minor to intercalate the calendar, he visited a Jewish community which did not possess the *Megillat Ester*, the Scroll of Ester. Meir wrote down the entire scroll – ten chapters, one hundred and sixty six verses – from memory!

Berurya's reputation as a scholar was also legendary. Her pronouncements on matters of purity had been praised by such luminaries as Rabbi Yehuda ben Bava and Rabbi Joshua. Once, Rabbi Yose, the Galilean, encountered Berurya and asked her directions to the city of Lyyda. She reprimanded him for transgressing the dictum of the sages: "Do not engage in lengthy discussions with a woman." She was alluding to the words of Yose, the son of Yohanan, who said: "Let thy house be open wide; let the poor be members of thy household; and engage not in much conversation with women. This was said regarding one's own wife, how much more so, someone else's wife." Obviously, the intent of the dictum was to limit any familiarity between men and women that might inadvertently lead to immoral behavior.

Berurya was disturbed that relations between the Romans and the Jews were still difficult. Although the religious restrictions which had caused the Jewish uprising had long ago been annulled, Roman authority was nevertheless greatly resented. Perhaps, Berurya thought, the problem resided in the fact that Romans and Jews didn't understand each other. The Romans ridiculed the Jews as a superstitious people which worshipped a deity who could not be seen. The Jews viewed their subjugation to Rome as the last of four subjugations referred to in their traditions. Berurya believed that when the Roman Empire crumbled, as did the Persian, Greek and Mede, Israel's star would ascend. It was just a matter of time.

It was late afternoon. Bilha was preparing the evening meal. Meir had just returned from the *Beit Midrash* with two of his students, who would stay for dinner. Berurya was teaching Bathsheva Torah. "'*VaYar' Elohim et kol asher 'asah, V'hineh tov me'od...* And God saw everything that He had made, and, behold, it was very good...' Do you understand what that means, Bathsheva?"

"I think so, Mother. It means that God was happy with what He created." She reflected a moment and then asked: "Does that mean everything in the World is perfect?"

"No, Bathsheva," Berurya responded. "There's a difference between good and perfect. The world we live in isn't perfect – God didn't intend it to be so. If it were perfect, we'd have nothing to do. I believe that God intentionally left Creation unfinished so that we would complete the task ... or at least improve things to the best of our ability. When the Torah says the world is good, it suggests that everything created has a purpose."

"Even flies and spiders!" exclaimed Bathsheva.

"Yes," said Berurya, "even spiders, scorpions and snakes! Everything in the world has a purpose and a reason for existing. Just because you're unable to understand what the purpose is, doesn't mean there isn't one."

Bathsheva thought about what her mother had just said.

"I think we can stop now," said Berurya, getting up. "We've studied enough for one day."

Bathsheva touched Berurya's arm. "Mother, will I know as much as you do when I grow up?"

"If it's important to you."

"Some of my friends say that you're the smartest woman in Israel!"

Berurya smiled. "That's quite a statement, dear, but it's not true! Besides, it's better for us to keep our minds on our studies, rather than getting involved in what our friends think." Berurya took Bathsheva's hand. "Come, let's see what Bilha's cooked for dinner."

"Do you need help?" asked Berurya in the kitchen.

"No, I can manage."

"Did you know, Bilha, that Bathsheva is doing well in her studies?"

"That's wonderful, Bathsheva! Let me give you a big hug. I'm very proud of you."

Bilha bent and wrapped the girl in her strong arms.

"Where's my father?" said Bathsheva.

"He's in the other room with students," said Bilha.

At that moment, Meir walked in; his students were a step behind. Meir turned and said: "Remember, then, 'The woman is acquired by three means: She is acquired by money, or by a writ or by intercourse. The school of Shammai says: By a *denar* or a *denar*'s worth; and the school of Hillel says: By a *perutah* or a *perutah*'s worth.'"

"Meir," said Berurya, "I thought you'd like to know that Bathsheva is doing excellently in her Torah studies."

"Hmmm..." Meir murmured absently. Without a glance at his wife or daughter, he continued his discourse: "Now, the Hebrew slave is acquired by money or by writ...."

Berurya observed Bathsheva. She was staring at the floor, obviously wounded by her father's indifference. Sensing her daughter's hurt, Berurya caressed her head. Then she reached down, grasped Bathsheva's chin gently, and tilted her head up. "Bathsheva," she said, "the answer to your question earlier about whether you'll know as much as I when you grow up is yes! And if you continue to learn as you did today, you'll know even more!" But Bathsheva did not smile. It was clear that she felt her mother was trying to make up for her father's lack of interest!

As they were about to sit down to dinner, there was a knock at the door. One of the students dutifully rose from the table.

"Who's there?" Meir called out.

"He says his name is Eliezer and that he was sent by the *Nasi*, Rabban Shimeon ben Gamaliel," replied the student as he came back into the dining room. Meir went to speak with the messenger himself. Moments later, he returned. He seated himself again and stared gloomily at his plate.

"What did the messenger tell you?" asked Berurya.

"I'm not sure what to make of it," muttered Meir. "Apparently, the Romans in Caesarea sent a strange message to the Sanhedrin in Usha. The message simply said: 'Send one of your *ksilophanos*.'"

"What is ksilo, kislo...?" Bilha stammered.

"The word is *ksilophanos*," Meir explained. "It's a combination of two Greek words: *Ksulon* meaning 'wood' and *Phanos* 'torch.' But why would the Romans ask the rabbis for a torch? The Sanhedrin understood the message – quite correctly I believe – to mean someone who could shed light on or illuminate Judaism."

Berurya's brow knitted. "Do you think it's an intentional pun on your name, Meir?" She gestured. "Meir – the one-who-illuminates."

Meir shrugged. "I'm not sure. It's entirely possible. What do you think? Should I go?"

"I think that we should both go," Berurya said without a second's hesitation.

Meir was surprised. "You want to go to Caesarea with me?"

"Yes."

The meal was concluded in silence. Meir wondered what was behind the unusual request. Berurya wondered if she should raise the issue of Bathsheva that evening and decided against it. "Perhaps Meir was simply preoccupied with his students." Berurya mused. But that was what she wanted to believe.

28
Caesarea

Meir and Berurya traveled leisurely to Caesarea. They journeyed from Tiberias to Sepphoris, and there lodged with Rabbi Yose. They continued on to 'Ardaskus, Tiv'one, Beit She'arim, and finally went on to Caesarea. While in Beit She'arim, they had spent time with Rabbi Judah, son of Rabban Shimeon ben Gamaliel: the son had inherited the title of Nasi from his father. His personality, however, was quite different from that of his father.

Ironically, Rabbi Judah had been born in the same year that the Romans murdered Rabbi Akiva. Judah studied under the tutelage of several of the best teachers of his generation: Rabbi Elazar ben Shamu'a and Rabbi Shimeon bar Yohai in Tekoa'. Then he studied with Rabbi Meir for a short time.

Rabbi Judah's reputation rapidly surpassed that of his father: he was acclaimed for his wisdom, sanctity, and humility, as well as his wealth. Rabbi Judah believed that it was imperative for the spiritual leader of the Jews to establish good relations with the Romans. In establishing such relations, he had succeeded as had no other religious leader before him. Unlike his father, Rabbi Judah resided in Beit She'arim; only in the latter years of his life did he move together with the Sanhedrin, to Sepphoris.

Though the Jews hated Rome, no one would deny that Caesarea was a beautiful city. White marble pillars looked like powerful arms supporting imposing structures. Caesarea's magnificent amphitheater, with its ascending tiers of seats, gave the spectators a breathtaking view of the Mediterranean and the harbor where ships unloaded their cargos. Even Caesarea's air seemed different from elsewhere, Berurya thought as she and Meir entered the city. Winds blew from the open water, and it was as if they bore messages from far-off lands. The sharp smell of the salt, the taste it left on the fingers, the sunlight dancing on the choppy, blue waves, the crashing of the breakers made it perfectly clear why the Romans had chosen this place as their home away from Rome.

Upon their arrival, Meir and Berurya were received by the Romans as visiting dignitaries. They were lodged near the administration buildings in the heart of the city. Meir was informed that a servant would call for them in the morning; he was advised that he and his wife should get a good night's sleep because the next few days might prove strenuous.

Early the next morning, a servant arrived. He conveyed them to a large, impressive building. As they walked, Berurya whispered: "Do you know what I'm reminded of?"

Meir shook his head.

"It reminds me of when we were in Usha and you had to face the Sanhedrin."

Meir smiled. "Do you think this'll be more challenging?"

"The sting of the scholar's tongue," said Berurya grimly, "can be as lethal as an enemy's sword!"

"In that case," Meir said, "let the Romans be forewarned!"

Inside the building, they were taken directly to their seats in a huge, crowded room.

Minutes later, the crowd rose to its feet as three Roman officials entered. Meir and Berurya rose as well. When the officials were seated, the audience sat once again.

Berurya carefully studied the faces of the officials. The man in the center seat on the dais was older than his associates. His face was full and rounded; the skin under his chin was flabby and he had bags under his eyes. The official to his right looked much younger. He had sharp features, with narrow eyes and thin lips that made him look cruel. The last official had a pleasant face. He had sober, intelligent eyes.

The official in the middle spoke first. "Rabbi Meir," he said, "first of all, let me express our appreciation to you for accepting our invitation. The Roman empire, as is well known, is unrivalled in the history of the world. Under the Roman banner, great advances have been brought to people everywhere. We have improved the quality of living in places which were backward and desolate before we came. We were more successful in some attempts than in others. Our greatest failure, I am sorry to say, has been with Jews. Our efforts here, sadly enough, are not appreciated and it appears that we are destined to be eternal enemies." The official paused for a moment and then continued: "It is with this in mind that we have called you here in order that possibly we Romans may come to understand you Jews better. This may well avert future misunderstanding and trouble...." The official lifted a hand. "The proceedings," he went on, "will be as follows: On the first day, you will tell us about your religious beliefs and practices. On the second day, Romans who possess some knowledge of your religion will question you. On the third and final day, we'll allow the audience to ask questions and finally permit you to make a concluding speech. Is that acceptable, Rabbi Meir?"

"Yes, it is," Meir answered promptly. Then he said: "Would you object if I were to consult with my wife on occasion?"

The official glanced at Berurya and then again at Meir. "You may consult with your very attractive wife," he said, "as often as you wish."

"Also," said Meir, "while at one time I was fluent in Greek, it has been several years since I've spoken the language. If, therefore, I should be compelled to pause and consider the precise wording of a phrase, I ask for your kind indulgence. Thank you." The official nodded.

Then Meir rose and walked slowly to the front of the room. He turned and scrutinized the faces in the audience. Then he drew his shoulders back and began: "We Jews believe in one God, who created the Heavens and the Earth. It was God who first spoke to Abraham in his home city of Haran, in Mesopotamia, and bade him to leave his country and family and journey to the land now known as Israel. God promised to bless Abraham – or Abram, as he was then called – and make him the father of many nations. And so Abraham took Sarah, his wife, and his nephew, Lot, and departed as God had bidden him.

"After years of Abraham being childless, God appeared to him in a vision and promised that Abraham would father a son, that his descendents would be slaves in a foreign land, and that they would endure great suffering and hardship before being freed.

"Sarah, barren for a decade, then gave her handmaid, Hagar, to Abraham for a wife. Hagar bore a male child who was called Ishmael. Then God gave Abraham, who was ninety-nine years old at the time, the commandment of Circumcision. Circumcision, you must understand, is a sign of the covenant between God and the Jew; every Jewish male is circumcised eight days after birth. God also revealed to Abraham that Sarah would give birth to a son and that He, the Almighty, would establish His covenant with this child and with his descendents. Then Sarah gave birth to Isaac.

"Throughout Abraham's life, God tested him to find out if he were loyal. The tenth and final test was the most difficult of all. Abraham was commanded to offer his son, Isaac, as a sacrifice. Though anguished, Abraham agreed to do so. His willingness to obey God, despite the terrible pain it caused him, demonstrated the strength of Abraham's devotion.

"Isaac was spared at God's intervention, and subsequently married Rebecca. They had twins: Esau and Jacob. Before their birth, the Lord told Rebecca 'two nations are in thy womb, two people shall be separated from thy bowels; and the one people shall be stronger than the other people; and the elder shall serve the younger.' As they grew, the boys' different personalities were evident. Esau, the elder, was a hunter; his father, Isaac, favored him. Jacob was loved by his mother.

"When Isaac was old and could no longer see, he asked Esau to bring him venison and said then, after he had eaten, he would bless him. Rebecca learned of this and schemed so that Jacob would receive the blessing instead. She made the food and wrapped Jacob's neck and arms in hairy animal skins so that he would be mistaken by Isaac for Esau, who was hairy. And the deception worked.

"On learning that Jacob had stolen the blessing Isaac had intended for him, Esau threatened to murder his brother. Rebecca sent Jacob to live with her brother, Laban, until Esau's wrath subsided. Jacob ended up marrying Laban's two daughters, Rachel and Leah. Between the two wives and their two handmaids, Jacob fathered twelve sons.

"Twenty years passed since Jacob's mother had sent him away. When he returned home at last, Jacob encountered Esau, who had formed a band of four hundred armed men. At this point, Esau could have easily exacted revenge. But God protected Jacob and the two brothers parted without incident.

"Jacob's life was twisted by turmoil, part of which he himself created. By showing that he loved one son, Joseph, more than all of his other children, he caused jealousy and hatred. Ultimately, the brothers sold Joseph into slavery and he was taken away to Egypt.

"In Egypt, God watched over Joseph and he prospered. At one point, Joseph was asked to interpret Pharoah's dreams. Pharoah saw how wise Joseph was and appointed him ruler over all of Egypt, second only to Pharoah himself. Joseph's wisdom saved Egypt from the ravages of a terrible drought and in doing so, saved his own family. When Jacob was told, after many long years, that his son Joseph was still alive, he took his family and went down to Egypt to sojourn there."

Meir halted, wiped the sweat from his brow, sipped some water, and continued to speak. Berurya gazed around the vast room as her husband spoke about Moses and the Exodus from Egypt. She saw that most of the crowd listened intently, especially when Meir described the plagues and the splitting of the Red Sea. "They're probably fascinated," she thought, "because they see the episode as one great battle!"

Then Meir described how Moses received the Torah on Mount Sinai.

"Excuse the interruption," said the Roman official who had spoken before, "but is this Torah something that you worship as holy?"

Meir shook his head. "We don't worship the Torah," he said. "We worship only God. The Torah is holy because it contains the Word of God. You see, when a Jew performs the commandments in the Torah, he is obeying the Will of God."

"Thank you," nodded the official. "You may continue."

Meir cleared his throat. "Jewish life is regulated by the *Mitzvot*, the commandments: those written in our Torah, as well as other laws and traditions transmitted orally to Moses on Sinai. The oral tradition is called Mishna. Generally speaking, Jewish law tells us how to behave toward our fellow-man and what obligations we have to God. Our festivals are based on historical and agricultural themes. The most important Jewish holiday is the Sabbath: every seventh day we are commanded to rest. All work must cease."

"That sounds like a lazy-man's religion," said the official with the thin lips.

"No, it isn't that at all," returned Meir. "We Jews have simply learned to work harder on the other six days!"

The retort brought smiles to many faces.

Meir continued his discourse for the greater part of the day. At length, he finished speaking and the assembly was dismissed. On the way back to their room, the Roman official whom Berurya had sensed was the most intelligent of the three caught up with them.

"Pardon me for intruding, Rabbi Meir," he said. "But I'd like very much to introduce myself. My name is Probus, and I just want to congratulate you on a fascinating lecture!"

"Thank you," said Meir.

Probus gestured. "I sincerely mean it, Rabbi Meir. I can only guess how difficult it was to present all of the history and traditions of the Jews cleanly and simply so that everyone in the audience could readily grasp it."

"Again, thank you." Meir glanced at Berurya. "However, my wife deserves much of the credit. It was she who advised me which subjects to include and which to leave out."

"Then both of you deserve my praise!" Probus exclaimed. He hesitated and then said: "I'm not supposed to tell you this, but tomorrow will be extremely difficult."

"In what sense?" asked Berurya.

"Those who question you are well-versed in Judaism and intend to embarrass you."

"It's beginning to sound interesting," Meir smiled.

"You're not concerned?" asked Probus.

"Not at all," replied Meir. "As a matter of fact, I'm looking forward to the challenge!"

"Will Jews be asking the questions?" asked Berurya.

"I'm not sure. Perhaps. Although, I'm inclined to believe they'll be Samaritans or Cutheans."

"It doesn't matter in the least," said Meir.

"You are very kind to warn us," Berurya said warmly. "May I ask who are the other two officials with you?"

Probus laughed harshly. "Iulianus, the man who sat in the middle, is reputed to be related to the Emperors Vespasian and Titus. To Jews, of course, these men are infamous – especially Titus, who oversaw the destruction of your Temple. We Romans see it in another light." Probus stroked his chin. "Iulianus," he went on, "got his fortune and position because of who he is, and little more. He's not terribly intelligent – neither is he a threat."

"And the other one?" asked Berurya.

"Gaius! Ah, Gaius is someone you should fear. He utterly detests Jews!"

"For some special reason?" Meir asked.

"None that I know of. They say that some of his comrades were killed in Israel ... here. But the man's hate runs far deeper than that. He's the one who wants to discredit you and your religion tomorrow."

"Interesting," mused Meir.

"I have to be going now," said Probus. "I have an engagement." He nodded his head. "Good luck tomorrow!"

"Thanks for the warning," Berurya said.

Meir and Berurya watched as the Roman strode away.

"What do you think, Meir?"

"If you're asking about Probus, he seems to be decent. He certainly doesn't conform to my idea of what a Roman is like. Gaius, on the other hand, fits the image perfectly!"

"Do you suspect anything, Meir?"

"I really don't know. But to be on the safe side, we'd better both respect and suspect the Romans."

The two of them decided to walk down to the shore.

"I love to watch the sun set over the water," Berurya said softly.

"What's that?"

"I was saying how beautiful this city is. Rome certainly has power and wealth!"

"And so did so many empires before her and so, I suspect, will so many empires after her! But inevitably they collapse. They are civilizations supposedly built as tributes to Man, yet their foundations rest on the suffering of the oppressed. They survive longer than those whom they subjugate. In the end, the Romans too will become victims. However, they'll realize it only when it's too late. Their search for immortality is always at the expense of morality. Rome," said Meir, "will fall not for lack of wealth, but for the wealth of what they lack."

He took his wife's hand. "You know, I think this is the first time the two of us have been alone in years."

"And we owe it all to Rome," Berurya laughed.

"I think a little bit of Bilha has rubbed off on you."

After their stroll, Meir and Berurya returned to their lodgings. It was getting dark. Meir closed the shutters and stretched out on the bed. Berurya sat at the mirror and freed her hair. Meir watched as she brushed it. "The Romans are wrong about one thing," he said.

"What's that?"

"They said I could consult with my attractive wife."

Berurya turned. "Why is that wrong?"

"You're not attractive – you're beautiful!"

Meir sat up and reached for Berurya's arm. "Come here."

"But I'm not finished brushing –"

"For now you are," said Meir, gently pulling her on to the bed. He lifted her dress, Berurya raised her hands above her head, making it easier to disrobe her. Meir took her chin and drew her towards him until their lips met. "Have I told you how much ... I love you?" he said.

"Not in a while. I was beginning to wonder."

"You needn't wonder – ever!"

Meir kissed her. He kissed her again and again, and put a hand on her thigh. Berurya closed her eyes. She sank back on the bed. Meir rose. He locked the door, blew out the flame in the torch, and returned to his wife.

Shortly after dawn, there was a sharp knock at the door. The servant who had accompanied them the previous morning was there for them again. As they walked through the streets, Meir inhaled deeply. "The morning air's wonderful!" he exclaimed.

"Did you sleep well, Meir?"

"Very well."

As was its custom, the assembly rose as one when Iulianus, Probus and Gaius entered. "Today," boomed Iulianus, "we have selected a number of individuals who will question you, Rabbi Meir. Is that clear?"

"Perfectly!"

A stout matron stood up. "Rabbi, yesterday you said that Jews subscribe to something called the 'resurrection of the dead.' I believe there is a reference to the notion in Psalm 72: 'May they blossom out of the city like grass of the earth.' To me, it seems fanciful but for the sake of argument, let's say it's true. My question is simple: When this resurrection occurs, will people rise up from their graves stark naked or fully clothed?"

The great chamber echoed with laughter. Iulianus slammed his fist on the table. "Silence," he bellowed. "We're not here for amusement – we want to learn something about the Jews!"

"How should I respond?" Meir whispered to Berurya.

"Someone obviously gave her the question. How else could she cite a verse from the Psalms? Use the reasoning behind her question when you answer."

Meir got to his feet. "May I ask your name?"

"You can call me Queen Cleopatra," sneered the matron.

Again, the crowd burst into laughter.

"Very well, Queen Cleopatra," said Meir calmly, "let me remind you that your analogy was to grass. I'll argue a posteriori. If, on the one hand, you take a naked grain of wheat and plant it in the earth and it sprouts forth fully-dressed, then isn't it a thousand times more likely in the case of the righteous who are buried in the raiments of their good deeds?"

There was silence in the room and Berurya smiled.

"That was an easy one," said Iulianus. "Ask the Samaritan to step forward."

The Samaritan entered and bowed to the officials. Gaius smirked. "I have three questions for you, Rabbi Meir," declaimed the Samaritan in a rich, bass voice. "The first is from the Torah, the second from the Prophets, and the third from Writings.

"The first question, good rabbi, deals with the second day of Creation. It is written in the Torah, and I quote: 'And God said, "Let there be a firmament in the midst of the waters, and let it divide water from water." And God made the firmament, and divided the waters which were under the firmament, from the waters which were above the firmament: and it was so.' Are we to believe, then, according to this quote, that the upper waters are suspended solely by the word of God?"

The Samaritan smiled smugly and glanced up at Gaius, as if to seek his approval.

Meir whispered to Berurya: "I have an idea." Turning to the Samaritan, he said: "In order for me to prove that God can indeed suspend water in the sky, I will need a glass-tube or perhaps a syringe or a water-clock."

Iulianus motioned to one of the servants. Within minutes, the servant returned with a water-clock.

Meir took it from the servant and declared loudly: "Now, if I place thin gold foil over the opening at the top of the glass, the water will still drop out from below. Silver foil does no better. However, if I place my finger on top of the opening like this – then the water doesn't drip any more!" His eyes blazed like burning coals. "Now, if I, a mere mortal, can keep water suspended with my finger, why would it be difficult for the Lord of the Universe to suspend water in the heavens!"

Iulianus guffawed. "You made your point, Rabbi Meir," he said. "Samaritan, ask your next question."

"Well," intoned the portly Samaritan, "the prophet Jeremiah says: 'Do not I fill heaven and earth? says the Lord.' If we are to believe that God fills all space, then how, when the Israelites were in the desert, did God speak to Moses from the small space between two staves of the Ark? Explain that, if you can!"

Meir shrugged. "I really thought you were going to ask me something difficult!" He gestured. "To show you how, I'll need two mirrors of different sizes."

Once again, Iulianus directed the servant to bring Meir what he had requested.

"What's your plan?" whispered Berurya.

"I'm going to show how one's reflection changes depending on which mirror one uses," Meir said. "If a human being can appear both large and small, why then shouldn't God be able to vary His own manifestations!?"

"Do you think they'll accept it?"

"It's worth a try," said Meir. "Obviously, the universe cannot contain God! But to use a metaphysical argument wouldn't work with these people."

Meir had reckoned correctly. As he demonstrated his proposition, it seemed to Berurya that he won the crowd's approval.

"My final question is a simple one indeed! Psalm 65 reads: 'The river of God is full of water.' Are we to imply from these words that since Creation there has been no loss of water!? To me, this is absurd!"

Meir leaned over to Berurya. "Well... any ideas?"

"Yes," Berurya said, with a smile on her lips. "One which I think Bilha would be proud of."

Gaius craned his neck. "May we ask the rabbi to respond to the question or will he admit that he doesn't have an answer!" he shouted, twisting his cruel lips around the words.

"Gentlemen, you agreed that I could confer with my wife. I assume that your word is still good."

"You may indeed discuss the question with your attractive wife," said Iulianus emphatically.

"Thank you," said Meir.

He listened attentively to Berurya as she outlined the plan. Meir stood up. "In order to respond properly," he announced, "we'll have to take a trip to one of your local bathhouses."

Gaius, Iulianus and Probus conferred over the request. Iulianus rubbed his chin. "Is there no other way?" he asked.

"I'm afraid not."

"In that case, we will accede to your request," Iulianus boomed.

Meir drew closer to Berurya. "I think it best that you wait back in our room."

"All right."

"Incidentally, how did you get the idea?"

"I'll tell you later."

Meir went with the Romans to a large, regally-appointed bathhouse. When all gathered inside, he asked: "Which steam-room is the hottest?"

"The one on the far left," the bath-attendant said.

"Good," said Meir. "Now, because the Samaritan has questioned whether God could prevent the world's waters from diminishing, I'd like to ask for his assistance in my experiment."

The Samaritan glanced over at Gaius. Gaius grimaced but nodded approval.

"Would you kindly undress?" Meir said.

The Samaritan was momentarily taken aback by Meir's request. He did not move.

"I'll ask you once again," said Meir evenly. "Would you please remove your clothes?"

Lowering his eyes, the Samaritan disrobed.

"Thanks," said Meir. "And now, if you don't mind, I'd like the bath-attendant to weigh you."

As the Samaritan waddled over with the bath-attendant, in the bathhouse other Romans joined the intently-watching crowd.

"I've registered his weight!" the bath-attendant called out.

"Splendid! Now," said Meir, "please go right into the steam-room. Someone will knock on the door when it's time for you to come out."

The Samaritan went silently into the steam-room. Meir began to pace back and forth.

A minute went by, then another and another.

The bath-attendant shook his head.

"It's very hot in there," he said. "I don't think he should be in there too long."

"Just a little longer," said Meir.

Meir waited several minutes and then told the attendant to open the door. The Samaritan emerged, beet-red and dripping as if he had just come out of a pool. His hair was matted; sweat streamed down his body; his breathing was hoarse. He cleared his throat. "Water," he rasped. "Water!"

The attendant brought him a jug.

Meir held up a hand. "Wait," he said. "Before you drink a drop, I want you to weigh yourself again."

The Samaritan stared at Meir in disbelief.

"Please," insisted Meir, "do as I ask."

The attendant weighed the Samaritan once more and registered his weight.

"Now, you may drink."

The Samaritan lifted the jug and thirstily gulped down the water; he drained it and demanded a second jug. The crowd murmured with amusement. When he had satisfied his thirst, the Samaritan – having become aware that all eyes were on him – quickly grabbed his clothes and put them on.

Gaius' face was dark. "May I ask what all this has proved?" he growled. "Or was it just a perverse attempt to ridicule the poor man!?"

"Not at all," rejoined Meir, "as you'll soon see." Meir faced the Samaritan. "You agree that you've sweated a great deal."

"Yes," the other said feebly.

"You've lost a considerable amount of water."

"I have," said the Samaritan.

Meir now turned to the bath-attendant. "Sir," he said, "you weighed this man before and after he entered the steam-room. What is the difference in his weight?"

"There is no difference," said the bath-attendant.

"Would you please repeat that more loudly so that everyone can hear?"

"There is no difference in weight!" the attendant called out.

"Then," declared Meir, "if your own pool of perspiration has not diminished – and you are mere flesh and blood – then how much more so in the case of the pool of the Holy One, Blessed be He! That's why it is written: 'The river of God is full of water.' As difficult as it may be for you, a puny mortal, to grasp, for God it is nothing." Iuliaus raised his hands: "I think that will be sufficient for one day," he said. "We'll meet again tomorrow."

Meir walked alone back to the room where Berurya was waiting. "How did it go?" she asked eagerly.

"You could say that I made the man sweat a bit!"

"You didn't overdo it, I hope."

"No, no. But I'm sure he won't forget that particular verse as long as he lives!"

"What did you think of today's questions?"

"I'm not sure," said Meir. "But if we're to believe Probus, they were meant to humiliate us."

"But why? What have we ever done to them?"

"Maybe it wasn't directed at us personally, but rather at what we represent? Remember the message to the Sanhedrin. It asked that a 'torch' be sent – someone who could shed light."

"It also referred to your name," said Berurya. "Surely you don't believe the phrase was accidental?"

"I don't know. Tomorrow is our last day. By then we'll be more clear about it." Meir paused and then said: "But tell me, how'd you get the idea of taking the Samaritan to the bathhouse?"

Berurya smiled. "Do you remember when Bilha and I went to the bathhouse in Tiberias? After we bathed, she complained that her skin was wrinkled and that she felt as if she'd been cooked alive! I said to her: 'Bilha, you've got to admit that the bath made you feel better.' And she said: 'The water was all right. But if I'd lost even one single ounce of weight in the steam-room, I'd more willingly have endured the torture!'"

Meir smiled broadly. "Let's rest now."

The next morning, the servant again rapped on their door. "Are you ready to leave?" he asked.

"Yes," said Meir.

"Follow me, please."

Meir and Berurya trailed silently behind the servant.

"Meir," said Berurya, "this isn't the same route as usual."

"I know."

Suddenly the servant stopped at a corner. "Wait here," he said, and hurried off.

"I don't like the look of this, Meir. Something's strange."

"What can we do?"

The servant reappeared. "Follow me, please." He turned the corner and led them into an alley. Someone was standing in the shadows. The thought that it might be the Samaritan bent on revenge or perhaps someone sent by Gaius to do harm flashed through Meir's mind. The figure reached for something tucked in his tunic and stepped forward. Meir's heart raced. He moved in front of Berurya. Suddenly, a shaft of light fell on the man's face: it was Probus!

"Probus," Berurya exclaimed, "you gave us a scare!"

"I'm sorry but I want to show you something." Probus held up a scroll of paper. "Have a look at this."

Meir moved into the light. He unraveled the scroll and saw a picture of himself! "What's this?"

Taking the paper back, Probus said: "Do you know that you're a wanted man in Rome?"

"That had happened so very long ago I've almost forgotten," Meir said to Berurya. He sighed. "After I left the brothel in Rome I returned to Flavius' house. It was just about dawn. I remember seeing a picture of me on a wall then. I realized that the Romans were looking for me and that I'd have to run."

"I believe that Gaius knows about your past," said Probus.

"But how could he?"

Probus shrugged.

"If it becomes known would I be arrested?" asked Meir.

"I'm not sure," replied Probus. "You've been invited here to represent your people. It would violate our code of honor to incarcerate an invited guest. On the other hand, accidents happen. When you leave the chamber today, you'll no longer be our guest..." Probus did not finish his sentence.

"You do have a choice, Meir," said Berurya.

"No, I don't."

"But you do, Rabbi Meir," Probus insisted. "You can go home right now and I'll make up some excuse. I'll say you got word that someone is ill or there's an emergency of some sort."

Meir shook his head vigorously. "I can't go until I finish here in Caesarea," he said.

Probus looked over to Berurya for support but instead she said: "He's right. Gaius isn't important. It's what all the people will think about Jews if we flee." Her brow knitted. "They don't have to like us. They may even hate us. But we'll have their respect – and they can't respect anyone who runs away because he's afraid! Furthermore, we don't know for a fact that Gaius is planning something. Therefore, we must stay."

"If you've made up your minds ..." Probus murmured.

"We have," said Meir.

"So be it," said the Roman. He turned and began to walk away.

"Probus!" Meir called after him: "Thank you – for everything! Don't misunderstand. We deeply appreciate all you've done for us."

"I only wish I could have done more!" the Roman called back.

Moments later, the servant reappeared. "After me, please," he said.

"I'm pleased that you agreed I should finish the job here, Berurya."

"It's the right thing to do, Meir."

"But then why did you say I had a choice?"

"There's always a choice, no matter what, Meir. Unfortunately, when people are in difficult decisions, most of them fail to see there are options. Somehow, they are paralyzed by the uncertainties, the choice of the mind is lost to the fear of the heart."

Meir and Berurya arrived at the hall and took their designated seats. A number of Romans approached and congratulated them on their presentations. As they spoke, Iulianus, Gaius and Probus were announced. The audience rose to its feet and sat when the officials took their seats.

"This is the final session," proclaimed Iulianus. "We'll ask questions, Rabbi Meir, and then you may summarize. Understood?"

"Perfectly," answered Meir.

"All right, then, I'll lead off. On the first day you spoke about concern for the poor, the widow and the orphan. If your God loves the poor, why doesn't He simply provide for them?"

Meir rose and moved forward a few steps. He stroked his chin, and glanced up at Iulianus. "Your question, sir, is an interesting one. It is the very same question once asked of my teacher, Rabbi Akiva. I'll give you the answer he gave: 'In order that through them – that is the poor – we might be saved from the judgement of Gehinnom, where the wicked are punished in the Hereafter.'"

Meir paused, advanced again and continued: "Obviously, God could remedy all the ills of the world but we Jews believe that He wants us to be directly involved. That's why there are so many commandments in Judaism which focus on those in need – be they fellow-Jews, or not." Meir gestured. "You see, human beings make distinctions about race and beliefs, but God makes distinctions when it comes to behavior. There's always a moral imperative in Judaism, demanding that we do what is just and right. And Judaism doesn't stop with the deed; it addresses the very intention itself. For example, a man shouldn't urge his friend to dine with him when he knows full-well beforehand that his friend will decline the invitation. Similarly, one shouldn't offer gifts when one knows in advance that they will not be accepted. What harm is done by such deeds, you may ask? The answer is simple: they are forms of deception. If you don't intend to do a kindness, then the pretense of doing one is wrong."

Meir shifted his weight from one foot to the other. "Regarding the poor, if there must be deception, then it should be for that person's benefit. If a poor person, for whatever reason, refuses your offer to support him, then you should give him needed money as a loan and then, after he's accepted it, inform him it's a gift. A deception of this sort, intended to help a poor man and, at the same time, allow him to maintain his dignity is commendable."

Meir thought for a moment, and then continued: "Perhaps, sir, I strayed from the subject, nevertheless I hope I've addressed your question." Meir wet his lips with his tongue. "Simply stated, sir, the principle is: 'Love your neighbor as yourself.' Now, your neighbor may be different. He may be rich or poor, intelligent or simple, strong or weak, but the common denominator is that he is like you and like me in that he, too, was created in the image of God and therefore deserves to be treated with respect, dignity and at very least, with compassion."

Meir coughed and sat down. Berurya leaned over and whispered: "That was superb."

"I have no other questions," Iulianus said. He turned his head. "Gaius, you may question the rabbi."

"Here it comes," Meir whispered to Berurya.

Gaius' cruel lips twisted. "I have two questions," he said in a harsh voice. "The first question should have been asked yesterday by the Samaritan; unfortunately circumstances didn't allow him to ask it."

"I told you he was behind the Samaritan," said Berurya.

Gaius pointed a finger at Meir. "You Jews," he continued, "are clearly born liars. Your religion is a lie; your ancestors were liars; and your Patriarchs were liars!"

As he heard the words, Meir felt his heart pound. "Gaius wants me to lose my temper," he thought. "I must remain calm."

"If you please," Meir interrupted, "would you be more specific? And what exactly is your question?"

Gaius smiled thinly. He seemed not to have heard Meir's remark. Leaning forward, he said: "The Samaritan tells me that according to your holy book – whatever it's called – the Patriarch Jacob promised God, and I quote: 'And of all that Thou shalt give me I will surely give the tenth unto Thee.' Since there were twelve tribes of Israel and only one, the tribe of Levi, was designated to serve your God, then obviously one out of twelve is not a tenth! Is it now!?"

Meir stared directly into Gaius' eyes. "Let me assist you with your calculation," he said in a level voice. "The Patriarch Jacob said: 'Ephraim and Manasseh, even as Reuben and Simeon, shall be mine.' Therefore, if you add the grandchildren, Ephraim and Manasseh, to the other twelve sons of Jacob, we now deal with fourteen descendents. Now, Jacob had four wives and each wife had a first born. According to Jewish law, the firstborn has a special holy status and one doesn't set holiness aside from what is already holy. Thus fourteen less four firstborn gives you ten! Jacob had fulfilled his promise!"

Meir sat down quietly.

Gaius was livid with rage and it took him several moments to calm himself. When he could control his voice, he continued: "I can never," he muttered shrilly, "make up my mind whether you are just liars... or shrewd liars!" Drawing out a handkerchief, he wiped the spittle from his knobby chin. "My next question," he said with patent sarcasm, "is very simple. I'd like a simple answer: yes or no." He grimaced. "Jews don't eat pigs. Is that correct?"

"Correct," said Meir.

"In your religion, it's a sin to eat the meat of a pig. Is that correct?"

"Correct," answered Meir.

"Jews consider the pig a loathsome animal – so much so, that the rabbis prohibit even the raising of pigs. Yes or no, rabbi?

"Yes," said Meir.

Gaius' eyes narrowed to slits. "Will you deny that Jews call us Romans 'pigs'?"

The room was deafeningly still.

"No," Meir said.

"Now," nodded Gaius, "we're getting to the truth at last."

Meir shot to his feet. "Hold on a second," he cried out. "Your questions are leading us in a certain direction; I must be permitted to comment at this point or everything will be misconstrued!"

Gaius, too, rose in his place. "Don't worry, Rabbi Meir," he snapped, "we know exactly what to expect from a man who is a hunted criminal!"

Now Berurya got to her feet. Her body trembled, but her voice was steady. "My husband," she said, "may be a criminal in the eyes of Rome. But you must know why he is considered to be a criminal. You must know the very hideous nature of his crime."

She drew a deep breath and went on: "My father was executed in this city, in accordance with Roman law. His death was slow and painful. Roman soldiers wrapped him in the holy Torah, moistened it, and set him ablaze. Roman soldiers burst into our house and slashed my mother with their swords until her blood flooded the floor, they raped my younger sister and dragged her off to Rome and a house of prostitution!"

Berurya's eyes flashed. "After all this horror, my husband, whom you, Gaius, now accuse, committed the terrible crime of bribing a guard in order to free my sister. For his despicable act, you've branded him an outlaw. And my father's terrible crime? Well, I'll tell you: he did no more than you have asked us to do here in Caesarea. He simply taught Torah! That's the 'crime' for which he paid with his life, for which my mother lost her life, and for which my sister suffered indescribably! Who then, I ask, is the real criminal?"

Meir took his wife's hand. When he spoke, his voice was firm. "To answer your question, Gaius, the pig, like the rabbit, the camel, and a number of other animals, is not permitted Jews as food." He lifted a hand. "But nowhere," he thundered, "are we commanded to pursue them, or torture them, or kill them! Yet all of these things you Romans have done to my people!

"In Roman eyes, the boar is a symbol of strength. I've seen the boar's image on the standards of your legions. You Romans yourselves make the association! But that's not the real issue." Meir wiped his brow with the back of a hand. "I'll tell you what the real issue is. The Hebrew word for pig is 'Hazir'. The three root letters are used to spell out another Hebrew word meaning 'return'. For Jews believe that, ultimately, sovereignty will return to its rightful owners: that will be the future of Rome and the destiny of Israel. I admonish you, Gaius, to remember this! And to know that when you spit at heaven, it falls back in your face!" Meir seated himself. "I have nothing more to add," he said quietly.

The huge chamber was hushed. "I, myself, have no questions to ask," said Probus. "I therefore recommend that we conclude the proceedings. I'd like to thank Rabbi Meir and his wife, Berurya, for answering the questions that were put to them. Our two peoples will most likely never be friends, but I hope we can at least learn how to respect each other."

Probus turned to Iulianus, who nodded his approval. Both rose and walked out. Gaius alone remained in his place.

In the courtyard, Probus came up to Meir and Berurya. "I want to apologize ... for what happened. I did my best to warn you."

"There's no need to apologize," said Meir. "I must confess that at first I didn't trust you. I am guilty of viewing all Romans as enemies. Obviously, it isn't true."

Probus' eyes filled with an expression of mingled appreciation and sadness. He was silent for a moment and then he said: "Before you leave, may I share a story with you. It is told," he went on, "that the Emperor Hadrian, while leading his troops to battle against a country which had rebelled against Rome, happened on an old man planting fig trees. Hadrian was fascinated. He stopped and asked the man how old he was and the old man answered: 'I am one hundred years old.' 'You're a hundred years old,' Hadrian exclaimed, 'and you bother to plant saplings! Do you really believe that you'll live to eat their fruit?' The old man shook his head and said: 'My lord Emperor, I plant and if I merit it, I will indeed eat the fruit of my saplings; but if I die, then just as those before me toiled for my benefit, so I have labored for those who come after ...' Hadrian said nothing, but dug his spurs into his mount's flanks and went off to war.

"Three years later, on his return, he found the old man in the same place. The old man saluted Hadrian, lifted a basket from the ground, filled it with the choicest figs, and handed the basket to Hadrian. 'My lord Emperor,' he said in his reedy voice, 'please accept these figs from your humble servant. I am the same old man who you encountered some years ago, while I was planting the saplings. God has allowed me to enjoy the fruits of my labor.' Hadrian smiled and said to an aide: 'Take the basket from the old man and return it to him filled with gold coins.'

"The story might have ended there, but it didn't. The old man went home that evening and related all that had happened to his wife and children. A neighbor was there, she listened with great interest and went back to her husband. 'Everyone else is successful but you,' she nagged. 'All you do is just sit around the house and daydream. Just this minute, I heard that our neighbor honored the Emperor with a basket of figs and in return received a basket filled with gold coins! Why not do the same thing – except bring a bigger basket and heap it with figs and an assortment of fruits. Go to the Emperor and bring me back gold, as our neighbor did!'

"The husband listened to his wife. He found a large basket, filled it with figs, and brought it to Hadrian. 'My lord Emperor,' he declared, 'I've heard that you love to eat fruit, and so I've brought you a basket of figs in exchange for gold.' The Emperor was furious;

he ordered the man to be stripped naked at once and the fruit he had brought thrown at him. The poor man was badly injured – he lost the sight in one eye and his face was seriously bruised. He went home with a heavy heart, weeping. When his wife set eyes on him, she was dumbfounded. 'What happened?' she said. 'The honor bestowed to me by the Emperor,' her husband replied, 'is an honor you deserved far more than I did!' The wife shrugged. 'You're always complaining,' she snorted. 'Be grateful you brought ripe figs and not hard apples!'"

Meir and Berurya laughed.

"The story's amusing," observed Probus, "but there's something to be learned from it. Firstly, Hadrian understood from the old man that one cannot live only for oneself. One must also consider future generations. The king gave him the gold coins because of the old man's humility and respect. Contrarily, the neighbor's wife completely misunderstood the old man's message. She was greedy, but she soon learned the bitter lesson that there are no short cuts to prosperity in life. Whereas the old man showed respect for the Emperor, the neighbor's behavior was disrespectful. In the first episode, the Emperor and the old man understood each other. In the second episode, the Emperor and the Jew clashed. The Emperor's honor was insulted, the Jew suffered physically."

"I understand the message," said Meir.

"Yes," agreed Berurya. "I, too, have learned that misunderstanding leads to hurt and pain on both sides."

"It's a wonderful story," Meir said. "Where did you hear it?"

"From a rabbi I knew and liked many years ago," replied Probus.

"What was his name?" asked Berurya.

"Elisha ben Avuya," Probus replied. "He was truly a great man. He taught me a great deal; he helped me understand Jews and Judaism."

There were tears in Meir's eyes and he averted his gaze.

29

To Attain Old Age

Meir and Berurya used a different route back to Tiberias. Instead of going north, they headed due west to Beit Shean. The distance was less than sixty kilometers, but the ever-winding road made the journey much longer. From Beit Shean, they would turn north, traveling almost parallel to the Jordan river until they reached the southern shore of the Kinneret.

During the first day's travel, they talked mainly about Caesarea and discussed their impressions of what had transpired. Meir could not get over the fact that Probus had actually known Elisha ben Avuya.

"I would've loved to have talked with him at length about Elisha," Meir said. "Listening to someone else speak of a deceased person whom you were fond of has a very special quality."

"What about Gaius and the Samaritan?"

"I detest Gaius," said Meir forcefully. "He stands for everything loathsome in the Romans. I feel no animosity toward the Samaritan. As a matter of fact, I feel nothing toward him. He tried to denigrate our traditions, but he failed miserably.

"Years ago," Meir went on, "I was involved with a Samaritan. The man was extremely wealthy. He made a feast and invited the entire town. I attended the festivities. If I say that he set out every food imaginable, I wouldn't be exaggerating! As a jest, I casually said to the host that I couldn't find a particular soft-shelled nut. I certainly had intended no insult but he reacted to my words like a madman! He began overturning tables and screaming at the top of his lungs! The dishes and platters he smashed in his blind rage were irreplaceable."

"Why did he carry on like that?"

"Actually," said Meir, "it was a clash of beliefs. The Samaritan said: 'You rabbis say that This World is ours – belonging to the Samaritans – but not the World to Come. If it's true, then I won't deprive myself of the pleasure in this world – even if it means one, single soft-shelled nut!' I was appalled and mentioned the story to a student, Dostai ben Yannai. I explained to him how the incident illustrated the last words of Proverbs: 'and the belly of the wicked shall want.' Wanton destruction is clearly an act of wickedness."

As they journeyed on, Berurya spotted a number of horsemen approaching from the south. "Meir," she warned, "they may be highwaymen. Let's find a place to hide."

"It's too late, Berurya. I'm sure they've seen us. If they attack ..."

"If they attack," said Berurya, "we'll defend ourselves."

Meir had not intended to say that, but he did not contradict her. The men galloped up to Meir and Berurya and blocked the road. The man on the lead horse pointed a finger. "Are you Rabbi Meir?"

"I am."

The speaker sat erectly on his horse: he was a powerfully-built man, with muscles in his arms and legs that bulged. His eyes were dark and his jet-black beard and hair gave him a formidable look. "Is that your wife?" he asked.

"Yes."

"You will both accompany us to our town."

It did not sound to Meir like he and Berurya had any option. Silently, the riders flanked them. The leader kicked his horse and headed down off the path.

"What does he want?" asked Berurya.

"I have no idea. But the fact that they haven't harmed us and know my name may be a good sign...."

"I hope he's not someone you've angered in the past."

Meir turned. "It's not a time for jokes," he snapped.

Ringed by the horsemen, they travelled in silence almost two hours.

"Are we nearly there?" Berurya shouted at length.

"Almost," said the leader over his shoulder.

"I don't think I can go on much longer, Meir," said Berurya. "I'm utterly exhausted. "

"We have no choice," said Meir. "Try to hold on, he said that we're almost there."

Suddenly, in the distance what looked like a city appeared on the horizon. "Meir, look!"

"Yes, I see."

As they entered the outskirts of the town, a large group of children ran up. They laughed and cheered. A few of the older ones dashed in among the horses and tried to touch Meir's leg. The leader shouted and waved the children away. As they rode into the center of town, Berurya realized that all eyes stared at them. The leader reined his horse in and motioned for his men to dismount. He dismounted himself. Meir and Berurya followed suit.

"Where are we?" asked Meir.

"In Mimla," the leader said. "Now, follow me."

"Meir," whispered Berurya, "I've noticed something very strange about this place."

"What is it?"

"Look around you," said Berurya. "There aren't any old people here! Everyone is young. Not one single person has even a strand of gray hair!"

"Berurya's right," thought Meir. "Everyone is young. Where are the old people of Mimla? Are they hiding? Have they been taken away?" A host of unanswerable questions flashed through Meir's mind.

The leader halted before a large tent and opened its flap; he motioned for Meir and Berurya to enter. Inside the tent, a man sat on a rug. Next to him sat a woman, cradling a baby in her arms. The man rose to his feet. "Rabbi Meir!" he exclaimed. "And you must be Berurya."

Meir nodded.

"Please sit down. May I offer you something to drink?"

Meir shook his head. "Why have we been brought here by force?" he demanded.

The man waved a hand. "Please," he said softly. "For that, I deeply apologize." Then, in an altered voice, he said: "My name is Pinhas. I'm the chief of these people. We wouldn't have brought you here if it were not absolutely necessary. We got word that you were in Caesarea for three days and took the chance that you might return by way of Beit Shean. Your reputation, Rabbi Meir, as a scholar and saintly man is unequalled. That's why we turn to you. I was the one who sent my brother, Hophni, to conduct you to our town. Again, I apologize from the bottom of my heart for any inconvenience we may have caused you and your wife."

Meir cleared his throat. "Your brother's name is Hophni and your name is Pinhas. I believe I know the problem," said Meir. "My wife had pointed out to me that there are no old people in this place. At first I couldn't understand why, but now I do: you are descendents of the house of Eli! Am I correct?"

"That is true," said Pinhas softly.

"It is written in the First Book of Samuel, second chapter, '...and all the increase of thy house shall die young men.' There are no elderly here because everyone ... is destined to die young! It is a punishment for the evil that Eli's two sons, Hophni and Pinhas, committed while they were priests."

"Do you understand why we need you desperately?" Pinhas said hoarsely. "I'm a young man. I'm healthy. But in a short while, like my father before me, and his father before him, I'll suddenly die. After me, my brother will die. And the baby over there – he's the

youngest of my children – he, too, will die young. I implore you. I
beg you. Pray for us ... so that we may live to old age."

Meir glanced from Berurya to Pinhas. "Please let me take my
wife outside and discuss the matter with her. We won't be too long."

"Take your time, Rabbi Meir, but please don't take too much! For
my people, the passage of time is different than for the rest of the
world. We can't afford to waste time because none of us lives to see
a single gray hair! Remember this while you confer."

Meir and Berurya went out of the tent. Hophni stood there with
his arms folded across his chest. Berurya now interpreted the stern
look on his features differently; she knew what tormented his soul.
His face was a cruel mask painted by a mocking angel of death!

"What'll you do, Meir?"

"I don't know," said Meir somberly. "Even if my prayers were
answered and God, in His infinite compassion, spared Pinhas and
Hophni it wouldn't help the others. Pinhas wants something I have
no power to grant."

They began to walk, each of them searching intensely for an
answer. They kept on walking, oblivious to the world around them.
Suddenly, Berurya halted in her tracks and clapped her hands. "Meir,
wait!" she cried out. "Pinhas himself has given us the solution!"

"What do you mean?"

"Remember when he said, 'We can't afford to waste time because
none of us will live to see a single gray hair?'"

"I remember, but how does that help?"

"Then remember Proverbs, chapter sixteen: 'The hoary head is a
crown of glory; it is found in the way of righteousness.' Meir, gray
hair is associated with doing *Tzedakah*, giving charity to the needy!
You must make them see that!"

Meir's face glowed. "You're right!" he burst out. "Let's tell them
at once!"

Pulling Berurya along with him, Meir rushed back to the tent.
"Hophni," he said. "I want you to come inside with us. It's important
for you to hear what I have to say as well."

The three of them entered the tent. Pinhas, still squatting on the floor, looked up. "Will you pray for us?" he said huskily.

Meir shook his head. "You don't need me, or anyone, to pray for you, Pinhas. Your salvation, my dear man, lies in your very own hands! Longevity, for the most part, is defined in terms of ancestors. Some people live a few years longer than their parents; some die a few years earlier. There are certain people whose lives, for one reason or another, break this pattern. Their lives might have been filled with great sorrow; certainly, this makes an impact. Some people, who spend their lives helping others, in performing acts of *Tzedakah*, seem to live longer." Meir sighed. "Living with the knowledge that you are destined to die young," he went on, "you people isolate yourselves from the rest of the world. You sit in your tents and wait for death to arrive! And your expectation never fails you! But I charge you now: change your lives! Go out into the world, and help others. Open your arms to the poor and needy and I tell you these, your acts of righteousness, cannot but help to extend your own lives...."

Meir's voice trembled with emotion. "Remember," he continued, "what God said about Abraham: 'For I know him, that he will command his children and his household after him and they shall keep the way of the Lord, to do *Tzedakah* and judgement...' And later on we read: 'And Abraham was old, advanced in years....'"

Pinhas got to his feet and gazed intently at his brother. Meir saw the tears in his eyes.

"You are truly great, Rabbi Meir," said Pinhas. "May the rest of that verse come to pass for you: '...and the Lord had blessed Abraham in all things.'"

Then Pinhas said: "Will you and your wife remain with us as our guests?"

"Thank you very much, but no," Meir replied. "We've been away from our home for too long and we're anxious to get back."

"In that case, Hophni will accompany you for part of the way."

Then Pinhas turned to Berurya. "You are very fortunate," he said, "to have a husband like Rabbi Meir." Berurya nodded but said nothing. As they rode out of Mimla, Berurya looked hard and long at the children: she prayed silently that they all would live to see gray hair.

30

Avnimos

Bathsheva and Bilha were overjoyed to have Berurya and Meir home again. Berurya described the events in Caesarea in detail. Bilha relished the account of the portly Samaritan sweating in the steam-bath. She kept saying, "If only I'd been there! If only I'd been there to see it!"

Berurya told them about Probus and how he had tried to help them defend themselves against the machinations of Gaius. No scene of the drama was omitted!

After the evening meal, Meir was about to leave for the *Beit Midrash* when he heard a knock.

"That's it!" exclaimed Bilha. "The entire time you were gone, we had quiet here. You're back just a few hours and already people want to talk to you."

Meir opened the door. A young man, whom Meir did not recognize, stood there. From the look of his clothes, he did not appear to be Jewish.

"Are you Rabbi Meir?"

"I am."

"I've come from the house of Oenomaus with sad tidings," announced the stranger. "His father has just died."

Meir responded with traditional words: "*Baruch Dayan Emet* – Blessed be the Judge of truth."

"What is it, Meir?" called Berurya.

"Wait here, please," Meir said to the messenger.

He went into the house. "Berurya, Avnimos' father has died."

"When?"

"The messenger didn't say. I'm going to leave now and spend some time with my old friend. Please take care of the *Beit Midrash* while I'm gone."

Meir departed and Bilha walked in. "Where's Meir?" she asked.

"He had to leave suddenly. Avnimos' father has died."

"Who is Avnimos?" asked Bilha.

"Avnimos, or Oenomaus, as non-Jews call him," replied Berurya, "is a famous philosopher – one of the greatest heathen philosophers of all time."

"And he's a friend of Rabbi Meir?"

"Yes, he is, Bilha."

"What a wide range of friends Meir has!" declared Bilha.

"I know what you're thinking, Bilha," said Berurya, "but in this case, you're dead wrong. This man has more knowledge of the Bible than most Jews! Meir once said: 'Even a heathen who preoccupies himself in Torah is like the High Priest.' Although he wasn't explicit, I'm sure he had his friend Avnimos in mind."

For a moment, Berurya reflected about her husband: "Meir," she thought, "differs in so very many ways from the rest of his colleagues. He will befriend an individual, whom other sages have disavowed, if he believes there is something special in the person. Indeed, some people will throw out a delicious fruit because it has a blemish but Meir will ignore the blemish in favor of the fruit! That's why he was Alisha ben Avuya's friend even after the man had been excommunicated."

"When will Meir be back?" asked Bilha.

"I'm not sure. Gedara isn't that far off and he could easily return in a day or two."

Bilha paused and then said: "You know, I was watching Bathsheva yesterday and thinking how very much she resembles you."

"If you mean she resembles me in looks, I can't see it at all. She reminds me of my mother...."

"That's true," observed Bilha. "But I remember you when you were Bathsheva's age and the resemblance is remarkable."

"Perhaps ..."

Bilha rose.

"Speaking of Bathsheva, I'm going to study with her for a while."

Berurya left the room and Bilha sat for a few moments. When she stood an intense pain shot through her side. Bilha bent and pressed a hand to the spot. Then she fell back into her seat.

It wasn't the first time Bilha had experienced such severe pain. Actually, the onset of the pain was becoming more frequent. She did not mention the pain to anyone. What good would it do to talk about it? She refused adamantly to see a physician, believing that often they did more harm than good. She had her own folk-remedies and they were fine.

"Life is queer," she reflected. "As I get older, I find it easier to recall experiences that happened long, long ago, while I simply cannot keep track of things from one moment to the next! I have memories from my childhood, whose details are so clear that I feel I'm living them almost for the first time ever...."

"One time I came home – I could not have been older than four," Bilha recalled, "and my mother's face lit up with incredible happiness. Apparently, I had wandered off and my parents feared something terrible had happened. When I walked in the door, my mother shouted my name and ran over and swept me into her arms. It was a hug I will never forget; it seemed to me that it would never end! Later, when my father came home, he, too, was overwhelmed at seeing me. But ... that memory of my mother's embrace will always stay with me always. How I wish my parents were alive today! How I wish I could be with them ... one more time."

Bilha groaned. The pain had returned. "Maybe ... I should call ... Berurya? No ... no, it'll go away by itself." Bilha rested her head against her arm. Once again, she imagined her mother holding her... hugging her.

Berurya finished with Bathsheva and descended the stairs. She called to Bilha, but there was no answer. "Strange," she thought, "maybe Bilha went outside? But why would she go out in the heat of the day?"

In the kitchen, Berurya found Bilha slumped on the table. Berurya's heart pounded. "Please ... no ..." She rushed over and touched Bilha's shoulder. "Bilha ... Bilha...."

Bilha lifted her head.

"Are you all right?"

"Don't fret – I'm perfectly all right. I must've fallen asleep. I dreamed about my mother. Yes, that was it. I was a little girl... and my mother hugged me." Bilha rubbed her eyes. "Berurya, if you don't mind, I think I'll lie down."

Bilha rose. She remembered the violent pain. But it was gone.

Berurya watched her as she slowly ascended the stairs. "I never realized," Berurya mused, "how much she's aged in the last few years, especially since Elhanan and Hananiah died. Her hair's almost all gray and she's stooped. She never tells me how she feels any more. What if something... should happen to her? I can't remember a day of my life without Bilha. She's like a mother, a sister, and a friend ... all-in-one! I hope and pray that she lives for a long, long time."

31
Leaving Hammat

After spending two days with Avnimos, Meir returned.

"How's he taking his father's death?" asked Berurya.

"It was peculiar. Years ago, when his mother died, he mourned deeply. I remember how he wept without control. Now, I could discern no visible sign of his grief."

"Perhaps he didn't have a good relationship with his father?"

"I assumed that. Then I decided to ask him. 'Avnimos,' I said, 'when your mother died, you mourned fiercely for her. Now, your behavior's different.' His answer was baffling."

"What did he say?"

"'Your observation is correct,'" he said.

"Is that all?"

"No," said Meir. "He cited the verse in the story of Ruth when Naomi says to her daughters-in-law: 'Go, return each of you to her mother's house.' He observed that it doesn't say, 'to her father's house.' For some people, a mother is more a central figure than a father. For Avnimos, the death of his father was inevitable while the loss of his mother was a bitter tragedy."

Meir reflected. "I've read that verse in Ruth all my life. It was only when Avnimos brought it to my attention that I understood what it meant."

"You respect the man," Berurya said.

"Very much. He's full of wisdom and knowledge!" Meir paused and stared at his wife. He took her hand. "But there's another reason I'm excited now."

"What is it?"

"I've been thinking about it for a long time: I want to move to Sepphoris."

The revelation momentarily stunned Berurya.

"Berurya, you'll love Sepphoris," Meir went on, squeezing her fingers. "It's a beautiful city, built very high up and overlooking vast tracts of land. Everything in it is centrally located. Like Tiberias, it's affluent: there are even homes which have their own ritual-baths! Only imagine – a house with its own *Mikvah*! There are deep wells in the ground there; a first-rate water-system serves the city's inhabitants. At one end, there's a beautiful amphitheater." He touched his wife's cheek. "Berurya, I know this all comes very suddenly. I only ask that you don't make a decision until you've had a chance to see the town and meet some of the people!"

"Why in the world do you want to leave Hammat? It's our home!"

"This isn't a capricious decision," Meir said soberly. "Quite the contrary. For years now, Rabbi Yose has been asking me to move there. Even the climate's better there. How many times have I heard Bilha complain that she can't endure the hot, humid summers here? In Sepphoris, the air's always fresh and salutary."

"Meir," said Berurya firmly, "tell me the real reason you want to go to Sepphoris."

"But I've told you why!" Meir said curtly.

Berurya looked taken aback. Regretting his tone of voice, Meir stared at the floor. "How can I answer your question, Berurya, when I don't know?" Meir looked up at her. "Perhaps, I'm weary of Hammat... the same routine, with this sedentary existence. I really don't know. The logical part of me, the part which I've always listened to, finds many reasons why we should remain here. But there's another part of me, deep within: it's like an ocean which looks calm on the surface but has treacherous currents in its depths.

I can't pin down what it is that's pulling me to go, but I fear it would be a grave mistake to disregard the feelings."

Berurya nodded. "The currents of emotion you speak of exist in each of us. You needn't fear them, Meir, but rather learn to use them for your own good. As you well know, the sages teach that in each human being there is a *Yetzer HaTov* and a *Yetzer HaRa* – a good and an evil inclination. That's one thing. But emotions which are felt to be undesirable per se, can enrich the human condition and better society. Emotions make individuals compete, strive, prevail, and have children.

"Who," Berurya went on, "hasn't been exposed to the sin of jealousy – the all-consuming passion which controls and ultimately destroys? Yet there are those who become master and not its slave! The emotion serves, not rules them. It can be made to build, not tear down; to create, not to destroy.

"Within us, Meir, is a world of contrasts: good and bad; intellect and emotion; weakness and strength; will and passivity. The strength of one in no way implies the weakness of the other. Shadows take on form in light, yet disappear in darkness. The Tzadik, the wholly righteous individual, can't be praiseworthy because he has never felt the desire to do evil. In the good man, the inclination to commit evil is strong: his goodness is a consequence of the struggle wherein righteousness prevails.

"Our conflict, Meir, is mighty. Intellect brings no promise of tranquility. On the contrary, as *Kohelet* says: 'For in much wisdom is much vexation; and he that increases knowledge increases sorrow.' Herein lies the dilemma. The tree of knowledge contains the seeds of its own destruction."

Berurya reflected. "My own life, Meir, has been a struggle between strength-of-will and weakness-of-emotion. Having been born a woman, I've been expected to behave as if I were an unthinking creature, subject to feelings over which I have no control. But I feel that my mind is my freedom; my body very often my prison. It would have been bitter enough had men only resented my teaching in the *Beit Midrash*. The greatest indignity, however, was heaped on me by women. Instead of appreciation, I got derision. Maybe that explains why, with the exception of Bilha, I haven't found other women's company particularly appealing.

"My strength-of-will is the wall I erected to contain sentiment and womanly emotions. The foundation-stone was when the Romans murdered my father! The second stone was when they killed my mother and a third stone for Penina's shame. And the deaths of our sons, Hananiah and Elhanan, of my brother, Elhanan, and all those close to me have raised the wall to such a height that at this point there is no pressure which could force through one single tear!"

Berurya sighed and smiled wistfully. "Meir, my husband, I love you – you know that. If it makes you happy, we'll move to Sepphoris."

"You won't regret it."

Berurya said nothing. Leaving Hammat, she felt, would be very difficult for Bilha and Bathsheva. Most major changes in life, she knew, were met with varying degrees of reluctance – even those which we clearly recognize as beneficial. Even before a mother can hold her own baby, the umbilical cord must be cut!

"When would you want to move?"

"In a month or two. There are a number of arrangements which I have to make first."

It was evident that Meir was greatly relieved to have Berurya's agreement. Berurya now had to convey the decision to Bathsheva and Bilha. Surprisingly enough, it was far less complicated than she had imagined. Bathsheva accepted her mother's description of the advantages to be gained by moving to Sepphoris. Bilha's reaction was highly unusual; she accepted the decision without a hint of protest.

"Living in Sepphoris has distinct advantages over living in Hammat," explained Berurya. "We'll still be close enough to visit friends here, yet we'll be near enough to see Penina and Menahem. We really don't visit them often enough."

Berurya suspected that Bilha's unqualified acceptance concealed some deep sorrow. Places always evoke memories. Sikhnin had been the home of their childhood. The house they'd leave behind in Hammat was the home where Hananiah and Elhanan had been raised. To depart was to close the door on memories. And that wasn't easy.

Berurya was determined to convince herself that Sepphoris was a door open to the challenges of the future. There would be many more students and they would have the opportunity to exchange ideas with and learn from other sages. Bathsheva would soon reach puberty. One day, she would marry and Sepphoris would then be the home of new memories dear to her.

During their last six weeks in Hammat, Meir seemed happier than he had been in a long time. It was almost as if he were starting his life all over again. He was like a new person. In the *Beit Midrash* he gave discourses on such topics as the importance of *Shalom* and the personality of Aaron, Moses' brother, who became a symbol for the pursuit of peace.

One Shabbat, basing the *drasha*, his exegesis, on the words of the prophet Malachai, "The Torah of truth was in his mouth, and iniquity was not to be found on his lips: he walked with me in peace and uprightness, and turned many away from iniquity," Meir expounded on how, when Aaron chanced upon a wicked person, he would greet him cordially and wish him peace. The next day, when this same man considered performing some sin or transgression, he would pause to reflect on Aaron's actions and think, "If I do this now, how will I be able to look Aaron in the eye? I'll be terribly ashamed of myself in his presence, especially after the respectful greeting he gave me." Consequently, the man would disavow his intent to sin.

"Aaron would also," Rabbi Meir expounded, "make peace between two people who argued. He would go over to one and say,

'Your friend, with whom you had a quarrel, I just saw him. He grieves at this very moment. He behaves like a person in mourning who tears his clothes at the mention of his loss. He says to himself, "I am so ashamed of my actions. How shall I ever approach my wounded friend? I have committed a great offense against him."' Aaron would sit with this man until he was certain that the bitterness had left his heart. Then he'd go to the other fellow and repeat the same words: 'Your friend, with whom you quarreled, I just saw him. He grieves at this very moment. He behaves like a person in mourning who tears his clothes at the mention of his loss. He says to himself, "I'm so ashamed of my actions. How will I ever approach my wounded friend? I have committed a great offense against him."' When Aaron was convinced that this fellow had also overcome his anger, he would leave. Ultimately, the two men would meet and embrace. As the sage Hillel used to say: 'Be of the disciples of Aaron, loving peace and pursuing it, loving thy fellow creatures, and drawing them near to the Torah."'

It was not only in Meir's lectures and discourses that Berurya saw a change but also in his behavior. When Meir learned of two people who habitually quarreled Friday afternoons before the Sabbath, he personally went to make peace between them.

Meir even found time for his daughter. He helped her learn Greek and listened with interest when she related the events of the day. Berurya was now happy – happier than she had been for many years. It was well worth leaving the old memories, if the future promised better ones....

During their last days in Hammat, many friends and neighbors had come to wish them well and tell them how much they'd be missed. Meir assured them that his disciples, those whom he had ordained, were extremely capable and could serve them well in his absence. Meir also emphasized the fact that it wasn't as if he were leaving forever: there would be many occasions on which he would return to visit and to lecture.

Old friends and new friends came to the house. Tamar and Yaddua were especially sorry to see Berurya leave. A few of the students whom Meir and Berurya had taught would join them in Sepphoris, but many more were prepared to continue on their own. Perhaps they'd attract their own students.

Tabi arrived the day before they were scheduled to leave. He expressed his master's sincere regrets for not personally being able to say good-bye but pressing business matters prevented Nathan from doing so. The truth was that ever since that day on the boat when Nathan had held the unconscious Berurya in his arms and realized that she would never be his, he decided that it would be best for him never to see her again. To yearn for what he could never have was far too painful for a man like Nathan. He said his farewell a thousand times in the empty echo-chamber of his heart!

The next morning Meir, Berurya, Bathsheva and Bilha went to the *Beit Midrash* for the last time. The room was crowded; there was an air of anticipation. Meir walked up to the front.

"I've known many of you for years," he said in a clear, ringing voice. "A teacher's students are like his children and each of you is precious to me. I've endeavored to transmit the traditions which I received from my teachers to you. What words will I leave you with?

"I've given this much thought. First of all, I want you to consider the following saying: 'The measure with which man measures will be measured out to him.' In other words, as you deal with life, so will it be dealt to you. There is balance. It may not be apparent at all times, but there is justice. Secondly, I want you to look at life as if with each *mitzvah* you perform, an angel is sent down to protect you. No one can achieve too much protection. Remember that with every *mitzvah* you perform, you enhance your name."

Meir's eyes were darkly radiant. "In life we have three names," he declared. "The first is given us by our parents at birth. The second is what our companions call us. The third is the name we make for ourselves, our reputation. The last is most important – always remember that. And finally, remember these words; repeat them so often they'll never be forgotten: 'Study with all your heart and with all your soul to know My ways and to watch at the doors of My law. Keep My law in your heart and let My fear be before your eyes. Keep your mouth from all sin, and purify and sanctify yourself from all transgression and iniquity, and I shall be with you in every place.'" Meir paused. "May the Lord be with all of you in every place," he concluded in a hushed voice.

Meir returned to the rear of the room and Berurya went to the front to address the crowd. "I'll restrict my words to a minimum," she said. "And I'll begin with a question: 'How do people differ one from another?'"

One student called out: "People differ according to appearance."

"Very good," said Berurya, "and how else?"

A woman whom Berurya had known for many years said: "People differ according to the sound of their voices."

"Excellent. And there is still one more distinction. Who knows what it is?"

Symmachus, one of Meir's ablest students, said: "We differ according to intelligence."

"True," agreed Berurya. "And now, let's consider the three: voice, appearance, and intelligence. The first two distinctions, voice and appearance, are most evident when differentiating between men and women. Women have high-pitched voices; men, for the most part, have deep voices. In regard to appearance, the anatomical differences between men and women are obvious: these distinctions of course, attract men to women. The third distinction, that of intelligence, does not separate men from women, but rather one from another. It's what makes us individuals. That's important to remember. Do not ever judge others without knowing them first. As Rabbi Meir once said, and I wholeheartedly agree: 'Look not at the flask, but at what it contains; there may be a new flask full of old wine, and an old flask that does not contain even new wine.' Judge another person as Your creator would judge you: not by the way He created you, but by the way you have created yourself! Look for the good in people and when you find it, you'll truly understand what God means when He tells us that we were created in His image. It is that image... which makes us all alike."

Having spoken, Berurya and Meir left the *Beit Midrash*. That afternoon, together with Bathsheva and Bilha, they departed from Hammat and did not once turn to look back.

32

News of Penina

Sepphoris was everything that Meir had said it would be: it was truly a beautiful city. Rabbi Yose bar Halafta invited Meir and Berurya to the *Beit Keneset* on the first Sabbath and praised them both before a very large crowd.

He described Rabbi Meir as "a great man, a holy man, a humble man." Of Berurya he said: "She is the only woman in all of Israel qualified to be wife of Rabbi Meir." Hearing his praise, Berurya smiled, but thought: "No matter who Berurya is, I've been known my entire life long either as the daughter of Teradyon or the wife of Meir! As if the name Berurya couldn't stand on its own!"

Life was good in Sepphoris. Bathsheva passed her twelfth birthday, when girls were considered to have reached the age of majority. Many girls were married when they were fourteen or fifteen. Like her mother, Bathsheva was blessed with both intelligence and beauty. With her mother's help, she surpassed many students whom Meir considered very fine scholars.

As Bathsheva came into her womanhood, Berurya witnessed Bilha's transformation. "The artist draws a face focusing on the clarity of line and the definition of features," Berurya reflected, "black and white were in sharp contrast. But age was created by blurring the lines and softening the features; black and white were blended into gray. So, Berurya mused, did God use the palette of time to create the portrait of aging."

Five months had passed since they left Hammat. It had been an uneventful period, except for one embarrassing incident involving Rabbi Yose. The rabbi had expounded the verse from Job: "In the dark they dig through houses, which they had marked for themselves in the daytime: they know not the light." He interpreted the line to mean that evil people had once devised an ingenious scheme to rob the wealthy: they had asked rich people to take balsam into their homes for safekeeping. The robbers knew it would be stored with other valuables and so, under the cover of night, they'd broken into the wealthy homes and by following the scent of the balsam discovered exactly where the valuables were concealed.

The rabbi's interpretation spread around Sepphoris and instigated a rash of thefts. Rabbi Yose was shocked when the townspeople blamed him for the robberies!

Meir said human nature was such that people who were not normally disposed toward crime could be enticed to become criminals if they believed they wouldn't be caught! He said to Berurya: "Few people are strong enough to withstand temptation. It all began in the Garden of Eden, with Eve's desire to taste the forbidden fruit and it has persisted down to our very own day. People, by and large, are unable to control their appetites for pleasure. Sometimes, Berurya, I feel only contempt for such people."

"I think you're too severe in your criticism, Meir. I don't deny that people very often succumb to temptation but that's part of being human. We stumble only to get up and try again."

"And stumble again," added Meir. He was silent for a time, and then asked: "Where's Bilha?"

"She said something about going to the well to meet somebody. Someone from Sikhnin."

"That woman's always listening to gossip," Meir said. He shook his head: "If it's not at the well, then it's at the marketplace! When does she have time for anything else?"

"Meir," Berurya said calmly, "what's troubling you?"

"Nothing at all. Why do you ask?"

"I'm your wife, Meir. I know you very well. You've been acting strangely the last few days. Why?"

Meir sighed. "Remember that in Hammat I once described the feelings I had – the ones that I said were like turbulent waters rushing beneath the surface?"

"I remember."

"I thought they'd gone ... but they haven't. For two days now, I've been unable to concentrate on my studies. It's as though I'm trapped inside myself!"

"Let me message your shoulders."

As she rubbed the muscles of Meir's back and shoulders, she felt his tension easing. "Does that feel better?"

"Yes. I guess you know me better than I know myself."

Meir had barely finished his sentence when the door flew open. It was Bilha – she was out of breath. "Bilha, what is it?" asked Berurya.

"Penina ..." she began.

"What is it?" Berurya asked with alarm.

"Penina ... is pregnant!"

Berurya could scarcely believe her ears. "Penina is pregnant!? Is that ... what you said?"

"Yes! That's exactly what I said! Remember I told you that I was going to the well to meet someone who just came from Sikhnin? Well, her husband is a friend of Menahem. Menahem knew that she'd be coming here, so he told her to tell me to tell to you."

Berurya swept Bilha into her arms. "That's the best news I've heard in years!" she exclaimed.

"I assume you'll be leaving for Sikhnin as soon as possible," Meir said.

"Yes," answered Berurya. "Is that a problem?"

"No," said Meir, "on the contrary, I was going to Akko in a few days. I'll leave tomorrow instead."

"But if you leave early, who'll travel with you?"

"Don't be concerned. I'm not traveling any great distance. I'll be fine."

"Are you sure?"

"I'm certain, my dear." Meir smiled. "Bathsheva will go with you, no doubt?"

"I'll ask her," said Berurya. "I'm sure she'll want to go along."

"I'm going to the *Beit Midrash* now," Meir said. "If you're asleep when I come back and I don't see you in the morning, give my congratulations to your sister and to Menahem! Wish them *Mazal Tov* for me!"

Meir sighed and went out of the room.

"What's wrong with him?" asked Bilha.

"I'm not sure, Bilha."

"He reacted to my news of Penina's pregnancy almost as if I were talking about strangers and not his sister and brother-in-law. Doesn't he care?"

"Of course he cares!" said Berurya. "Something's bothering him. When we get back from Sikhnin, he'll be a different person. Wait and see."

Later on, Bathsheva came home.

"Bathsheva," Berurya laughed, "I have wonderful news!"

"Penina is pregnant!" Bilha blurted out.

Bathsheva glanced at her mother and then at Bilha. "That's marvelous!" she said. "When will we see her?"

Berurya looked at Bilha. "Do I know my daughter?"

"Tomorrow," replied Berurya.

"I'm so very happy for her!" Bathsheva grinned. "She must be ecstatic!"

"If she's only half as excited as the two of you," said Bilha, "she may not even wait the nine months!"

After the evening meal, Berurya and Bathsheva sat together and studied, but neither could really concentrate so they called Bilha and the three of them talked late into the night. At length, Bilha suggested they go to sleep since they had a full day ahead of them. Bathsheva asked when her father would be back. Berurya said that he'd be studying late and not to wait up for him.

Meir returned very late that night and quietly went up to sleep. He undressed in the dark, his mind still filled with his studies. Often, when he hadn't resolved problems, Meir would lie in bed for hours and consider various solutions. Tonight was no different. He turned over and gazed at Berurya as she slept. He reached out to touch her cheek, but checked himself. "I won't disturb her," he thought. He rolled over and stared intently into the darkness.

When Berurya awoke the next morning, Meir had already left. "He probably went to the *Beit Keneset* to pray at dawn, and from there he'll be off to Akko."

Berurya prayed in her room. When she had finished, she went downstairs. Bathsheva and Bilha were already waiting and anxious to go. "Is everybody ready?" asked Berurya.

"Ready!?" Bilha burst out. "I've been ready for more than fifteen years!"

33

The Temptress

It was the second day of Meir's journey to Akko. So far, the trip had been uneventful and he was grateful. Berurya was absolutely right about his traveling on his own. It was dangerous. Meir himself always advised his students to travel in groups of at least three. But he put the thought out of his mind. He reckoned he would continue for another hour or so and then rest for the night.

In the distance, he discerned what he thought was a river. He hoped the recent rains had not raised the level of the river so it would be difficult to cross. If that were so, he would have to search for a bridge downstream or else find a spot that was shallow.

He reached the bank of the river and dismounted. For some moments he stood and surveyed the situation: it didn't look good. The river was high, far too high to cross at that point. If there'd been a bridge, it had been washed away. His only choice was to walk along the bank in hope of finding a spot where he could cross in safety.

He kept walking, thinking as he went how peaceful everything was. It was a calm and beautiful day. Suddenly, he stopped. He thought there was someone on the far side of the river. "Maybe he'll help me get across?" he murmured aloud. He called out and waved a hand to get the man's attention. But the other did not respond. Meir quickened his pace. "I have to get his attention before he leaves! If I can cross here it'll save me hours of travel."

Meir ran until he was out of breath. "Hello there!" he shouted. The figure on the other side turned in his direction. It wasn't a man at all – but a woman! "What would a woman be doing out alone?" he wondered. "Hello!" he cried out again. By now, he had come close enough to discern the woman's features. He could not believe his eyes; never in all his life had he seen a creature as beautiful as she! He swallowed and felt how dry his throat was. The woman was magnificent! She was striking, voluptuous. Even from a distance, he was mesmerized by her incredible beauty.

The woman smiled at Meir seductively. He felt the blood surge through his body. His heart pounded. All he could feel was an overpowering desire to embrace her, to hold her in his arms, to ...

Suddenly, gripped by the fear that she might go away, Meir looked frantically around him. How could he cross the river? He hurried back to his horse. "If there was a bridge there once and it was carried off, maybe I can still find one of the ropes?" Slowly, he edged his way down the slippery embankment. He had been right! There was a rope tangled up in the rushes. He hauled it in. He hoped the woman would still be where he had left her when he got back. To his relief, he saw her. Meir lashed one end of the rope to a tree, weighted the other end with a stone and flung it across the water to the other side. The woman bent and picked it up and tied it to a tree there: "Now," he thought with fierce excitement, "she's only minutes away from my arms." Gripping the rope tightly with both hands, he slowly made his way across the swirling stream. So intense was his desire that he felt superhuman strength!

Suddenly, mid-way across, the rope tightened and snapped and Meir plunged into the cold swiftly-running water. Desperately, he clung to the loose rope as the current sucked him rapidly downstream. With every ounce of strength he had, he pulled hand-over-hand on his lifeline. At last, soaked to the skin and exhausted, he managed to drag himself back onto dry land. He spat up mouthfuls of water and, teeth chattering, flung himself in total collapse onto the earth....

He opened his eyes and realized he must have been unconscious for hours. Where was he? How had he gotten there? Frantically, he tried to remember. Then, in a flash, it all came back. The ravishing woman on the other side of the river.... Meir raised himself on an elbow and stared across. The woman had disappeared. Had it been a dream? Meir looked down at his hands. They were raw and bleeding from contact with the rope.

Suddenly, he was overwhelmed by an appalling realization. "If the rope hadn't snapped, I would surely have committed a terrible sin!" His breath was in short, harsh spurts. It felt as if a heavy weight pressed down on his chest. His sense of guilt was staggering! He sat on the wet earth and buried his face in shaking hands. "What have I done?!" he moaned, repeating the question again and again.

He clenched his fists, shut his eyes tightly and bit his lip. But he could not obliterate the image of the woman. When his guilt was too much to bear, he screamed "God!" into the still air. For hours, filled with remorse, he sat there and prayed for forgiveness.

34

A Feeling of Guilt

Instead of going on to Akko, Meir decided to return to Sepphoris. During the tedious journey back, he reviewed what had transpired from the time he arrived at the river until the instant he awoke from unconsciousness. The more he thought, the more questions came to mind. But there were only questions and no answers. Who was the tantalizing woman? How was it she had been there alone? Why hadn't she spoken? Where had she gone?

"Maybe," he thought, "she wasn't really a woman? Maybe it was Satan, who had changed himself into a seductive woman to make me transgress? That, at least, would explain some of the unanswered questions. Then God had intervened and stopped Satan from seducing me. But it didn't really matter if the woman were real or Satan: I yielded to my passion, I acted in a way I never believed I would!"

When Meir got back to Sepphoris, he was relieved to find the house empty. He wasn't ready to face Berurya. "I'll go to the *Mikveh*," he murmured aloud. "Yes, I'll immerse myself and purify myself physically and spiritually. And then I'll spend the rest of the day in prayer and repentance."

Meir felt it would be best to return to his daily routine as soon as possible since he didn't know how long Berurya intended to stay with Penina. The next day, he went to the *Beit Midrash* to instruct his students. Standing anxiously before them, he thought: "I wonder if any one detects a difference? But ... that's silly: how could anyone possibly know!?"

Meir's secret was safe, yet he was uneasy and felt that even the questions had hidden inuendoes. He decided to conclude the lesson with the words: "When a man commits a transgression in secret, the Holy One, Blessed be He, proclaims it in public. How is this done? God turns the eyes of the world into mirrors so that the sinner can perceive only the darkness of his own soul. That is the worst punishment of all!"

At length, Berurya returned with Bathsheva. Bilha had remained behind in Sikhnin to help Penina.

"How was the trip to Akko, Meir?"

"To Akko?" muttered Meir: "It was ... uneventful." He paused. "How is Penina?"

"How very happy she is! She actually radiates joy! It's so good to see her this way!"

"And Menahem?"

"Menahem is the perfect husband. He watches over Penina as if she were some fragile creature, like a bird. She's been through much in her life: she deserves someone like Menahem." Berurya stared at her husband. "Is there any other news?"

Meir swallowed hard. "Can she know?" he thought. "Can she see something in my expression?" He gestured. "What could be new?"

Berurya shrugged. "Your students, your colleagues ..." She touched her forehead. "Oh, that reminds me! I've regards from an old friend."

"From whom?"

"From Yehezkel!"

"Yehezkel," Meir exclaimed. His face beamed. "How is he?"

"He's lost all of his hair and put on a lot more weight; aside from that, he hasn't changed. Unfortunately, his wife died a year ago."

"I'm sorry to hear that."

"They loved each other very much," Berurya observed. "I don't think he'll ever remarry."

"Yehezkel," Meir mused. "Do you remember that night I met you in his house?"

"Very clearly, Meir."

"I was running from the Romans, and ... you came into my life. I remember that I was totally captivated by you."

"Were you?"

"Of course," said Meir. "Why else did I volunteer to go to Rome to help your sister? From the moment I saw you, I knew I wanted to marry you."

"Even in the dark!"

Meir hesitated, and then said softly: "Berurya, come out for a walk with me."

"Now? In the middle of the day? But I have a hundred things to do!"

"They can wait."

Meir and Berurya strolled slowly through the streets of Sepphoris. A number of people stopped to greet them. At last, they reached the outskirts. "Look down," said Meir. "Is there a more beautiful sight?"

Berurya shook her head. A breeze sprang up and whirled grains of sand into the air.

"Berurya, I haven't said it in a while, but I love you. I want you to know that."

Berurya smiled. "I love you too."

Meir reached for her hand and held it as the two of them stood and gazed out at the mystical beauty of the Land of Israel. They went home and Meir was especially attentive to his wife all that day. That night, he studied at home instead of going to the *Beit Midrash*.

35

In a Moment of Wrath

Life in Sepphoris was different from life in Tiberias. It had advantages and disadvantages. Sepphoris had a far better climate. The summers were less humid than those in Tiberias and the winters did not bring the bone-chilling dampness that came with living at the shore of the Kinneret.

However, Sepphoris was a much smaller community. Homes were generally smaller and crowded closer together than they were in Hammat. The gang of boisterous, unruly young men who routinely gathered in the vicinity of Meir's house was particularly irritating. Try as he did to concentrate, Meir found the noise extremely distracting. At first, Meir sent a few of his students to ask the youths to quiet down. His request fell upon deaf ears.

Meir himself went out to deal with them. He requested politely that they show some consideration. As a rabbi and scholar who very often studied until the early hours of the morning, he needed quiet. Not only was his request ignored but the situation worsened. When the members of the gang spotted Rabbi Meir, they mocked and taunted him. At night, they intentionally made a tremendous racket.

Meir lost his patience. One evening, as he sat at the dinner table, he brought his fist down with all his force. Startled, Berurya stared at him. "I've had it with those hoodlums!" he cried out. "They've pushed me too far!"

He stood up abruptly and began pacing back and forth across the dining room. He shut his eyes and he twisted his hands together.

Berurya knew very well what he was doing. "Meir, stop!" she hissed.

Meir opened his eyes.

"You are praying for their deaths!"

"Yes," Meir answered, with blazing eyes. "They've tried my patience long enough! They deserve to be punished!"

"What gives you the right to ask God for someone's life?"

"What right have I?" Meir exclaimed. He paused for a moment and then said: "In the Psalms it says: 'The sins will be consumed out of the earth...' Those hooligans are sinners and they deserve to be wiped from the face of the earth!"

"Meir," said Berurya calmly, "the same verse you've just quoted ends with the words, '... and the wicked will be no more.' Consider that the psalmist uses the word 'sins' and not 'sinners'. He asks for the sins to be put to an end, so that the wicked will be no more! Don't pray for their deaths, Meir, pray that they repent and change their ways. Ask not that they die – ask that they become good."

Meir paused. The wrath was gone from his eyes. "You're right, as usual," he said quietly. "I'll pray for God to have compassion on them and for them to mend their ways."

He walked into the other room and began praying.

Meir's outburst had surprised Berurya. Never had she seen such a look in his eyes. For a moment, he reminded her of the Prophet Elisha when he was jeered at by the boys; greatly angered, the prophet had cursed the boys in the name of the Lord. Two bears had emerged from the woods and slain forty-two children. "I wonder what would've happened," Berurya thought, "had Meir cursed them and prayed for their destruction?"

36
Sisters

Months went by. As Penina's pregnancy advanced, Berurya's trips to Sikhnin became more frequent. Now, it was only a matter of days. Bathsheva would stay in Sepphoris; Berurya and Bilha would travel to help Penina.

Penina was ecstatic. "To tell the truth, Berurya," she said, "I never dreamed God would allow me to become a mother. I had given up all hope. I had accepted my fate. Now, I feel like a different person."

"Dear Penina," said Bilha, "you look like a different person!"

Berurya and Penina smiled.

"I've gained a great deal of weight," said Penina.

"Are you uncomfortable?" asked Berurya.

"A little. But I'm not complaining," she smiled. "The midwife believes that I'll give birth in a couple of days."

"What do you think," asked Bilha. "Will it be a boy or a girl?"

"Bilha!" admonished Berurya, "That's silly! What God wishes it to be is what it will be."

"That's all right, Berurya," remarked Penina. "I've given it a lot of thought: boy or a girl, I'll give my child all the love I can."

"What does Menahem want?" Bilha asked.

"Menahem? He says that he doesn't care. But I think he'd be happier if I had a boy."

"Have you discussed a name?" asked Bilha.

"No. We'll decide on a name after he's born."

"He!" Bilha echoed. "That proves it! You're going to have a son."

"How do you know?" asked Berurya.

"It's a sign. Rachel, the old lady from Tiberias, used to say that when a pregnant women says something inadvertently, it's a sign it will come true."

"I think Meir's right," said Berurya. "You're chock-full of superstitions and old wives tales."

The three of them laughed.

"If you don't mind, my dear ladies," said Bilha, "I'm not quite as young as I used to be. I'm going to sleep now. Wake me early in the morning and I'll make breakfast."

Penina and Berurya wished Bilha a good night's rest.

When Bilha was gone, Penina said warmly: "She really is special."

"I know."

Penina rose. "Feel like walking a bit?"

"Sure. The night air'll do us both good."

The sky was vast and clear and the stars flashed with silver fire. "I miss Sikhnin," Berurya said. "Whenever I come back here, I'm comforted. It's hard to explain. I look all around me and I'm reminded of things that happened in my childhood. When I step into this house, I remember Father and Mother. How they'd have loved to be here to see little Penina give birth!"

"Do you think of Mother and Father often?"

"Sometimes," Berurya said. "To be honest, I think about Father more than about Mother. I suppose ... I was closer to him. That's not to say that I didn't love Mother. I did. But Father made a greater impact on my life."

"It's strange ..." said Penina. "I think of Mother more. Remember the doll she made for me when I was a little girl? I still have it. It's a part of her and it will always stay with me."

They walked on quietly for some time. "Berurya," said Penina, "do you remember the time you were pregnant and I said all those nasty things? I do hope you've forgiven me."

"I forgave you when it happened. I'm surprised you even thought about it again."

"All sorts of odd thoughts come to mind. Did it happen when you were pregnant?"

"Not that I remember."

"I guess the most important thing I want to say ... is how much I love you, Berurya. You're a wonderful sister! You rescued me when I was a captive in Rome. You helped me with those horrendous nightmares. You ..." Penina began to weep.

Berurya embraced her. "Come on, little sister," she said, "I think we'd better be getting home now. Maybe this wasn't such a good idea?"

"I'm fine," Penina said. "It was important to me to tell you what I told you. I've wanted to do it for so many years."

"Then I'm glad you got it out. I want you to know ... I feel the same way about you."

The two sisters walked back. Berurya kissed Penina's forehead. Then she went to her old bedroom and closed the door quietly behind her.

Penina went into her room and found Menahem fast asleep. She went over to close the shutters and gazed up at the heavens. "Such a beautiful night to be a star!" she murmured. She swung the shutters shut, blew out the candle, and lay down to sleep.

37
Complications

Several hours later, Berurya was wakened by a piercing scream. She jumped up and ran to Penina's and Menahem's room. Menahem was standing by the bed.

"What is it?" asked Berurya.

"I don't know!"

Penina was curled up, holding her stomach.

"She's in pain. Menahem, get the midwife quickly."

Menahem hurried off.

Bilha was now in the doorway. "What's the matter?"

"I think Penina's in labor."

"I'll bring some water."

Bilha bustled down the stairs.

"The pain, Berurya! The pain!"

"Menahem's gone to bring the midwife. You'll be fine, Penina." Berurya held her sister's hand tightly. Again Penina cried out.

"Where's that midwife?" thought Berurya. "Why is it taking so long?" She pulled the blanket down and saw that Penina was bleeding. At that moment, Bilha returned with a jug of water.

"She's bleeding, Bilha. What should we do?"

"I'll try to find the midwife myself. She'll know what to do." She turned and left.

Berurya sat down by her sister. One hand held Penina's hand; the other caressed Penina's forehead. "Please, God," Berurya prayed, "if it is Your will that she lose the baby, please don't make her suffer. She's been through too much already."

At that instant, Menahem and Bilha entered with the midwife. Berurya rose to her feet. "Can I help?"

"No," said the midwife tersely. "The other woman will help. You and the husband should wait downstairs."

"It'll all be fine!" Bilha said to Menahem.

Berurya and Menahem waited downstairs. Except for a few reassuring words they passed the time in silent prayer.

Berurya knew that prayer responds to our hopes and fears. In moments of crisis, it recognizes the frailty and vulnerability which makes us human. She knew that prayer cannot be measured by the number of words. Endless requests might be no more nor any less effective than the earnest petition "Please God heal her!" She felt that prayer, like the smoke of ancient sacrifices, carried with it no promises as it ascended to heaven. The only hope, she felt, was that God's will and our prayers are one and the same.

An hour later, Bilha came unevenly down the steps. Her eyes were red and swollen; her entire frame shook.

"The baby must have died," Berurya thought with horror. Bilha moved slowly over to Menahem, she opened her arms as if to enfold him in them, but then froze. "Penina!" she rasped. "Our darling Penina is dead!"

Berurya's mind reeled; Menahem raced up the steps.

"How?" Berurya cried out. "Why?"

"The midwife did everything she could to save her," sobbed Bilha. "There was so much bleeding, so ... much bleeding."

Berurya's knees buckled; she felt as if her insides were being ripped out. She tore at her hair. If she were to scream, the sound would surely echo from one end of the world to the other. As she had done so often in her life, Berurya seized the fabric of her robe and tore the cloth – the sign of mourning. Convulsively, her fingers tore again; it was as though she tore the very fabric of her heart. Slowly, with bitter emphasis, she began to recite the words, *Baruch Dayan Emet*: "Blessed is the Judge of truth."

38
The Eulogy

Although she knew it would be a terrible task, Berurya insisted upon delivering the eulogy at her sister's funeral. She gazed directly into the eyes of the assembled crowd and spoke: "Yesterday, the soul of an infant came into this world ... and the soul of my sister departed from it. When a child is born, his hands are clenched, as if to say 'all the world is within my grasp. I shall inherit it.' And when a man dies, his hands are open, as if to say, 'I take nothing with me from this world.' All of us know that the days of our years are numbered and yet, even with this knowledge, we continue to pass the time in pursuit of things that have no lasting value.

"My sister, as many of you know, had more than her share of sorrow. But she never dwelt on it. Her favorite saying was one she heard from my husband, who in turn heard it from Rabbi Akiva: 'All that God does is for the good.' She not only said it – she lived it."

Berurya lifted a hand and went on: "What my sister wanted in her life was to become a mother and to raise a child. She wanted the chance to give that child the kind of love and affection she had received from her mother.

"My sister, Penina, never cared for possessions. The only possession she ever really treasured was a doll which our mother had given her when she was a little girl. It didn't look like anything, but it meant everything to her. I know she would want her daughter to have the doll; as the child grows up, the doll will be something for her to hold on to, a memory of a mother she never knew....

"I will always try to remember Penina as she was during the last days of her life. Undoubtedly, they were the happiest of all. The prospect of becoming a mother made her bloom, made her radiant. God, in His wisdom, must have had a reason for taking my sister at this time. It is a reason I cannot fathom."

Berurya stretched her arms out. "May her soul find rest with our father, our mother, our brother, my two sons, and all the righteous of Israel." She intoned: "The Lord hath given and the Lord hath taken away. Blessed be the name of the Lord."

39

Another Mourning

Berurya remained in Sikhnin for a month. She and Bilha helped Menahem with little Rachel. Menahem had chosen the name for his daughter simply because he liked it: he hadn't realized that Rachel was the Matriarch who died in childbirth.

Penina's death was a devastating blow to Menahem. During the first three days of *Shiva*, it seemed as though he hadn't fully grasped what happened. He spoke of Penina as if she were still alive. He could not hold his infant daughter – merely to look at her caused him to burst into tears. After the prescribed week of mourning, he went back to work. He hoped his work would preoccupy his mind, but his heart wouldn't allow it. At night, his heart and his mind were one. Both grieved as one. The price Menahem had to pay for his love was the pain of his loss. He was strong, but his love was stronger.

Whenever Berurya felt a need to be alone, she would climb the slopes of the mountain she had often climbed as a child. There, her special tree awaited her.

It was under that fig tree that she had pretended to be the Prophetess Debra, who judged the children of Israel; messengers from all over the land came to seek her advice and counsel. As she grew older, the tree became a patient, understanding friend. She sat alone, beneath its branches, for hours, completely absorbed in her thoughts.

Now, she was utterly alone. Her brother... her father and mother...Hananiah and Elhanan... and now, Penina... As names are carved into the bark of a tree, so were the names of her loved ones carved into the living tissue of her heart.

After the month of mourning, Berurya returned to Sepphoris. Bilha insisted on staying on in Sikhnin. Menahem told her he'd be fine, but Bilha would not go.

Berurya at once plunged into studies. The study of Torah had always been the balm that soothed the wounds of life. Like some miraculous drug, its words healed even the most savage anguish of her soul.

40
Blessed With Everything

More than a year had gone by since Penina's death. For Menahem, the task of raising a daughter, the pressures of work, and worst of all, his intolerable loneliness were more than he could bear. At the constant urging of friends and family, he remarried. His new wife was a kind and decent woman. She cared for Rachel sincerely and well. But for Menahem, nothing and no one could dull his longing for Penina.

In Sepphoris, an event of great joy was being planned: Bathsheva was betrothed to Zivvtai, a young and promising scholar of whom both Berurya and Meir approved heartily. The date of the wedding had been set for just after Bathsheva's sixteenth birthday. But there were still months to go until intense preparations were begun.

One afternoon, Berurya went to the *Beit Midrash* to talk with Meir about Bathsheva's wedding. When she arrived, Meir was in the midst of his discourse. Not wishing to disturb him, she sat down unnoticed on a bench in the rear of the room.

Meir was explaining the words, "And the Lord blessed Abraham with everything." The verse reminded Berurya of Pinhas and Hophni and the inhabitants of Mimla. She wondered if, through *Tzedakah*, they had at long last found the longevity they desired so devoutly. Those words, "And the Lord blessed Abraham with everything," were the words with which Pinhas had blessed Meir on parting.

Berurya thought: "I am the one who gave Meir the idea and he's the one who merited the blessing."

Berurya listened to Meir's interpretation. "What does it mean," he expounded, "when the Torah tells us 'And the Lord blessed Abraham with everything'? Before these words, we learned of the death and burial of Sarah. Following these words, the Torah tells us that Abraham sent his servant to find a wife for his son, Isaac. Possibly, the verse refers back to the time when Isaac was born but was included in this section to indicate that Abraham's life was not fully complete until his son married. I believe that being 'blessed with everything' alludes to Isaac's future inheritance and to the continuance of the family's traditions.

"How then do we interpret these words, 'and the Lord blessed Abraham with everything?' To me, it means that God did not give Abraham a daughter: that, in and of itself, was a blessing."

"That's absurd!" murmured Berurya to herself. "To suggest that God would bless someone by not giving him a daughter! That means I wasn't a blessing to my father and Bathsheva hasn't been a blessing to us." Berurya was infuriated. She got to her feet and strode out of the room, but not before uttering the word 'ridiculous' loud enough for everyone to hear.

When Meir came home, Berurya was still agitated.

"Why did you leave the *Beit Midrash* so abruptly?" he asked.

"You don't know?"

"No."

"Well, it was your interpretation of the words, 'And God blessed Abraham with everything.'"

"Be more specific."

"God did not give Abraham a daughter – that was a blessing!"

"Is that why you left?" Meir said. "But you've disagreed with my interpretations before. Why make such an issue out of this one?"

"You still don't understand!" Berurya said acidly. "Meir, I've been fighting with you over the interpretation of that verse all my life! It reflects your attitude toward your daughter, toward me, and toward all women."

"My attitude!?" Meir rejoined, raising his voice.

"Yes. In your eyes, women were created to bear and raise children and to care for the needs of their husbands. Apparently, you believe that their role in life includes little more."

Meir stared at her. "Do you really want to know what my attitude is? Well, I'll tell you: I think women are frivolous, garrulous, vain and simple-minded. They are inordinately jealous and spend hours gossiping. Worst of all, they're incapable of controlling their emotions."

Berurya was tight-lipped. "Is that what you think of me?"

"No, of course not! You're the exception; you're different from other women. Ever since I first met you, I've marvelled over and over again that you so rarely display emotion. No matter what, you're always in control."

He gestured. "Most women, however, aren't like you. They weep on the slightest provocation. Just look at a woman askance and she cries. Women are slaves to the heart; men live by their minds."

"Is that... what you really believe, Meir?"

"Absolutely!"

Berurya's face was solemn. "I don't think we have anything more to discuss," she said bitterly. "I've misjudged you, Meir. It's taken me a long time to arrive at the realization, but I have. Maybe, as you say, it's because I am a woman." She paused, and then went on: "Once, I believed you were different than other men. But, I'm sorry to say, I was mistaken. You're not different. More intelligent, but not different." She waved a hand. "Maybe you should go back to your students now."

Meir was about to answer, but instead decided to leave. As he walked to the *Beit Midrash*, he thought angrily: "She's wrong and I'll prove she's wrong! But how? How will I demonstrate that women are weak-willed and prisoners of their emotions?"

He walked slowly, pondering how best to prove his point. Suddenly, a wild idea came to mind: he would bring his most handsome student home for the express purpose of seducing his wife! Of course, the student would not actually seduce her, he'd only bring her to the point at which she was ready to respond to his advances. When Berurya admitted she had succumbed to temptation, Meir's assessment of women would be wholly vindicated!

When he arrived at the *Beit Midrash*, Meir carefully considered each student. His choice had to be perfect. The student had not only to be physically appealing to Berurya, he had to be intelligent and charming as well.

"Reuben, come with me," he called out. "I want to talk to you."

Reuben had recently come to Sepphoris and had already made a very favorable impression on Meir.

Once outside the *Beit Midrash*, Meir explained his plan to the student. Reuben was shocked. He refused outright.

But Meir pressed the issue. "I'm not asking you to do anything immoral, Reuben. You're to stop the instant you sense the slightest response to your advances. That's not a transgression."

The student was flustered and agitated; he protested again. But Meir would not accept no for an answer. He badgered and cajoled and finally persuaded the reluctant student.

"All right, rabbi," stammered Reuben, "I'll do it. I don't like it, but I'll do it."

"And you must promise not to divulge any of this to anyone, at any time, ever! No one else must ever know. Understood?"

Reuben nodded. The next evening, Meir brought Reuben home for dinner. Meir managed the conversation so that the student talked extensively about himself and his background. After Reuben had left, Meir continued to talk about him. "Well, what do you think of him?"

"He seems like a nice young man," said Berurya.

"I think he'll turn out to be a really exceptional student! He's extremely intelligent and he has what it takes to be a scholar. Plus the fact that he's compassionate, kind, and gentle."

Berurya did not comment.

"Since he has no family here," said Meir, "do you mind if I invite him to dinner again?"

"As you wish," said Berurya. "The only problem is that with Bilha gone for the next few days I have a lot to do in the house."

"I have a solution: I'll tell Reuben to stop by tomorrow and help you out."

"What about his studies?"

"Don't be concerned. I'll see to it that he doesn't fall behind."

"In that case, I'd certainly appreciate the assistance."

The next day, just as Meir had promised, Reuben arrived.

Later that evening, Meir met Reuben in the *Beit Keneset* and took him aside. "Well, how are matters progressing?" he asked the student.

Reuben's eyes shone. "I find your wife a very unique woman," he said. "I'm intrigued by every word she utters! I've never met anyone so intelligent, so charming and ..."

Meir was somewhat annoyed. "I didn't ask you about what I know already," he said with irritation. "You'll have to spend more time alone with her. I'll arrange somehow to make sure that everyone'll be away from the house for two days next week. I'll tell Berurya I asked you to stay with her in my absence. I'll suggest she assist you in your studies. That will make it completely credible. You'll test her then."

"Won't you reconsider, Rabbi?"

Meir shook his head vigorously. "Definitely not!"

41

The Final Test

On Wednesday night, Berurya cleared the dishes from the table. Reuben stood up and offered to help her.

"Thank you, Reuben, but that won't be necessary."

The student watched her as she went about her work. "Berurya," he asked, "are you happy?"

"Happy? That's a peculiar question. What exactly do you mean by 'happy'?"

"Define it any way you want," Reuben said.

Berurya put down the plate she was holding. "Happiness is a concept that resists definition. It reflects a state of being which people want to attain but that few are able to recognize, even when they actually experience it!" Berurya smiled wistfully.

"One problem is that other people often define happiness for us. They tell you what, supposedly, will make you happy. Wealth, for example, is one common criterion for happiness." Berurya thought of Nathan. "But I don't believe that happiness can be defined by material possessions. Some people have unimaginable wealth but they're still unhappy. Others have little, almost nothing, yet they claim they're content. Scholars seek fulfillment through their studies. Are they happy? Some are; others are jealous of their colleagues' achievements. Then study's no longer a question of knowledge for knowledge's own sake, but rather a competitive struggle. Envy certainly destroys a scholar.

"Reuben, please don't be offended but the question 'are you happy?' is meaningless." She reflected and then continued: "I see the first two psalms of King David as a single one. The psalm begins with the words, 'Happy is the man that hath not walked in the counsel of the wicked...' It ends with 'Happy are all that take refuge in Him.' If you can live these words, you may be able to grasp the meaning of happiness. If not, don't seek happiness, but pursue peace instead."

As Berurya spoke, Reuben listened intently. Here was a woman, he thought, of true renown and intelligence! A woman whose reputation was unequalled in all Israel. He shivered as he realized that he could not possibly continue with the deception. "There's something," he murmured hoarsely, "that's been weighing very heavily on me and I must tell it to you...."

"Please do, Reuben."

"It's not by chance that I'm here tonight." Reuben flushed, swallowed hard and went on: "You're actually being tested by your husband! Rabbi Meir ... said that I was to attempt to seduce you and that the moment you responded, I was to leave."

"Who else... is a part of this so-called test?" asked Berurya incredulously.

"No one," mumbled Reuben. "No one else knows." He put a hand to his moist eyes. "Believe me when I tell you that I wanted no part of this," he said haltingly. "But Rabbi Meir insisted. He's my teacher; I felt I had to obey him. But I can't continue. Please forgive me ... I beg of you!"

Berurya trembled. "Come with me," she said with sudden ferocity. She pulled the student into the bedroom and slammed the door shut. Then she undressed. Reuben stood there and shuddered, like a frightened child. Naked, Berurya got into bed. She extended her arms...

42

Atonement for All My Sins

As soon as Berurya heard the front door close, she dressed and went out. As Sepphoris slept peacefully, she walked on and on for hours. "What was the purpose of the test, Meir?" she thought. "What did you hope to prove? Did you suspect me of being unfaithful? No? Then what was it? Perhaps it was the argument we had? Yes, that must be it! That's when you first brought Reuben into our house. You told me how impressed you were with him. You wanted me to like him." She sighed. "Yes, now it all makes sense. You wanted to show that if I succumbed to his seduction, it would prove that women are slaves to their emotions! But, Meir, your test proved only one thing: that we have failed each other! How could you have done this? Why didn't you consider all the years that I put my feelings aside for you? What greater test was there than when our darling children died and you weren't there when their lifeless bodies were brought in? At that horrific moment, I thought of you. To ease your pain, I doubled my anguish! I permitted myself no tears, no weeping, but rather searched for the words with which to console you. I've always been beside you. When Rabban Shimeon ben Gamaliel sought to excommunicate you and you were ready to accept defeat, I made you fight back. I was in Caesarea with you. When the Romans tested you, was I not tested as well? I supported you, Meir, as always. I've delighted in your achievements; I've strengthened you in your trials.

And I did it all for one reason: my love and respect for you. If only you'd respected me half as much!"

Berurya walked until the sun came up. Along the way, she stopped to say her prayers as she'd done every morning of her life. This day would be no exception.

Moving on, she saw a little girl rolling a hoop along the dirt path. It reminded her of the time she was a little girl growing up in Sikhnin. "Those were such wonderful times," she thought. "Father would lift me to his knees and hold me as he taught me Torah. Whenever I study, I feel his arms around me. I hear his voice: 'Berurya, you're such an intelligent child. I'm so proud you're my daughter. So very proud ...'"

Berurya remembered her father's death. She had been utterly helpless. What could she have done when the flames ate the parchment of the Torah? If only she had been able to embrace him that one, last time! The unutterable pain of that indelible moment had made her vow to be strong and never cry.

As Berurya walked on, she heard the delicate chirping of birds. She saw fledglings in their nest. "Quiet, little birds," she murmured aloud, "your mother'll return with food soon. You must be patient."

Berurya drew closer to the tree and saw the reason for the fledglings' commotion. At the base of the tree, the mother lay dead. Berurya bent and picked up the dead bird. "Why did you have to die?" she whispered. "Your children need you. You've no right to leave them like this. They need you; I need you. I'm left alone, all alone. My little sister, Penina, was as fragile as you. A fragile bird who shouldn't have suffered as she did! Ah, one hand gives... and the other takes away! To know that she could have a child but not to live to see that child. Ah, the bird who died should have lived."

Holding the bird in her hands, Berurya wept. Tears coursed down her cheeks; the mighty wall she had built to withstand flood-waters had been breached by a tiny bird! Sobbing, Berurya knelt and gently set the bird on the earth. She dug a tiny grave and placed the dead bird in it. Then she covered the grave and intoned: "Rest in peace, my little one ..."

When she brought Reuben into the bedroom, Berurya had made a decision. Committing adultery meant there was no turning back for her. Very soon, she would join her sister, father, mother, brother, and two children in a world far kinder than the one she was in. The difficulty lay not in death, but the pain of leaving loved ones behind.

Berurya thought of Bathsheva; tears welled up once again in her eyes. "My precious daughter," she thought. "I'm afraid I won't see you marry. How I'd have loved to be there! You've brought me so much happiness, more than you will ever know. I wish you a family of your own – children to love as I've loved you."

Berurya wiped her eyes. Her throat had closed. "Bilha, I'll miss you," she thought. "You've been like a sister. We grew up together and I hoped that we'd grow old together. Now ... that's not possible. Take care of yourself, Bilha. May God grant you a long, long life."

Berurya felt she was ready. She walked quickly home. Once inside, she looked around her for one, last time. She felt she might weep again but didn't. There simply were no tears left. She took a rope and entered her bedroom. As she fastened it to one of the beams in the ceiling, her last thoughts turned to Meir.

"Good-bye, my beloved husband," she murmured. "I know in my heart that your name will be remembered for thousands of years. The light of your wisdom will illuminate the way for untold scholars yet to be born. If I am to be remembered, then let me be remembered as your wife. Your wife who loved and adored you. I hope that my death does not bring you too much pain; this is the one time, Meir, that I won't be able to stand beside you."

A final tear fell from her eye. Berurya did not wipe it away.

"God forgive me for what I am about to do," she said aloud, "and may my death be atonement for all my sins..."

Epilogue

As Berurya had predicted, Meir achieved greatness. When Judah the Prince compiled his Mishna, many of Meir's rulings were incorporated in the great work. Rabbi Meir's teachings have affected Jewish life profoundly throughout the ages.

According to plan, Bathsheva married Zivvtai. They had three children: two girls and a boy. Bilha lived with them until she died at eighty-three.

God had allotted Meir many years. He died of an intestinal ailment on a journey abroad. Realizing that he only had a short time left, he asked that his bier be left on the shore of the Mediterranean so that the same water which touched the Land of Israel would surround him. His body was brought back to Israel; his death was mourned by multitudes.

On one of his writings, Meir's students found next to the Hebrew words *V'hineh Tov Me'od*, "Behold it was very good," the emendation *V'hineh Tov Mot*, "Behold, death is good." Meir carried the pain of Berurya's loss until the very end. There was only one person he had considered his equal and he had loved her with all his heart.